Praise for
THE AWAKENED WOMAN

Winner of the 2017 NAACP Image Award
for Outstanding Literary Work—Instructional

"*The Awakened Woman* empowers women to access a fearlessness that will enable community progress."

—*Essence*

"Remarkable."

—*O, The Oprah Magazine*

"Trent's energy and conviction are evident throughout the book, and her story is invigorating, revitalizing, motivating, and encouraging.... An empowering story coupled with easy-to-navigate steps that can help any woman achieve her full potential."

—*Kirkus Reviews*

"Any time anyone tells you that a dream is impossible, any time you're discouraged by impossible challenges, just mutter this mantra: *Tererai Trent*."

—Nicholas Kristof, Pulitzer Prize–winning journalist and #1 nationally bestselling author of *Half the Sky*

"Against the gripping backdrop of Dr. Trent's beginnings in war-torn, patriarchal Zimbabwe, *The Awakened Woman* shines as a beacon of hope to women everywhere. She invites the reader to sit around a sacred fire of sisterhood with her, guiding us on a powerful personal journey and stoking the embers within us all to reclaim our voices to heal our souls—and the heart of the world."

—Danica McKellar, actress and
New York Times bestselling author

"A soul-shaking and potentially life-altering read filled with stories, guidance, and rituals to help readers realize their sacred dreams."

—*LA Yoga*

"In *The Awakened Woman*, Tererai Trent weaves her riveting story with that of other women to inspire us to dream as boldly as she dared to, then holds our hands and walks us through each crucial, practical step to achieve those dreams. Tererai calls us to remember the foundation of who we are and reminds us of the rituals that ground us. This powerful, interactive book is a perfect gift for your girlfriend, your daughter (or yourself!) when you want to say: BE YOU. BE BOLD. BE CREATIVE. YOUR LIFE MATTERS. And what could be more important than that?"

—Lisa Bloom, civil rights lawyer and
New York Times bestselling author

"A mesmerizing and inspiring story of an amazing woman's remarkable journey. It was more than a coincidence that two strong, passionate young women from opposite sides of the world met briefly in a southern African village, exchanged life-changing words, unwittingly documented the encounter with a photo, and years later crossed paths again in the United States, bonding as sister activists and cherished friends for life, and this is just one of the jaw-dropping stories told throughout Tererai's journey to becoming Dr. Trent."

—Jo Luck, former president and CEO of Heifer International
and 2010 World Food Prize Laureate

"I am amazed at how eloquently Dr. Trent has shared her story of trials and triumph. It has inspired me to live out my truth and encourage my sisters to do the same. I believe we all need to be awakened from the past that keeps us held back from living the greatness inside of us."
—Patrice Register, CEO of PLR Services, LLC

"Provocative. Illuminating. Delightful. In *The Awakened Woman*, Zimbabwean-born author Dr. Tererai Trent creates a bridge between unlikely worlds—weaving precious wisdom of Africa with modern-day research, she enlightens women on how to be midwives to their own sacred dreams. Her passionate insight presented through the lens of her amazing life's journey makes this book a unique and rare treasure."
—Melissa Cara Rigoli, creative designer and musician

"The power of her new book, *The Awakened Woman*, is in its wisdom, its simple advice for all women.... Never has there been a more critical time for women to lift each other up, learn from each other, explore new ideas, and take leadership in world order. *The Awakened Woman* is truly a life-changing guide for every woman looking to explore her best self and give meaning to her life. No one but Tererai could have written it, and it has changed my life forever."
—Terry Hernandez, executive director of the Chrysalis Foundation

"*The Awakened Woman* is a call to action for humanity. Tererai taps into deep wisdom, reminding us that our sacred sisters can help us to bring forth our dormant dreams. It's only when we come together, awakened, that we can truly live our purpose."
—Vicki Saunders, founder of SheEO

"Compelling, insightful, gracious, loving—Tererai lights a candle for the world and inspires us all to light ours!"
—Theresa Gattung, leading New Zealand business personality, author, and philanthropist

Also by Tererai Trent

CHILDREN'S

The Girl Who Buried Her Dreams in a Can

THE AWAKENED WOMAN

A GUIDE FOR REMEMBERING &
IGNITING YOUR SACRED DREAMS

DR. TERERAI TRENT

Foreword by Oprah Winfrey

Published by kikki.K Pty Ltd in agreement with Enliven Books,
a division of Simon & Schuster, Inc.

All rights reserved, including the right to reproduce this book or portions thereof in any form whatsoever.

This publication contains the opinions and ideas of its author. It is intended to provide helpful and informative material on the subjects addressed in the publication. The author and publisher specifically disclaim all responsibility for liability, loss, or risk, personal or otherwise, which is incurred as a consequence, directly or indirectly, of the use and application of any of the contents of this book.

Copyright © 2017 Tererai Trent, PhD

Interior design by Kyoko Watanabe

Manufactured in China

We would love to see and hear your stories of you achieving your dreams.
Share them with us.

@kikki.K @tereraitrent #101milliondreamers

ISBN 978-0-646-80659-4

kikki.K Pty Ltd

ACN: 092563249

204/120 Bay Street

Port Melbourne

Vic 3207 Australia

www.kikki-k.com

Dedicated to you the dreamer, the beacon, and the generous light that enables others to shine. You awaken the world, giving us hope, and a compass reference that *indeed, it is achievable.*

"But still, like air, I'll rise."

—MAYA ANGELOU, "STILL I RISE"

CONTENTS

Foreword by Oprah Winfrey	xiii
Introduction	xvii
1. Find Your Great Hunger: The Call to Awaken	1
2. The Women the World Forgot: Reclaiming Your Voice	13
3. Midwife to Your Sacred Dreams: Sowing Fertile Seeds	39
4. Be Your Own Storyteller: Creating New Pathways	65
5. Validate Your Body's Knowing: Harnessing Your Sensuality	85
6. Let Your Spirit Take Root: Believing in Your Dreams	107
7. Be Courageous, Not Silent: Inspiring Action and Opportunity	141
8. The Sacred Sisterhood: Cultivating Your *Sahwira*	177
Conclusion: It Is Achievable!	197
Your Sacred Dreams Journey: Ten Essentials	221
Creating Dream Circles of Sacred Sahwira Sisterhood	227
Recommended Resources	239
Acknowledgments	245
Notes	247
Bibliography	255

FOREWORD

I invited Tererai Trent to appear on the final season of *The Oprah Winfrey Show* as my "favorite guest of all time." That was quite a proclamation, considering that from the fall of 1986 until the winter of 2011 I had interviewed more than 37,000 guests. I've listened to the wide range of stories of the human diaspora, despair, self-destruction, dysfunction, loss, victory, achievements, and triumphs.

I'd first heard Tererai's story two years before she appeared on my show for the first time. Her hunger to overcome ingrained obstacles and daring to create a vision for a better life resonated deeply with me. Her life's journey embodied the essence of every lesson I'd shared in my own work for twenty-five years: Hope—believing in something greater for yourself. Understanding your thoughts create your reality. Gratitude—appreciating what you have no matter what it is. Knowing it doesn't matter where you come from. Keep reaching for your dreams. And above all . . . you have the power to change the course of your life with education. Her story—from being a barely educated child bride and mother in remote Zimbabwe to achieving her dream of an education in America by being awarded her PhD—is one of such resilience and courage, I knew she would inspire anyone open to hearing her.

When she walked out onto my set, there was an immediate and deep spiritual connection at work. We locked eyes and stood still for just one or two breaths. In that short moment of time I could feel something powerful. Woman to woman. I see you. I know you.

I know who you are and I know what it takes to do what you have done.

It was a holy moment, a profound experience of looking at someone and with every fiber of my being feeling the fullness of who they really are, and instantly knowing they feel my fullness, too. You see and are seen. Completely.

One of the most inspirational people I've met in all my years of interviewing, Tererai has a personal story that will bring you to tears—and make you cheer. Her perseverance, commitment, and hopefulness are a salve to even the weariest of spirits.

Yet Tererai, in all her wisdom, knows it has never been just about her. There has always been a "we" behind her success, and the way she knows and honors this deep down in her soul is Tererai's true gift.

What I felt that day on my set with her was a way of being in the world, a practice of awakened sisterhood that I have also experienced with my girls in South Africa at the Oprah Winfrey Leadership Academy for Girls (OWLAG). Following the tradition of their ancestors, I hear the echoes of their greetings as they pass each other on their way to class: "*Sawubona*"—"I see you"—and in response, "*Ngikhona*"—"I am here." It's something we can cultivate. I see you, I am here. It's a power we can create and nurture.

This is the book I have been waiting for from Tererai because it embodies that feeling she and I exchanged that day on my show. With memoir, myth, ritual, and poetry Tererai inspires us in *The Awakened Woman* to tap into our deepest longings and to grow from them a sacred dream, a dream that satisfies what she calls our "Great Hunger"—our desire for meaning, purpose, and community. I see you, I am here. Woman to woman.

Part memoir, part inspirational blueprint for how to make a better world, part love letter to our mothers, daughters, and ourselves, *The Awakened Woman* reminds us of the power of belief and how it inspires us to create and transform our world and those around us. Her words pierce the deepest parts of us, the place where all our longing and loneliness reside. She invites us to stop anaesthetizing those parts with material things, and instead to listen to our longings and allow them to wake us up to our true potential.

All the beautiful writers, storytellers, entrepreneurs, grandmothers, and mothers who speak in this book—from Maya Angelou to Toni Cade Bambara to Audre Lorde to Tererai and her mother—are the home that's waiting for us, inviting us to step into their arms and their wisdom. They call out for us to take our place among them as dream seekers.

If you've ever had a dream, a longing, a desire, but thought to yourself, "No way, I could never. I don't have the time/money/resources/skills/courage . . ." this book is for you. If you've ever looked at the world and felt an aching for one of its many hurts or injustices, this book is for you. If you know the power of sisterhood or need to know its power, this book is for you.

—Oprah Winfrey

THE AWAKENED WOMAN

A GUIDE FOR REMEMBERING & IGNITING YOUR SACRED DREAMS

DR. TERERAI TRENT

Dr. Tererai Trent's story of dreaming is, without doubt, the most amazing I have ever come across. She is living proof of the power of dreaming big and believing the seemingly impossible is possible. As one of the world's most acclaimed voices for women's empowerment, Tererai has created this book as a call to action for all women – to awaken their hearts, recapture their dreams and find their true voice.

I found this book really empowering and, as you read through the chapters and discover the many practices and rituals throughout, I hope you feel as empowered as I did. Tererai's approach to awakening our true selves is so inspiring – it's no wonder she was named Oprah's 'favourite guest of all-time!'

Also, don't forget to grab a copy of the beautiful The Awakened Woman Journal we have created. It's the perfect companion to this book, designed to help you put pen to paper as you absorb as much of Tererai's wisdom as possible. Available in store and online at www.kikki-k.com.

Kristina Karlsson
kikki.K founder and stationery lover

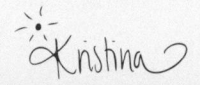

Kristina

kikki.K

INTRODUCTION

A woman in harmony with her spirit is like a river flowing. She goes where she will without pretense and arrives at her destination, prepared to be herself and only herself.

—MAYA ANGELOU

I grew up in a cattle-herding family in rural Zimbabwe, a member of the Northern Shona or Korekore people. My village, Zvipani, is in the Hurungwe District, which was named after a famous sacred mountain known as Urungwe.

During harvest seasons, before our community was devastated by the Second Chimurenga War that shaped Zimbabwe's struggle for liberation, the people of the Zambezi Valley performed their rainmaking ceremonies in the shadows of this great mountain—a potentially active volcano—its size a source of pride and dignity for all the people in the fifteen thousand or so households that make up the Hurungwe District. When earthquakes hit the region, and the mighty Urungwe rumbles, the people of the valley drop to their knees in prayer in awe of its power.

The Shona have inhabited Zimbabwe since at least the eleventh century, when the ruins of Great Zimbabwe, a city center for trading where many artifacts of art, politics, and culture have been found, are dated. Shona people are divided into five major clans, each with its own *mutupo*, or totems defining lineage and family. I was born into the Moyo—the Heart—*mutupo*, among the Korekore in the northern region, which has traditions steeped in such ancient art as fabric painting, sculpture, and music practices—beautifully giving voice to the human condition in ways that transcend geography and time.

The Korekore people are indigenous farmers with a rich spiritual culture. We believe that our world and all that exists begins with the Supreme Being and Creator, an invisible spirit presiding over heaven and earth whom we refer to as Mwari, Musikavanhu, or Nyadenga, which in translation generally means: "He Who Is"; "God, the Great One"; "the One who created people" or "the Great Spirit." Individuals cannot access God, and so our elders seek advice and guidance from God through *vadzimu*, ancestral spirits. These invisible guardians, our ancestors, are the cornerstone of our spiritual life as well as a source of comfort and protection, especially during illness. It is these ancestors to whom we pray for protection when the Urungwe rumbles.

Like most native Zimbabweans, the Korekore way of life is organized around our belief in collective duty for the survival of all. There is an unspoken rule that obligates individuals to a moral responsibility to work for a common goal. All things being equal, the community and the ancestors protect individuals and their rights.

As children, we learn early that we belong not only to our families but also to our neighbors. As such, neighbors have the same rights and responsibilities as family members to instill good manners in village children. It is believed that an individual's behavior, good or bad, affects the wholeness of the society. As children, while having so much adult supervision has grave consequences when we misbehave, it also gives a sense of security and belonging. Very often, neighbors bring food or cook for children when their mother is away.

Despite the beauty of our collectiveness, other powers within the environment threatened our way of life. The British colonized Zimbabwe in 1888, and communities like ours were forcibly resettled from our ancestral homes to this incommodious territory when the harsh terrain was determined to be unsuitable for European colonists. Demarcated by the European settlers as a "native" reserve in 1913, Hurungwe became one of the largest and poorest African Reserves in Zimbabwe. Today it is known as the Mosquito and Tsetse Fly Belt. Our village has struggled with disease, poverty, and a lack of basic resources—clean water, electricity, health care, education, and at times, food—for decades.

I have seen how volatile things happen when poverty, war, and an oppressive colonial system interlock with existing norms of a traditionally patriarchal society. Women and girls, although powerful keepers of our wisdom and collective memory in Korekore culture, were devalued by a clan system that gave men power over disputes and decision-making and marriage practices like polygamy and wife inheritance. Onto this reality, the oppressive colonial system layered the denial of our dignity and sources of subsistence, shaping and extending inequality among the community. We were sitting on a powder keg.

When the war for liberation broke out during my youth, my people, who were already strained by these patriarchal and colonial forces, grew divided. Families were forced to divulge family secrets, communities were torn apart when they disagreed on which side to support, or based on whose children had joined either the freedom fighters or the Rhodesian army. Women and girls became casualties of a war that started before some of their mothers were born. While all women and girls were in danger of sexual violence as soldiers passed through their homesteads, unmarried young women and girls were the most vulnerable. Rather than have their daughters sexually abused, fathers and clan leaders forced very young women into marriages as a kind of protection.

It was within this milieu that I, hardly fourteen years of age, had my first child. By eighteen years of age, I had birthed four.

You see, I come from a long line of women who were forced into a life they never defined for themselves. I had lived my whole life in a poor rural village and had seen how poverty and a lack of education deeply entrenched women in a life of servitude and took away their self-esteem. My own mother and the women before her could only endure their husbands' infidelity, because men are held to a different standard than women. Promiscuity among men is regarded as part of the norm.

Despite my own early and abusive marriage, the determination and brilliance of the women around me, who moved through life with stoicism despite the hardships they faced, planted a seed that stirred a deep hunger in me for a different life. Yet it was not that easy to change my life.

A chance opportunity came when I encountered a visiting American woman who assured me that anything was possible. She reawakened my dream for an education, and for the education of all girls and women in my village. At my mother's urging, I wrote down my dreams, planted them deep in the earth, and prayed they would grow.

They did. With steadfast determination, hard work, and belief in my dreams, I eventually earned not only a PhD, but also a prominent global platform from which I could address world leaders and international audiences, where I could lead the charge in the fight for quality education and women's rights.

In 2012, I founded Tererai Trent International (TTI), an organization working to improve and provide universal access to quality education in rural communities in Zimbabwe. With Oprah Winfrey's generous donation and a partnership with Save the Children, my foundation has impacted nearly six thousand children who are receiving quality education and getting an early start on learning.

We have trained many teachers and built classrooms, and today girls are sitting in classes not only in greater numbers, but also with confidence in a better future. In almost fifty years, no child from Matau School in my community went on to attend university after completing primary and secondary school until my organization was on board. Now the Matau community can boast of several students in different colleges, including one at the University of Zimbabwe, one of the best academic schools in the country, and another at a university in Algeria where he is pursuing a career in medicine. But I am getting ahead of myself.

Long before I landed on Oprah Winfrey's stage as her "favorite guest of all time," before the founding of my nonprofit organization, and before I was a two-time keynote speaker at the UN Global Compact Leaders' Summit, I was simply a woman from humble beginnings who had a sacred dream that was only waiting for me to awaken in order to realize it.

Around the world, women are awakening as in no time in recent history. In January 2017, surrounded by 750,000 people, I marched in the streets of Los Angeles as part of the Women's March. Globally, three million women, men, and children marched that day.

"Do you hear that?" my friend asked as we made our way to the rally. It sounds like a plane, I thought, unable to place the sound. "It's people," she said, tears welling up in her eyes. "It's people!" I reached for her hand, chills of emotion running through me. Soon we could see for ourselves where the hum originated: pulsing throngs of women in a sea of pink hats and brightly colored signs, smiling and chanting together as one. Across the United States, and on every continent that day, women came together with the battle cry of justice and love on our lips.

Afterward the question I heard most was "What now?" We saw what we could do together and now we longed for a blueprint for what to do next, a handbook for manifesting our vision of a better world in big and small ways. This book is that blueprint; from traumatic beginnings, I manifested my vision for a healed world. I offer the storytelling and practices in the pages that follow from my heart to yours in the hopes that they will nurture your awakening as a sacred sister ready to make waves.

Sacred Dreams Manifesto

My sisters, *we women are a massive, untapped, global resource for healing the world*, and we are now rising up all over the world—in the streets, in the home, in the political arenas formerly run solely by men, in academia, in corporations, in the media, and in service to the world. And yet so many of us have, for one reason or another, set aside our deepest wisdoms, our most precious skills, and our most sacred dreams. The events of my early life silenced me, and I know many of you have suffered silences, too. I also know, like me, you can and will awaken and live your *sacred dreams*—a cosmic purpose lying dormant within that waits for you to arise and speak its name. This book is your guide to do this, to uncover and reignite that which is most sacred to you—the dream in your heart and the connection to your global sisters.

Women have a unique capacity to inspire, create, and transform. My mission is to ignite your sacred dreams by providing accessible, intimate, and evocative guidance that encourages you to reexamine your dreams and uncover the power hidden within you—power that can re-create our world for the better. I will tap into the dreams in your heart, give you permission to claim your greatest purpose, and provide you with the tools to forge a brighter path—for all.

This is the movement of the awakened woman, the circle of sacred sisters.

In these pages, I will tend the fire of resilience glowing within you. I will be your companion as you reclaim your potent voice, filling in the past silences. With poetry and storytelling, I will give you the courage to nurture your deepest hungers and discover your sacred dream, to plant and tend the seeds of who you were meant to be, and to align your life in harmony with the greater good.

Poised between the ancient and the modern, a rural village in Zimbabwe and major cities in the United States, I offer you a global perspective on the root causes of women's social devaluing, and our connection across geographic borders. This book is for those women who harbor forgotten or untapped dreams, unheard and overlooked, from the global south to the global north. It is meant to help us remember that we are our own and the world's richest resource.

We need to be remembered—and we need to remember

ourselves—if we are to release this life- and world-changing power. Far too often society does not understand who we are as women. It misreads us. We must come together to proclaim that we are a global matriarchal collective of healers and dreamers. The spirit of this collective can heal nations.

I know that you have a desire in you: a desire to be seen, to be heard, and even to hear yourself more clearly. A desire to dream. I hear those longings. This book will rekindle—or set ablaze—the flame within you. Not only will you see and hear yourself more clearly, but you will also see and hear others that have a burning desire to remove what silences them.

This book harnesses all the lessons and stories I've learned in my own life and in my experiences as an internationally recognized voice in women's empowerment; it will give you the tools to name and manifest your sacred dreams. Weaving indigenous wisdom from my land and people with contemporary research, I hope to bring a unifying and expansive perspective to what it means to become an awakened woman in our modern times.

Now more than ever, when we as a global community face complex problems too big for easy solutions, the world needs the vision, creativity, and voice of the women of the world. We can no longer afford to live our lives cut off from our sacred and collective purpose. The world needs a cadre of *awakened women*—women in touch with the divine in them, women empowered by their femininity, women cultivating their sacred dreams and by doing so nurturing the sacred purpose in all women.

In the chapters that follow, we'll go step-by-step, hand in hand to awaken your sacred dream, spreading out into the fullness of your body, mind, and spirit; proclaiming your worth and your dignity, healing your soul wounds, and empowering you to dream boldly again.

To get the most out of the stories, wisdom, and rituals in this book, I recommend starting a sacred dreams journal in which to chart your insights and growth along the way. You may even want to collaborate with friends or create a reading circle. I have outlined ways of doing this at the end of the book, "Creating Dream Circles of Sacred *Sahwira* Sisterhood."

I also want to mention that each chapter ends with a "Sacred Ritual" for you to practice on your journey to achieve your dreams. Why ritual? Because rituals give strength and direction to a journey. They are what give meaning to an unpredictable world and its forces of silencing. They are the actions we need to walk the path to our dreams with confidence, knowing we are guided by something bigger than we are. Many religions, tribes, and families have their own faith rituals, which they practice without fail to provide meaning to their existence.

This is also true among my Korekore people, for whom rituals are the sacred actions that bind our collective power, grounding our ancient connections to earth and life wisdom. They guide us in how we treat the earth and express our gratitude for the sources of our healing and well-being. My grandmother always reminded her grandchildren that while rituals guide us in achieving our dreams, we should not forget that rituals are the highest platform from which to show our gratitude.

Rituals have been used since the days of the cave dwellers. And my people believe they carry and deliver profound messages from our ancestors and the universe. They not only give meaning to our lives here on earth, but also connect us to the mysteries of the world that the human mind has yet to understand. I live my very life by rituals in honor of those connections. Every breath and action I take is guided by these rituals, as they help me celebrate the joys of my existence while providing me with a mirror through which I can understand loss, sorrow, and my healing. They need to be practiced with humility—they are that important. And *you* are that important. You have the power to practice rituals that will strengthen your belief in yourself and your sacred dreams.

Together, through a mix of indigenous wisdom rooted in sacred experience and generations of lives, modern research, and sacred rituals, we will walk the path to your sacred dreams, a path of joy and discovery as you make your way to your fulfilled self. With each page, each story, each question, I call you to take action: to find your great purpose, reclaim your voice, embrace your body's yearnings, nurture your spirit, and claim your place among the sisterhood of sacred dreamers.

This sacred dream journey is the path of the awakened woman, my sisters. Your dreams are a place where the divine resides. In order to awaken, you must unearth them, nourish them, and walk toward them in body and soul. Once awakened, you embody the divine, capable of healing your own soul and the heart of the world.

THE AWAKENED WOMAN

1

FIND YOUR GREAT HUNGER: THE CALL TO AWAKEN

> *We cannot expect to change what's in the world unless we first awaken what lies deeply within.*
>
> —TERERAI TRENT

We sit barefoot and cross-legged around an open fire. My mother, my grandmothers, my aunts, and all the women and girls of my village are there. The men and boys, who eat separately, have already been given the food we prepared for them. Now, free to say the things we dare not say in the presence of men, free to be ourselves and not simply wives or daughters, we pass around dishes of *sadza*, cornmeal, and the vegetable relishes each of us has brought, and we eat.

Later, after our bellies are full, we begin shelling groundnuts. The moon is round, casting a cool, shimmery halo of light down upon our circle of women while the flames of the fire brighten our faces and bodies with warmth from below. The soil below us is reddish and chalky. I feel it caked on my feet and under my fingernails. A cool night breeze rustles the bulrushes in the fields surrounding our circle.

The day had been long, like many others. Up at sunrise to bring the cattle out to graze. I'd returned at midday to milk the cows, and then it was back out into the fields until dusk, when I'd returned home, hungry and weary. But now the sun has set, and I am warm from the food and fire with the moon rising high in the vast night sky.

Tonight there are no sounds of gunfire from those who are fighting for our independence, or from the white minority who have ruled since the late nineteenth century. And so we women and girls sit, muscles and tongues loose in the comfort of our togetherness, and, as my people have done for generations, we sing songs and tell stories. As the stories warm our hearts we momentarily forget our pain, our struggles, and the impending danger of war. We are enshrined in a circle of healing.

On this night, my grandmother tells a story that was to become part of my psyche even then as a young girl, binding itself to me at the deepest cellular and spiritual level of my being. "The indigenous hunter-gatherer people of Southern Africa from the Kalahari Desert," my grandmother begins, and I nestle the weight of my hips and thighs down deeper into the earth and lean closer to her in anticipation of her tale. "They believe that there is more to life than the material world," she continues. "The men and women there describe two kinds of hunger: the Little Hunger and the Great Hunger."

In the storytelling tradition of my people, stories were not told only once, but were repeated often. New details emerged with each telling and listeners caught different insights as they met old stories as different selves. The story of the Great Hunger, which I heard many different times from many different tellers, grew in me until there was no separation between the story and me. It forever ebbs and flows in my being.

"In my village," my grandmother says, her voice radiating out into the circle, "two sons of a very powerful man were given money to buy the best clothes and toys. Unlike many, their household could also afford plenty of delicious food. Despite a lavish lifestyle, the boys always demanded more money to satisfy their addiction to drugs and alcohol.

"One day, the father asked community elders to help him figure out how to make his sons behave more responsibly, more like other teens in the village.

"The elders determined that the boys were unhappy because they hungered for meaning in their lives. Surprised, the father said, 'But my sons are very happy! I make sure they have everything they want.' The elders pointed out that 'wants' are based on ego and greed, not on needs. When not met, a *need* may result in inequality, poverty, or oppression. 'Wants,' on the other hand, are something we, as human beings, consciously desire, but if 'wants' are not met, life still goes on without negative consequences. 'But I also give my children money so they can meet their needs and can feel good about themselves,' said the rich man."

A few of the women edge toward the embers of fire, stocking the wood to increase both the flame and warmth. My grandmother waits a few moments as the women go about their tending, and then she begins again, "The elders pointed out that money does not create happiness, nor does it build self-esteem. Responsible children are created with empathy, love, and respect, not by giving them stuff. It doesn't nurture our children to flood them with money and expensive gifts that we equate as the expression of a good life. Unfortunately, our wants are often driven by Little Hungers that create a false sense of self."

My grandmother pauses for our attention as she prepares to conclude her tale, although she does not need to do so, for we are enraptured. None of us wants to let *Chikara*,* the Little Hunger, entrap us in its grip and consume us. We sit in anticipation, rocking from side to side on our hips as the story works its way into our skin and down deep into the marrow of our bones. As my grandmother would say, "A story is like a dress, it can either fit perfectly, well defining the contours of our body, or it can have some parts that mismatch those contours, leaving one unhappy." It is up to us, the listeners, to find the

---
* The Shona I use in this book is old Shona. It is still spoken but cannot be found in today's dictionaries.

best parts to wear, to find what best resonates with the soul. In the quiet between her words, we were each trying to find the part of the story that we can wear for life.

"The rich man was silent," she finally said. "He had never thought about 'needs and wants' or happiness in this way. He was advised to send his children to work with others in the community, to have them repair old homes, mentor orphans, to contribute to the welfare of their neighbors. So the boys went to work.

"Not long after, they began to receive compliments for their contributions. They soon began organizing community services and rallying other youths to rebuild the community school. Once their hunger to do good was awakened, these two boys never looked back." The listeners nod and call out "Amen" or let out a trilling cry in response to this tale. We are thrilled by the boys' transformation, longing for the Great Hunger to be awakened in us as well.

My mother, Shamiso, or Grandma-Gogo as the children called her, would say, "*Ndi Chikara akubata*"—"Like a magnet, forever we remain trapped in Little Hunger's grip and become its slave, unless we reflect on the meaning of life's purpose." The Little Hunger can never be satisfied. It always demands more, leaving us exhausted as we try to cope with its unending desires and demands. We become unhappy, vulnerable to risk, and still, we want more. Little Hunger not only leads to dissatisfaction, it also makes us envious, competitive, ungrateful, and anxious. Many unhappy lives and homes are filled with the havoc and damage caused by Little Hunger.

But the Great Hunger—the greatest of all pangs—is the hunger for a life with meaning. The Great Hunger is liberating and energizing; it enables us to move beyond immediate gratification and toward fulfillment. The Great Hunger inspires us, leading us to discover new ways to grow, give, and help others. If you tap into the Great Hunger, you will awaken your sacred dream. With the awakened consciousness of a sacred dreamer, you will come to know yourself as a part of the larger circle of woman, the sacred sisterhood. Your whole life will be a ritual in the service of this great purpose, this togetherness.

My sacred sisters, regardless of our differences, perhaps shaped by class, race, gender identity, and geography, ultimately there is one thing that makes human beings profoundly fulfilled—it is life with meaning.

Unfortunately, the reality of living a contented and fulfilled life is elusive to many of us. Today we live in a society driven by the Little Hungers that overshadow our true happiness and stifle our self-esteem. The voices that define, discourage, and silence us also propel us toward the "wants" of life that are shaped by the Little Hungers rather than the "needs," which are shaped by the Great Hunger. Want status, want wealth, want fame, want beauty, want "likes" and "followers" and "retweets." Oh, my dear sisters, we must gather the strength to go deeper than that.

What is it that you are truly hungry for?
What does your soul need?

There is a deeper hunger that lies within us, waiting to be discovered. It is the innate, human hunger to support one another, though our material desires often mask it. Your task is to listen for the stirring of an insatiable hunger begging you to connect to the world in a new way and to align your dreams with this yearning. The power of the Great Hunger leads us to a different path, a path of the true, authentic self. Once we find our Great Hunger, then the voices that silence us, the names that others use to define us, and the fears that lurk in dark corners, become diminished—and an electrical surge of purpose fills us. Our Great Hunger becomes the source of our calling.

You will know you've found that place when you are aligned with a purpose that makes you come alive, when you feel harmony between your Great Hunger and the needs of others. When we find this place of deep contentment where the Great Hunger resides, then we have awakened our sacred dream and we find abundance and great joy.

I am not saying that once we find our Great Hunger all becomes well. We need healing and we must do the hard work of nurturing our positive traits—resilience, courage, empathy, compassion, loyalty, conscientiousness, and openness. In turn, these traits will nourish us in times of doubt and distress. Tapping into your Great Hunger is not the end of our healing, it is the beginning—the beginning of our collective waking up.

It can be so easy to wear other people's faces: the face of the "committed to commitment" wife, regardless of her unhappiness; the face of the selfless mother, stifling her own dreams; the face of the impoverished "Third World" victim, weighed down by words and terms others put on her with no awareness of her true self; and on and on. What we need more than anything is to feel exuberantly comfortable wearing the face of our true, authentic selves, and this has major consequences for our ability to contribute to the world.

When we are not deeply tapped into our authentic selves, we become divided from ourselves, and as a result, we grow to be divided from one another, from our sacred purpose, and from the world. The world is depending on you to name your Great Hunger, for indeed, awakening to your sacred purpose is a radical, social act. It is time to let your sacred purpose come forth. Like a river flowing, let your Great Hunger pour from you and let it flood the world.

Hear it from the echoes of my own silencing and how that changed once I found my Great Hunger. I can tell you this: without a burning desire to change the trajectory of my life and move toward a purposeful life, I would still be leading an unfulfilled life in my village.

Come sit beside me, dear sister. Smell the burning wood, feel the relief of an evening breeze on your skin after a long day of toil. Despite our struggles, the danger in our environment, and the fear shaped by years of stifling our true selves, let us come and be one in this collective circle of sisterhood. Let us loosen any restrictions on our feminine energy and band together with greater focus. Let us look up at the stars together as the sound of women's laughter dances across the flames. Let us continue this ritual of storytelling that not only allows us to express our joys and sorrows but also awakens the call of our souls.

It is our turn now to be part of the circle, you and me, in our sacred space. May this ritual make us lean in close, strengthening our voices as we build stronger alliances of interlinked networks that know no geographic, racial, ethnic, or economic division. The storytelling ritual will make us celebrate each other, wipe each other's tears, and bring healing to our communities and the world at large.

Let me initiate you into the community of awakened dreamers, the sacred sisterhood. Let us discover and call out your sacred dream, your Great Hunger, knowing that your sisters, hand in hand, are holding you forth.

SACRED RITUAL FOR FINDING YOUR GREAT HUNGER

The most powerful practice for finding your Great Hunger is to ask yourself this simple question: *What breaks my heart?*

Let this question become like a heartbeat: as you wash dishes, rock your child to sleep, commute to work, walk the dog, and breathe in and out, allow this question to pulse within you.

It is not a once and done thing, this Great Hunger of yours, and it is not only for the oppressed and downtrodden. You don't have to feel sad or unfulfilled to have Great Hunger, although I have found that it often most loudly asserts itself during difficult times. Perhaps this is because when life is most challenging it is obvious that we need healing and purpose. But even those of you who may have achieved every goal you ever set for yourself, or found every happiness you ever imagined, have a Great Hunger. As long as there is a need for your voice and talents, the hunger persists.

When you watch the news or when you think about the state of the world today: *What breaks your heart?*

Forever, your Great Hunger continues to call you to become the person you were always meant to be, to reach your full potential, and to heal yourself by caring for your community, even if you're not sure exactly who that person is or how to do it. For me, my desire for an education stemmed from my belief that all the girls in my village, including me, were capable of learning and contributing equally with boys. I had no idea what my life would look like if I followed my Great Hunger, all I knew was the shape of its longing.

You don't have to start big. Just ask yourself: *What breaks my heart?*

I shared this practice with three friends. One immediately said, "I feel heartbroken when I hear of puppies being abused. I feel I can contribute to the well-being of these animals." She quickly mobilized to become a foster home for abused dogs, the ones who rarely get adopted from shelters. Today she helps heal, train, and find good homes for them.

Another said, "My heart hurts when I hear of parents who are cheated by unscrupulous agents when they try to adopt children from foreign countries, but don't know what to do about it. Their stories and pain break my heart. I find myself not sleeping thinking about each situation. I have been there and I'm sure I can help."

The third friend said, "But I don't feel at all silenced or disempowered. I feel I have everything I need and do everything I can." I asked her if she would explore the question anyway. A few days later she called me, stunned and amazed. "I worry about a lot of issues these days, but the answer that came up again and again in response to this question is the Syrian refugee crisis," she said. "That is what most breaks my heart right now. But as soon as I had the thought," she continued, "I felt, well, there's nothing I can do. So I prayed and held it in my mind, not really knowing what to do."

Then she got an email. It was a volunteer request forwarded from a neighbor: a local organization that helps refugee families adjust to life in the US itself needed help. It turns out my friend lives near one of the largest Syrian refugee communities in the nation. "I realized that I did feel disempowered without even knowing it," she reflected. "I assumed I couldn't do anything to ease the pain in my heart and the pain in communities so far away from me. I was wrong. I had way more power than I knew."

Today she has a whole family of new Syrian friends whom she takes grocery shopping, helps learn English, and job search, among other things. She has eaten the best Middle Eastern food of her life, and even hosts potluck dinners to inspire others who would like to help but don't know how. All this happened by naming an unnamed longing in her heart. This is the awakening of our consciousness. When we listen to what makes us ache and breaks our hearts, we find our Great Hunger, our sacred purpose.

If an answer doesn't arise, here is a practice to aid in your asking. Find a quiet place free of distractions, someplace where you can close a door and shut others out, or a space separate from the busy noise of everyday life; this will be your *masowe*, your praying place for your sacred dreams journey. Sit or lie down in a comfortable position, feeling attentive and awake, but also calm and relaxed.

Take a few breaths to wash off the cares of your day so that you are truly present. Take three breaths in through your nose and out through an open mouth, and then a few more, which will aid in circulation, relax the nervous system, and increase oxygen to your lungs.[1] Hear the sound of your breath and notice how your body moves. Notice your chest rising and falling, perhaps even your stomach expanding and softening.

Feel the breath expand into the front, back, and sides of your rib cage as your breath deepens. Let the skin on your forehead melt down toward your nose and let your inner eye and your outer eye sink back.

Notice where your body meets the ground, floor, or chair beneath you. Allow the ground to support you, trusting that you are carried and held by its strength. Breathe into that trust, that support, allow your heart to expand up and out of it, your back straight, your chest slightly open to the space in the room.

After a few moments of quiet, deep breathing in this position, ask yourself: *What breaks my heart?* If it helps, you might also ask: *Where do I look in my community or in the world and feel my heart aching with some lack, pain, or injustice?*

What does my heart long for?

Repeat the questions if you need more time with them:

What breaks my heart?

What in this world makes my heart ache?

What does my heart long for?

While still in your comfortable position in your quiet space, take a few moments to say your answer aloud, even if only fragments or phrases emerge. You may not know what to make of the answer. You may have two, three, or more answers. The answer may not make complete sense to you at this time. All of this is okay. The answer, even if only partially formed, is the beginning of your sacred dreams journey. Be open to anything that surfaces.

No matter what arose in you this is a time for celebration. Take a few breaths of gratitude for the opportunity to explore these questions.

Before returning to your day, I encourage you to write down what you have discovered. Now is a good time to start a journal or keep a notebook to chart your revelations as you read and practice these awakening rituals.

Over the next couple of days, read or state aloud what you discovered in response to the question *What breaks your heart?* Allow yourself to let the responses turn over and float through your daily thoughts and feelings. Begin making connections between your heart's longing and your life. How might your heart's desire become a dream you can achieve? Do you see a connection to something beyond your own personal goals? How? Can you explain it to yourself and to a friend?

Most important, ask, "Do these desires not only heal the past but also uplift generations to come?" Remember, you are not an ordinary dreamer, you are a sacred sister and you dream with a purpose for the greater good.

You will know if the desire in your heart is the kernel of a sacred dream, because it will energize you, invoke your spirit of resilience, un-silence the once silenced voice, speak to issues that matter most, and implore you to encourage other women to do the same. The Great Hunger expects you to honor the greater good with your gifts. This is what gives meaning to life.

Your unique gifts are longing to be expressed, and the Great Hunger will keep on nudging (or pestering) until you respond to the call. The whispers of the Great Hunger are always encouraging us to unlock what is within. Release your Great Hunger and you will be led by it with grace.

2

THE WOMEN THE WORLD FORGOT: RECLAIMING YOUR VOICE

*Words set things in motion. I've seen them doing it.
Words set up atmospheres, electrical fields, charges.*

—TONI CADE BAMBARA

A woman in her late fifties followed me into the restroom after a talk I gave at West Virginia University. I'd talked about family cycles and the pain and shame that poverty, abuse, and poor education disproportionately bring to women and their children. "You brought it home," this woman, Nikita, told me. "That cycle of shame runs deep in my family."

Nikita then tearfully traced for me her matrilineal heritage of poor, uneducated women. Denied an education, Nikita's great-grandmother married young and gave birth to a daughter when she was just a teenager. That daughter, Nikita's grandmother, dropped out of school after eighth grade, married young and also birthed a little girl, whom she raised mostly alone while her husband spent many years in jail; after his release he abandoned his family altogether. Nikita's mother, like her mother and grandmother before her, grew up in poverty. She dropped out of school in seventh grade, barely able to read or write. She eventually turned to selling drugs and prostitution.

Into this cycle of poverty and poor education, Nikita was born. Her script, and that of her children and her children's children, was written for her: before completing high school, Nikita told me, she gave birth to two daughters. Both daughters are serving five-year sentences for dealing drugs. Nikita supports four grandkids, the children of her incarcerated daughters.

Nikita said that my talk opened up a deep stirring in her, a place she had not wanted to visit before. This was the first time anyone had openly named the legacy of lost dreams that brought shame and grief to the women in her family. It had long been a guarded secret, a burden she carried all the time.

"We were really smart people," she reflected. "My mother could listen to a blues song and the next thing she had created something similar, but deep. Both my daughters were math wizards," she remembered with a glow of nostalgic pride and more than a strain of sadness.

At fifty, Nikita's dreams weren't much more than a memory, her longings haunted by the lost dreams of her mother, grandmother, and great-grandmother before her. We hugged, and as I was about to leave the restroom, Nikita whispered through her tears, "I come from generations of silenced and forgotten women." And before I could recover from how she had combined those two words to define herself, Nikita continued, "Though inside, I do not feel broken. Deep down inside me, I can still feel my hopes and dreams."

Silenced yet unbroken; the fire of resilience remains.

Not all women grow up in homes like Nikita's, of course, but most of us grew up in a world that in one way or another stifled our dreams. As girls we have so many ideas and dreams and we are filled with such promise, a hunger for something more than what our ancestors or our mothers had. And whether it's through an impoverished childhood, abuse, or the bias and discouragement of a culture that disapproves of feminine power, women get very good at putting those dreams on the shelf. We promise ourselves we'll come back to them, but often they become distant memories, faded and cracked like old photographs.

I meet these women all across the globe; they tell me their stories in the hopes that someone will hear and see them, at last. A career woman who worked her way up a male-dominated corporate ladder only to discover that what she really wants is to move out to the country and spend time with her kids. An intelligent African grandmother thrilled to see her granddaughter learn to read, but secretly harboring shame because of her own illiteracy. A mother of four who is repeatedly told that she is "too old" to finish her college degree yet yearns to learn. A forty-year-old teacher who has achieved her professional and personal goals but can't help wondering, "Isn't there something more?" A thirty-seven-year-old writer who wonders, "At my age, am I still allowed to change my mind, to shift my life course?"

Every day I hear of stories and experiences like these, stories that merge and weave into my own story. Although it looks different at different times and in different places, and they emerge from the realm of religion, politics, education or lack thereof, or even our own families, the problem of women's silencing is a global one.

There are messages coming from all directions that say: you are not good enough as you are; you are not of much use to the world; you do not have the resources to be empowered; you are too old to be in the public eye; you are too ignorant to understand the world around you—even things that concern your own life; you are not pretty enough to be useful. "The heart of a woman goes forth with the dawn," as Harlem Renaissance poet Georgia Douglas Johnson wrote.[1] But as far and as confidently as it roams, searching for a world willing to meet it in its full glory, a woman's heart returns in the night, Johnson tells us, dreams deferred, breaking against the bars of injustice, or invisibility, or fear.

And you, sister, what are the words that define or limit you? What are the words you do not yet have? What silences your dreams? Are there deafening silences in your life? Where have you hidden your girlhood hopes and dreams? Can you still hear them? What is the "more" buried deep inside you that you are afraid to ask for? What is your Great Hunger?

Many of us have lost touch with our dreams. We are afraid to speak them, as I was, because we feel certain those words will fall on deaf ears, or worse, that we will be mocked or sneered at. Perhaps no one bothers to ask us our dreams anymore. Or we are afraid to proclaim that the socially sanctioned dreams we have achieved—the big career, for example, or a glamorous wedding—are not as satisfying as we were told they would be.

We might be more silent than we were built to be, but we are certainly not broken. In the face of doubt and questioning our voice, and in a profoundly divisive world, we can create a global choir of transformation, unity, and healing if we gather the courage to speak our truth.

Our Silencing

I am intimately familiar with how it feels to be a woman forgotten: devalued, dismissed, and disempowered by social forces beyond my control. My story may be very different from women across the globe who have also experienced silencing, but I hope that from telling my story, and the stories of others who have shared with me, I can shed some light and try to make sense of what our collective silencing looks like so that we can give shape to our absence and heal our voicelessness. It is one of my passions to investigate the root causes of this silencing because it is through understanding that we can imagine ways of reclaiming our voice.

At the end of 1979, just as the War of Liberation, the civil war that had raged for over fifteen years in my country, was coming to an end, I was pregnant and, in the New Year, when I was hardly fourteen years of age, I gave birth to my first child. My mother named him Tsungai, which means "persevere," indicating the long road I was going to travel, the same pathway that generations of women before me had traveled.

By eighteen years of age, I had given birth to four children, one of whom died as an infant when I was unable to produce enough milk to feed him. I was a child myself. I felt invisible in my marriage; the clinking of dirty dishes, the sound of rags scrubbing the floors, and water sloshing as I washed baby diapers were the sounds that swallowed my existence. I would clean the house, take care of the children, and do all the chores—things culturally delegated to women—as my husband did not help with such things.

He would be away from the house for long periods of time, I knew not where. Rumors would reach me that he was having many affairs. Afraid to ask him for the truth, I would refuse to share a bed with him, which led him to beat me since he expected his conjugal rights, as he had paid a cow in exchange for our marriage and me. Although I despised my many marital obligations, there was also a part of me that wanted to belong, to be a good wife despite the silencing of my soul that my marriage demanded. Every time I yielded to the voice of belongingness, I felt myself slipping further into invisibility.

In my culture, all people are known through their *mutupo* (totem), an ethnic clan identity represented by an animal or animal body part. Individuals within the clan are addressed by their totems, such as Nzou, the Elephant; Mhofu, the Eland; Shumba, the Lion; Hungwe, the Bird; Nyati, the Buffalo; Soko, the Monkey; Moyo, the Heart; and so on. Although men and women share totems based on patrilineal ancestry, male family members carry the totem while a woman adopts the totem of her husband's family when she marries. A totem serves as a family emblem that encompasses social identity and collective pride, as well as a bond of unity within the group. It was a curse to have fatherless children or children with different *mutupos*, and so I felt stuck.

The sexual trauma of my early marriage damaged me for life. My culture had a strong code of silence around such trauma. These issues were not openly discussed, although it was made clear that "good" girls remain in their marriages no matter what. Like many young women, while I did my best and tried to behave like a good woman, my husband's promiscuous behavior was held to a different standard. When I shared my concerns with my in-laws or with his sisters, I was told that this was part of the marriage.

I realized some of my friends accepted such marriages and that society expected women to remain in these relationships for the sake of the children. I quickly learned that it was expected for men to have multiple, concurrent sexual partnerships. Sexual abuse, rape, and coerced sex occurred frequently, and yet many in my society blamed women for this abhorrent behavior.

Around this time, during the middle of the war, I got a surprise visit from my brother Tinashe, who had run away from the fighting. He arrived at my husband's community in the middle of the night, slept at a nearby store, and showed up at my in-laws' home early in the morning. He found me sweeping the yard, and before I could see him I heard his voice. "Tererai, is that you?" he said with tears streaming down his face.

We spent the day talking about the war and the suffering it brought to communities and families. The following day he left without a word. I was later told that he took the first bus very early in the morning. I was deeply saddened. Little did I know that he had been so concerned with my situation that he rushed back home to tell my mother how he found me. My mother took advantage of one of my father's many disappearances and dispatched my cousin, Sekuru Munemo, to bring me back to my home village. Sekuru arrived at the home of my husband's family just a few days later to find a sad and skinny girl in a torn red dress. I will never forget the first words out of his mouth: "Sekuru Munemo has come to take you home to your mother."

Leaving my marriage cast me as a pariah. Even relatives and friends whispered behind my back, "*Aiwa rangove gaba, nyuchi ne hunchi hwadzo zvakaenda kare*"—"Eh, she is now an empty can—valueless." Single women are considered unstable, with the belief that only marriage gives a woman stability and worthiness. "The bees and honey are long gone," they say, meaning that I am no longer a virgin, and now I am called *mvana* or *nzenza* (unchastely, a slut). I had a ninth-grade education and no source of income, three young children, and the mark of shame upon me.

Nevertheless, I believed that I could find work. At the age of twenty, my first job was as a cleaner for a local bus company in Chinhoyi, a midsized town between Harare and Karoi toward the Chirundu border, an immigration border post that demarcates Zimbabwe and the Republic of Zambia. The Harare-to-Chirundu bus route is busy, which meant that I was at work in the early morning to clean toilets, dishes, and floors left dirty by night drivers and conductors. Because the owner of the company made constant excuses on payday, I hardly got paid. He was notorious for sexually abusing female workers, and many victims became his wives. I could not stand this man and stayed as far away from him as possible, but I was desperate to keep the job so I would tread lightly. Those who married him were hostile to new girls who joined the company. That there was so much mistrust among women seemed a pity to me.

I had this job for almost a year when the owner told me that he could no longer afford to pay me. When I asked about being paid for work already done, he invited me to discuss this in his chambers. Instead, I packed my stuff and ran home to my children.

Without a job, I began to feel desperate. Around this time I met a man named Zuda and we quickly became friends. Zuda seemed different, and as friends we confided about our past lives. He actually took some responsibility for his previous failed marriages and was understanding about my own past. After a year of courtship I thought he would be a great husband. It suited my patriarchal family fine that my second husband paid a bride price befitting a "damaged" woman, which was enough to buy a cow.

In marrying again, I was comforted with the knowledge that I had a place to rest my head, as did my children. But three months into the marriage I learned some difficult truths about my husband. He was prone to violent mood swings, using controlling behavior and demeaning language in order to get what he wanted.

When he told me I was worthless, I believed him. When he told me I would be an embarrassment to my family if I dare thought of leaving him, I believed him. When he whispered to me that, after all he had found me "used," and not a virgin, and that leaving him would tarnish my image, I believed him. I put stock in stories I heard from older women about how their husbands changed over time. I bought into the traditional notion that children need a father and a mother living in one home. I joined with other young women as we prayed together, hoping that our husbands would change someday, too.

Then one day, I found Zuda in bed with a young girl. "How could you do this to me?" I asked him. He became enraged that I dared to confront him, flailing his arms in the air and shouting so close to my face that I could feel his spit as he enunciated each word.

"You have no right to challenge me," he sneered. "You have no right to stop me from sleeping with any woman I want." And then, as if to completely undermine me, he added, "I fulfilled my responsibility to you by paying a bride price to your parents. If it doesn't suit you, give me back the cow I paid to your people."

One morning, I went to the local clinic with some stomach pain only to be told I had a sexually transmitted disease. When I confronted my husband, he accused me of being promiscuous. Terrified and hurt, the painful warts further shaming me, I accused him of bringing HIV, a terrible disease that was running rampant in our community, into our family. He beat me until I could hardly stand. With blood pouring from my mouth and from the delicate skin of my thighs, which were already bruised from previous beatings, Zuda stood over me hurling insult after insult down at me. "My children," I thought to myself, and my eyes scanned the room until I saw them. They were cowered up against the wall, holding tightly to each other, fear darkening their bright brown eyes.

Then the voices of our neighbors standing around outside reached my ears. They had heard us. It was a further embarrassment to me to have another woman witness my own beating. Women are supposed to preserve the sanctity of marriage at all costs and remain proud to be married. As though reading my fear, Zuda kicked me so hard that I was hurled outside for the world to see how despicable and unworthy of a wife I was. The neighbors gawked at the sight of me as they witnessed the insults. My daughter, Sibo, hardly eight years old, walked slowly toward me with an old dirty cloth. She leaned down and wiped away the tears, which were now mingling with blood from a forehead wound.

Overwhelmed with the task, she sat down next to me, crossed her arms over her tiny knees, and let her head fall forward onto her arms. She was so close that I could smell the dust on her dress. I longed to reach out and curl her into my arms, but I was afraid I might further infuriate my husband and place my daughter in danger. Shame and isolation made its way into the pit of my stomach and settled there.

Hurting and too embarrassed to seek help, I tried to nurse my own wounds, but the gaping slash just below my knee would not heal. In the days that followed, I developed a fever that I could not get rid of. Then the wound below my knee began to turn green. One morning, my neighbor found me lying outside in the sun, shivering and sweating with a pounding headache. She immediately found me a car that took me to the hospital. As I sat in the hospital being cleaned and sewn back together by the nurse and a doctor, my mind wandered back to my public humiliation, the insults, and the faces of my children. I left the hospital with antibiotics and, having nowhere else to go, I returned to my abuser.

A few days later, I woke up nauseous and vomiting. It was a struggle to focus. Food tasted different and I developed a terrible craving for the residue created by bark-eating termites on nearby trees. "Oh," I moaned. "I must be pregnant." Part of me thought having children with this man might make me a good wife. As I sucked soil from a termite mound, I wondered how on earth I would support my children. Deep down, I knew that with each pregnancy, I slipped further and further into poverty and dependence on a man.

In that moment of grief and hopelessness, a story I'd recently heard about a woman who ended her own life surfaced and took hold of my thoughts. After years of enduring backbreaking labor growing cotton, the woman learned that her husband used all of her earnings to bring home a third wife instead of supporting his existing wives and children. Shattered, the woman killed herself by ingesting the same toxic pesticide commonly used to control cotton bollworms.

I pushed my body up against the tree, the taste of soil still fresh in my mouth, and considered ending my life, too. Another toxic marriage, another child brought into a world of violence and pain, another life that I could not support on my own—it was too much to bear.

Much to my surprise I felt a stirring in me for my own mother, Grandma Gogo, Shamiso. My longing was not for death, I realized, but for the woman who gave me life. Instead of suicide, I would go to the only place I had left to go: back home to my mother.

I knew I had had enough.

I did not sleep at all the night before I left. I was too nervous. My neighbor helped me by holding on to a few of my belongings like cloths for my children and myself. In the morning, she sent her young kids over to invite mine to play at her house. As soon as Zuda left the house for work, without even a chance to bathe, I ran to my neighbor's, retrieved my children and my few possessions, and we ran all the way to the bus terminal. I could see my own fear reflected in my children's eyes as they looked back, afraid that someone might see us and alert Zuda.

The journey was long, even though the bumpiness of the ride suggested the driver was in a hurry, too. In order to avoid the large potholes on the tarred road, the bus driver swung the tires out left and right, and the knot in my stomach twisted as we careened through the traffic. After almost three hours, the road became dusty and we left paved roads behind us. The bus gathered speed and a thick red dust flew through the vehicle's broken windows, painting the passengers' hair and eyelids red. The dust on the road made it difficult to tell where we were, but almost an hour later, we knew we had arrived at our destination when the bus conductor shouted the name of the homestead adjacent to the terminal, "*Noti, Noti.*"

My rural childhood home is not far from the bus station. I could see both my mother and Mbuya Mafukeni, my surrogate grandmother, winnowing bulrushes for grinding. The kids ran to greet their grandmother and I followed more slowly behind, limping from my wound. Both women stood still looking at me as though rooted in one place.

I made my way to them; unable to keep my composure as they walked toward me, I felt tears begin to stream down my cheeks. We approached each other and my grandmother reached out her hands to me as she said, "*Yahwe, usacheme, misodzi yako unoshungurudza vana nevanga risingapore*"—"Child, don't cry, please don't, your tears will trouble your children and leave a permanent mark on their heart, please don't cry." I fell into my mother's arms while my grandmother took my bags from my shoulders. I held on to my mother's shoulder as I listened to my grandmother telling me that just this morning my mother told her of a dream she had about me. Both women suspected something was wrong. "In my dreams, you were crying" is all my mother said.

We settled in my mother's kitchen. Mbuya Mafukeni went outside and came back with some aloe vera leaves, guavas, and other herbs. She quickly boiled the concoction and then applied it first to my wound, then giving me the rest to drink. I didn't have to tell the story, as the kids had already shared what had happened to me. I could tell by the look on my mother's face, as she listened, that the news of my treatment brought her unbearable pain. "This is home for all of you," she said, comforting us, her voice soothing and firm. "Stay as long as you want."

Over the next few weeks, my leg began to heal, but although I was in the presence of my mother, my grandmothers, and my aunts, my spirit remained troubled. My situation had improved, but I was still stuck in many ways. Poverty, lack of education, too few jobs available, and children to mother—these things still weighed heavily on me.

One afternoon my mother and I went off to fetch water together. It was springtime and the forest made many offerings of fruit and nuts. Our fingers ran across the familiar stems and berries, gingerly harvesting as we walked.

From above us, grebes, freshwater diving birds, swooped down for food in the river where we collected our water. We talked as women often did, of our situation as women, of the changes we had begun to see in our newly independent country, of the past and our hopes for the future. "You are following a path that has existed for generations, Tererai," my mother told me. "It comes from a blindness shaped by ignorance, ignorance that grows out of poverty, war, and lack of education."

I nodded my head as I listened, too deflated and hopeless to say anything in response. "We all know this," she continued. "My mother knew it and her mother before her. We speak to each other and we stand up for ourselves when possible, but for the most part, we are silent. We say to ourselves, 'This is our culture and our tradition. It is just the way things are.' But this is not true. It will not always be this way. Someone needs to break the cycle."

The river gurgled powerfully by as we paused for a moment in the shade. "Who will break the cycle?" I wanted to ask, but remained silent.

Soul Wounds

We might think that the easiest thing to do in the face of so much silencing would be to put our hope in future generations. But this struggle does not end with us. The vicious cycle of silencing women is not only in Nikita's or my ancestral village, it's global, and it forces women to make drastic decisions that further marginalize them, which in turn seals their fate at various levels of trauma to the soul.

Dr. Bertice Berry, an award-winning comedienne, motivational speaker, and sitcom star of *The Bertice Berry Show*, crystallized the viciousness of intergenerational family cycles when she said that with no intervention we stay trapped in these negative cycles, as our parents and their parents before them were. In her book *The World According to Me*, Dr. Berry describes this generational curse: "Your parents were running a relay 'round a track and when you came along, they passed you the baton. You never really got to ask if this was your race. . . . The pressure to keep going in the same direction, as fast as possible, is intense."[2] No one can end this race without a powerful intention to change direction.

My mother realized that if someone in our family and community was to break the cycle, she was going to have to achieve an almost impossible dream, a dream that would right the wrongs of generations and tear down barriers for girls. It was going to take a bold dream. And I had one—an insatiable hunger for education and for change to come to my village. Perhaps the most important gift my mother ever gave me was this: she made it clear to me that I had the right to dream, no matter the circumstances of my life.

The truth is, if we don't make it our mission to speak our truths in the face of so much silencing, we may not be putting our hope in the next generation, but instead passing down our silences to them. Lakota social work professor Maria Yellow Horse Brave Heart calls this "historical trauma": "the cumulative emotional and psychological wounding over the lifespan and across generations."[3] She also uses the phrase "soul wound" to explain this phenomenon.

Researchers have long thought that descendants of people who have lived through hardship are likely to pass on their trauma by way of socialization cues like sharing their own fears, anxieties, and depression. But cutting-edge research now shows that this intergenerational wound is also an embodied one. Science is now helping us see that trauma is not only transmitted through social and cultural expressions, but that social experiences of suffering actually permeate our biological makeup—past traumas of our families are stored *in our cells*. Experts call this "epigenetics."[4]

If science is right, certainly my body and thus my mind got my share of a full load of traumas from both my maternal and paternal grandmothers. While these women were strong in their own right, they came from their mothers' wombs carrying some deep wounds, some more visible than others. While the women on my maternal side seemed to have more resilience, a drive to improve their lives despite the silences, the suffering of my paternal grandmother and her mother before her felt more visceral to me. My father's mother, Ambuya Muzoda, was a very quiet woman. She was married to my grandfather, VaKabayashe, an emotionally abusive husband, and my paternal grandmother learned early to assume a submissive role during her many years of suffering.

To understand the depth of her struggles and why she allowed this level of abuse in her life, one must understand something about the man she married. VaKabayashe came from a polygamous family with many sons. He only married six times, but because a man is expected to inherit the wife and children of his deceased brothers and nephews, it is said that he fathered approximately forty children with as many as ten different women. Coping with a polygamous life is never an easy thing. Jealousy among co-wives and backbiting to seek attention from the man is rife. Ambuya Muzoda's pain was unbearable, and as a young girl and mother, I would often hear her say, "*Maivavo-inga barika moto unopisa*"—"Hear me, mother, truly polygamy is like a hot charcoal that burns your soul."

From Ambuya Muzoda I learned that gender inequality has the power to crush a woman's spirit. She firmly believed that young wives will only get into trouble by speaking out. She often said, "It is best to keep quiet and avoid saying things that trigger insults or beatings from a husband." Ambuya Muzoda suggested that I pretend to have a mouthful of holy water that cannot be swallowed and can only be spit out at the end of an argument. In other words, keep quiet! She says this is the best way for wives to keep the peace at home. After all, one wouldn't want an abuser to have the satisfaction of seeing a woman's tears. To my grandmother, the suffering of women was a curse with no solution.

I did not agree with my grandmother's water strategy, but I also refused to let a husband see my tears. Early in my own first marriage, my husband encountered my stubborn refusal to cry. During fights, I wouldn't speak or fight back. I showed no emotion at all. I wouldn't give him the satisfaction. Instead, I'd bite my lower lip to hold back tears just as I did as a child working in the fields. This infuriated him and caused such incidents to escalate into assaults. And then blood and tears would begin to mingle. But to me, blood was better than Ambuya Muzoda's approach. Although I admired her dignity, I did not want to live a passive life if I could avoid it.

My grandmother was a beautiful, dignified woman, but she passed down to me the trauma of being a woman in a patriarchal culture. She passed down her soul wound. She did not know any other way to protect and guide me.

Perhaps we haven't all experienced such profound trauma, but I'm willing to bet that you've suffered silences, indignities, sexism, or lost the pull of your girlhood dreams. What are your soul wounds? Can you afford to give those wounds to the next generation? "Our ancestors dreamed us up," writes educator and poet Walidah Imarisha, "and then bent reality to create us."[5] What can you dream up for yourself and the world for the good of generations to come?

What all of these stories and experiences of silencing show is a world in which we are too often stripped of our full humanness—our dignity. I know that the women in this chapter do not struggle in exactly the same way, nor do all of you who are reading this book struggle in exactly the same way. Yet I feel a deep connection with all women living in patriarchal cultures (and that's pretty much all of us *still*). Even though we come from different circumstances, I recognize the pattern repeating in its various incarnations, whether on social media, in boardrooms, or even on the floor of the US Senate.

Any message, whether overt or subtle, that tells you that it is your job to be pretty, to remain young or else stay out of the public eye, to stay in abusive relationships, to stay subordinate in relationships, to be quiet, to focus on your clothing and hair at the expense of your political and economic and intellectual power—this is the status quo biting back at your emerging empowerment, trying to make you feel smaller and weaker and incapable. We might think that things are getting better and that without our active involvement the world will still become a better place for our daughters and little sisters and nieces. But if we do not claim our full human dignity, do not find our purpose and awaken our sacred dreams, we will pass the loss of ourselves down to the generations that come after us, as my grandmother tried to do with me.

Whether you are a wealthy, highly educated female politician in the US, an Iranian woman lawyer, or a poor illiterate woman in Zimbabwe, there are forces telling you: stay quiet, be meek, focus on your hair or your weight rather than your wisdom, your creativity, your intelligence; be young and pretty or be invisible. Isn't it a shame that men's worth is measured by their intellectual acumen, how much money they are making, or their contributions to society, while women's worth is measured by their physical appearance or their reproductive capabilities?

The messages are there—in the form of sexist words from colleagues, or from invisibility in the media, or poverty, or religious ideology, or sexist partners, and in many other ways. But that doesn't mean we can't do something about it—in fact, as an older woman, I feel it is my responsibility and that of others like me to do our part to stop the intergenerational trauma of feminine silencing. You do not have to march in the street (but if you do, I'll see you there!). You do not have to have a lot of money. But you do have to do the work it takes to awaken—to be courageous enough to name the

Great Hunger within you and to claim your right to give voice to your sacred dream.

Split the World Open

Well-known and much-loved poet Adrienne Rich once wrote that fellow poet and political activist Muriel Rukeyser "was one of the great integrators, seeing the fragmentary world of modernity not as irretrievably broken, but in need of societal and emotional repair."[6] And what was one of Rukeyser's most frequent prescriptions for societal and emotional repair? If even one woman "told the truth," she wrote in one absolutely stunning poem, "The world would split open."[7]

When sleeping women wake, goes an old Chinese proverb, mountains move. It is important for us to know that we are never irretrievably broken, but simply in need of social and emotional healing, a healing that comes when women wake up—when we tell the truth about our lives.

This is what I call the sacred dreams movement. It is pioneering American feminist Gloria Steinem celebrating the bright abundance of many torches carried by women young and old: "At my age," Steinem reflects, "in this still hierarchical time, people often ask me if I'm 'passing the torch.' I explain that I'm keeping my torch, thank you very much—and I'm using it to light the torches of others. Because only if each of us has a torch will there be enough light."[8]

It's Laymah Gbowee, who won the Noble Peace Prize in recognition of her efforts to end war in Liberia by leading the Liberian Mass Action for Peace, a coalition of Christian and Muslim women who sat in public protest of their ruthless president and rebel warlords. It's also everyday grandmothers, mothers, students, nurses, teachers, accountants, and more, who dare to awaken and in awakening are capable of splitting the world open.

It's Muriel Rukeyser's question writ large: What would happen if every woman—whether barefoot or stiletto-clad—told her truth?

It's you and me, and everyone in between, harnessing our inner light, reconnecting with our dreams. Then, surely, our collective stories will split the world open and make it anew.

I also hear the voices of resistance to my words. There is no need for a "movement" to empower women to achieve their dreams, they say. Women and men are already equal, in the US and other countries in the global north, at least. Everything is fine, no need to make changes. It's true that we have reached a point in history when women are entering professions formerly accessible only to men. And while women in politics, women-centered films, and women in the workforce are inspirations to us all, there is often a darker side to these achievements. We see, time and time again, that women who harness the full power of their voices are often targets of misogyny.

For example, Lindiwe Mazibuko, parliamentary leader of South Africa's Democratic Alliance (DA) from October 2011 until May 2014, was subjected to near constant sexism from the African National Congress, the DA's main opposition party. During a 2013 parliamentary debate, one male MP rose and said: "While the Hon[orable] Mazibuko may be a person of substantial weight, her stature is questionable."[9] Other male MPs have demanded during a debate that "she must explain to this house what has she done to her hair" and remarked that she had been "arrested by the fashion police" for her "bad fashion taste." Mazibuko knows she's not alone. "It happens all over the world," she reflects. "If it's not Julia Gillard [Australia's first female prime minister] or Hillary Clinton, it's somebody else."[10]

And just recently, we in the United States saw Senator Elizabeth Warren censured by the majority male Senate from reading, on the floor of the Senate during the confirmation hearing of Senator Jeff Sessions as attorney general, a letter by civil rights leader Coretta Scott King. Mitch McConnell's words ring out all too familiarly to women everywhere: "She was warned. She was given an explanation.

Nevertheless, she persisted."[11] Several of Senator Warren's male colleagues read the same letter the next day without a word of complaint or protest from the other senators.

"Mom, what will it take for American women to be treated as equals in politics?" my daughter asked me on the phone just a few days after news of Warren's silencing spread. The weight of her sadness took the air out of my lungs. I could feel the feminine, and the feminist, in her wavering. My daughters came here with the strong belief that America, their mother's choice country for an education, was a place for women to thrive. The foundation of this belief was shaken to the core.

The battle for equality is still very much alive in one of the most powerful countries in the world as much as it is elsewhere. This is not the first time a woman in power has been silenced. But it is not only happening in political platforms; we have experienced it in ourselves, we have seen it in the corporate world, and sometimes we have seen it in our own girls.

The silencing of our sisters as they rise to power is our collective silencing, just as we suffer along with our sisters as we watch the media objectify women and make profit from our devaluation. The need to awaken not only our own dreams but those of other women as well is just as urgent now as it ever was. I have traveled the world and seen much sadness and listened to many people—I know the hunger in women is there; the need is there. I know of my own hunger and I know it is shared; I know its depths and its longings. Women silencing their dreams are real.

On the other hand, people say: But there is so much oppression and inequality and suffering that we can't possibly do anything about it. It will never end, what can I do about it in my little part of the planet? The answer to this I have also seen and heard: individuals, in their own big and small ways, on their own little patches of earth, recovering their own light and sharing it with the world.

Indeed, Mazibuko says that however depressing this treatment may be, to her it's also a good sign: "It's a signal that we're a force to be reckoned with," and only strengthens her "resolve to root out sexism in the house and also make sure I keep doing what I do to make sure a woman in a leadership position in a political party in parliament is no longer seen as some kind of aberration."[12] Similarly, Senator Warren's silencing on the Senate floor was not only a source of outrage for many American women, it was also a rallying cry. Simply because she persisted: for herself, for Coretta Scott King, and for justice for all people.

Consider Brazilian tattoo artist Flavia Carvalho's simple yet profound "A Pele da Flor" (The Skin of the Flower) project: the artist offers free tattoos to women who want to cover scars they received from domestic violence or from mastectomies.[13]

A love of art combined with an education in biological sciences led to scientific illustration, and from there Carvalho began working as a tattoo apprentice. After a client sought her out to tattoo over an abdominal scar—the client had been stabbed by a man she had rejected in a club—Carvalho realized the power that her art and her craft could offer survivors of abuse or illness. She makes beauty on the skin in places where once there was only evidence of suffering. She turns wounds into brightly colored flowers and birds and goddesses.

And this one idea, by this one woman, working in what many would consider a very average, unglamorous job, has caught the attention of nongovernmental organizations (NGOs), and Carvalho is partnering with the Municipal Secretariat of Policies for Women in Brazil to serve an even broader community of survivors. This is the sacred dreams movement in action: Carvalho followed her dream of being an artist and now she is helping to heal the world in her own unique way.

There is no limitation to what you can do when you learn to listen to the stirrings of purpose inside of yourself—and when we all live that truth, we make up a mighty collective indeed.

When I was young, ten to fifteen of us girls in my village would play a game. We'd form a big circle and hold hands and sing. Two girls would stand in the middle of the circle clapping to our song, which dared the two in the middle to break through any part of the circle they thought was not strong. As we sing we move with the rhythm of the song, circling the two girls in the middle. They in turn move in the opposite direction as they follow the circle looking for a weak link. Our voices rise as we sing our lungs out, our bare feet dancing in unison, and our watchful eyes never leaving the two girls in the circle.

In call and response, we of the circle sing *"Apa pakasungwa nehutare"*—"This part of the bond is tied with metal chains." The girls in the center sing in reply *"Apa zinyekenyeke ke?"*—"Could this be the part of the chain that is loose, and how very loose is loose?"

As the song's rhythm increases, our hands clasp more tightly together, forming an even stronger bond. The anticipation of succeeding is palpable. No one in the group wants their part of the chain to break because if it does, this destroys the whole chain. We are guarded, each knowing her purpose. Our ultimate goal: never to break the chain.

Each member of the group strengthens the chain. Blame for breaking the link is never on the individual level; we believe there is a surge of blood running through the circle, and as each person receives their dose, they pass it on to the person next to them. Our little palms are the conduit for channeling this life-giving blood, this energy. If the chain breaks, it could be due to a weak flow of blood anywhere along the circle, not necessarily at the spot where it occurred. We are all responsible for the circle as a whole.

On the sidelines, a few adults clap to the rhythm of the song, cheering for the strength of our unbreakable bond. And if the circle does break, they are also there to remind us that it is reparable. If one of the two girls inside the circle manages to break through the circle, then the pair whose small fingers let go of the hand clasp leave the circle and go for "repair"—in other words, to refresh their strength—while their place is taken by those who are standing by.

As part of the circle, this game reminded each girl of the purpose of our bond: that we have the power to conquer whatever comes our way. We gripped each other so hard that our hands often turned red, and this little pain reminded us of the part we play in the collective bond. We all longed to play our part in creating the strongest possible circle, our existence validated by the simple, playful act of doing our small part.

When we forget what we can accomplish by holding the hands of other women, we can lose our sense of purpose and that of our power. The sacred dreams movement happens when we remember what we can do. By reclaiming our part in the collective circle, and by joining this circle, we share our courage with the world around us.

SACRED RITUAL FOR RECLAIMING YOUR VOICE

Every journey begins with a dream. How do we get in touch with dreams if we have let them sit idle or procrastinated on them for years? If we have listened instead to the voice of "reason," doubt, or societal pressures that have seemingly required or asked us to ignore our deepest longings? It's simple, you take back your power and begin again—by *reflecting* on your heart's deepest longings.

Embolden yourself now to name your dreams. To do this you must get over anything blocking them from surfacing in your body and soul. Ask yourself this question: *Do you truly believe you have a right to dream?*

What is your first response to that question? What immediately comes to you? There's no need to judge or analyze your answer, just acknowledge it. Spend a few moments either writing your responses down or speaking them aloud.

Achieving your heart's desire and reclaiming your truest, most authentic voice are grounded in the belief that you have a right to dream and that you deserve complete fulfillment. Know that your dreams are precious. They are yours to ignite and develop. No one can take them away. No matter your circumstances, your dreams are valid.

In celebration of your right to dream and in a battle cry against any hurdles you may continue to face, whether in your own heart or in the world, I invite you to ululate to claim your voice. Ululation is an ancient sound, practiced not only by Africans but by many ancient cultures, including the Greeks and the Egyptians. It is a loud, high-pitched sound, like a cry or a song. It has been used for thousands of years the world over to express grief or to celebrate rituals. It is primarily a sound made by women.

There are as many different ways to ululate as there are cultures that practice it, but here are my simple instructions: make a high-pitched sound of "lulululululu" as loud as you can as you wag or trill your tongue side to side in your mouth. If you feel embarrassed by the thought of this ritual, or are worried you will do it "wrong," just notice those feelings. Choose to use your voice anyway. Seek to fill the room with your voice. If it wavers or cracks, just keep going. Use your whole diaphragm to make sound. You do not have to hit any key. You just need to let the force of your voice ring out from deep in your belly to the corners of the room. Laugh and try again.

Sit in the quiet that remains after your ululation and let the sound of your voice still reverberate in your ears.

With your notebook or journal reflect on the following:

+ How have the present and past shaped you?

+ What soul wounds are you carrying? Are you what had happened to you? Is that what you choose to become?

Take a few moments to write down your thoughts. Dear sister, it is important to be conscious of who we are, and to face the shadows of our past so that we can move to a place of self-acceptance, forgiveness, wholeness, and love.

- What is the purpose bigger than yourself that your desires are aligned with?

- Do you see your right to dream aligned with the needs of others?

Write down your thoughts to these questions. As you write, feel yourself tethering your heart's desires to the greater good, growing in confidence that you have a right to dream as a birthright of your humanness, and that your dreams are part of a collective whole. Allow your heart to fill with the knowledge of your right to dream, having named your limitations and obstacles, and then overcome them with a shared purpose greater than any voice of doubt or any hardship.

Now turn your focus inward, linking your inner voice with your outer voice. Imagine creating your life in tune with the deeper, inner authority of your soul. This inner knowing is your true guide to your sacred dream.

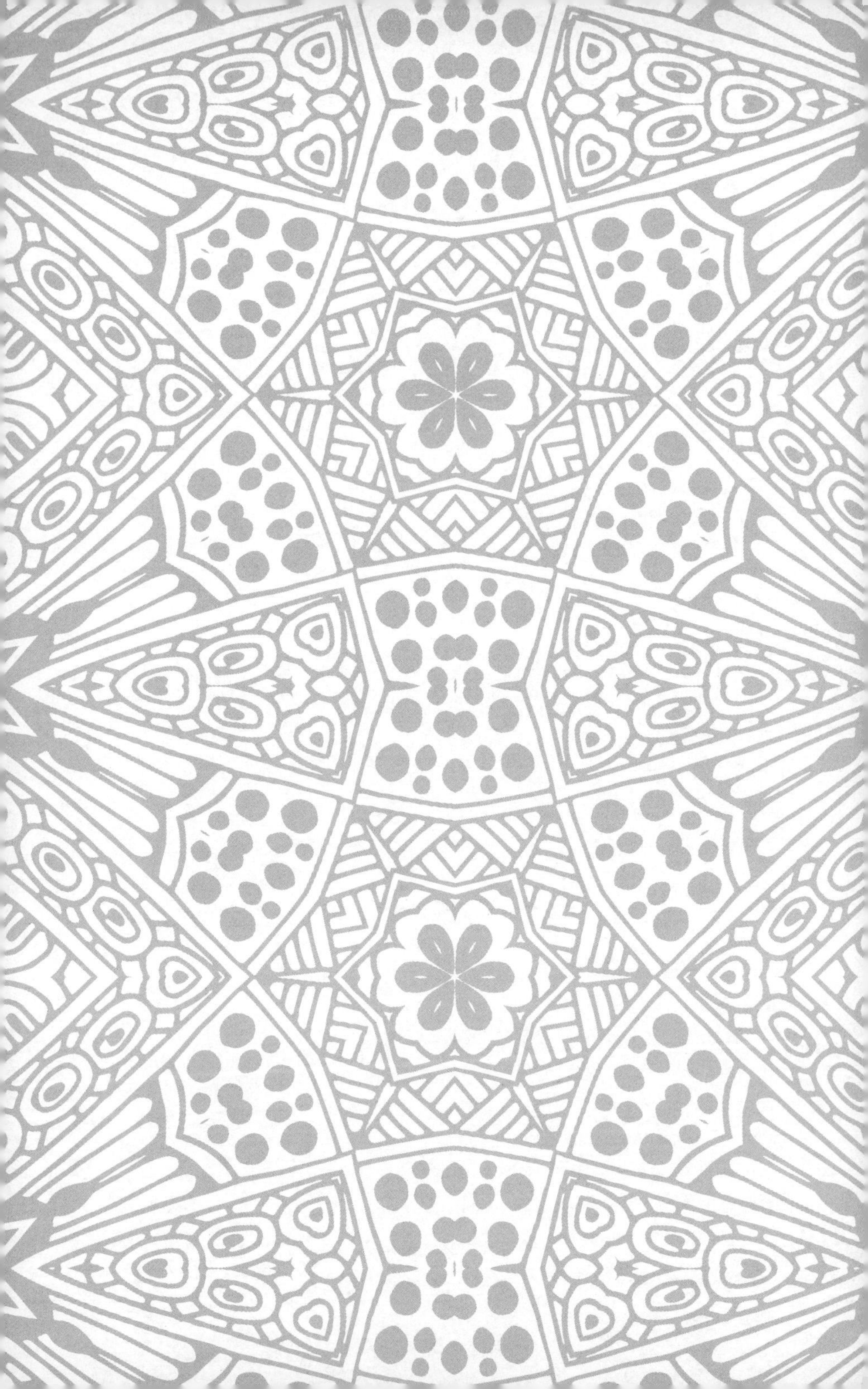

3

MIDWIFE TO YOUR SACRED DREAMS: SOWING FERTILE SEEDS

> *Only in the fever of creation could*
> *she recreate her own lost life.*
>
> —ANAÏS NIN

I hear our voices calling out to be heard; we are resilient and not irretrievably broken, only in need of our collective awakening.

Everywhere I go, on my lecture tours and in my humanitarian travels, I'm listening. I'm listening to the world waking up to the sound of women's collective crying out, to the call for women's empowerment. I hear it from women themselves, especially from older women who can no longer suffer their own silences, or the history of silences that came before them.

These older women call out loudly and clearly—no matter if it is illiterate women in my home village, or the PhDs I rub elbows with at events like the Emerging Women Conference. I hear it from women I meet in Cedar Rapids, Iowa, and in Palm Springs, California. I hear it in Birmingham, England; in Abu Dhabi, UAE; and in Istanbul, Turkey.

I want to be a midwife to this awakening; I want to sweat and coach and comfort and guide this global empowerment of women into its fullest life; I ululate at every first breath.

My grandmother was a midwife, a *nyamukuta*. My culture, the Korekore people of Zimbabwe, takes an expansive and inclusive approach to childbirth, and thanks to my grandmother's role as a healer, I was introduced to our birthing customs at a very young age.

Ambuya (or *Mbuya*) means grandmother in the Shona language, but it also refers to women related to one's grandmother through totems. In addition to my maternal grandmother, VaHarusekanwi, who died before I was born, I grew up with two other grandmothers. Ambuya Mafukeni was an adopted grandmother, related to me through my mother's clan, and Ambuya Muzoda, my father's mother. Although neither grandmother could read or write, both were strong and wise. They knew how to unleash the medicinal power of every bush, and they could identify the sex of a baby prior to birth by observing the mother's behavior and cravings during pregnancy.

I was initiated by Ambuya Mafukeni into the ancient tradition of midwifery when I was a young girl. Often dragged from her sleeping mat in the middle of the night, Ambuya Mafukeni delivered hundreds of babies in our village and beyond. She was highly sought-after for her skill at healing illness and disease. If she'd had the opportunity to be educated, I've always thought that she would have been the best gynecologist of my country, if not the whole world.

This is not to say that Ambuya Mafukeni's many talents were entirely overlooked. The community so revered my grandmother's skills as a birth worker and a healer that she became our village's heirloom seed keeper—or the seed curator, the one who keeps the old seeds so they don't become extinct as they play an important role in our well-being and all our rituals. This is high praise, indeed. To us, indigenous crops such as *rukweza, zviyo, njera,* or *rapoko* (finger millet), and *mhunga* (bulrush millet or pearl millet) are much more than merely subsistence grains. We believe these plants have special medicinal and nutritional value and that they are intrinsically connected to birth and death.

For centuries, finger millet, bulrush millet, or sorghum have been brewed into beer used in rain ceremonies or to summon spirit mediums when disease or death are near. When death is imminent, village elders prepare thin finger millet porridge for the person's final meal. Likewise, bulrush millet is used to ease the birthing process. To be a seed keeper, like being a midwife, means bearing sacred witness to transitions: to growth, change, and loss—all the many powerful forms in which transformation occurs. To appoint Ambuya Mafukeni, midwife and healer, as a seed keeper was to acknowledge her for the powerful role she played in partnering my community through life's most profound transitions.

Early one morning, a messenger arrived at Mbuya's home, out of breath and worried. "Will you come?" he managed to say between gulps of air. A young woman named Paida, who was expecting her fifth child, was having a terrible time during a prolonged period of labor.

My grandmother looked at me and I knew what to do before she had to say anything. *"Gadzirai bota renjera, ndirimunzira"*—"Have them prepare a thin porridge from *rapoko* millet. I'm on my way"— my grandmother tells the messenger, who runs off ahead as I rush to collect her medicine bag. We know we are nearing Paida's homestead when we hear the messenger shout, "Prepare thin *rapoko* porridge! Mbuya Mafukeni is coming!"

Paida's grandmother sighs with relief as we enter her homestead. The yard is empty of men except for a few boys playing near a mango tree. We can hear the groans of a woman coming from a nearby cooking hut, and so without a word or the usual greetings, we quickly rush into the hut. Paida is sitting on the floor with one leg stretched toward the door. Her big belly is exposed and one hand rests on the side of her back. The color is drained from her lips, leaving a whitish ring.

I glance around the room and notice a pile of red anthill soil nearby and know she has been eating it. Due to malnutrition and iron deficiency, pregnant women in my community tend to crave soil from anthills. In a few years' time, I would find myself doing the same thing while pregnant. Only later did I learn that this practice of eating iron-fortified soil or dirt is called geophagia.

Paida's eyes are tightly closed, and I can see each wave of pain roll through her as she twists her mouth from side to side. Though I am quite young, my intuition and my experience tell me there is something different about Paida's groans. Each groan is weaker than the one before and she sweats profusely. Paida's grandmother joins us. She sits near her granddaughter, dabbing her forehead with a towel. There is concern and fear in her eyes.

When a cousin brings the porridge, Paida's grandmother feeds it to the struggling woman. I keep staring at Paida's big, exposed belly, until Mbuya Mafukeni runs me outside to go play with the other children. I go but I remain near the hut, knowing that Mbuya will call me when she needs assistance or medicine from her bag. After all, she is going blind and it takes her forever to find what she needs. I camp near the door, where I can peep inside without the elders seeing me.

"I'm worried she is too exhausted," Mbuya Mafukeni tells Paida's grandmother. "Would you make more porridge?" Mbuya fears that Paida won't have the energy to release *chavakuru* (the placenta) or produce milk. The porridge, she explains, will induce lactation, which is needed in case the placenta gets stuck.

In observing Paida, Mbuya Mafukeni predicts the birth of a baby girl, and after a few more hours of labor, it is so. When the child is finally born, Mbuya Mafukeni quickly brings the baby to Paida's breast. Talking softly, my grandmother welcomes the baby into the world and begs the newly born daughter to suck her mother's breast. As the baby sucks, my grandmother kneads Paida's belly and her placenta is released. Sighing with satisfaction, Mbuya Mafukeni says, "*Nyadenga atinzwa*"—"The One who resides in the heavens [God] has heard us."

After what seems like a long time, Mbuya Mafukeni ties the umbilical cord, leaving a piece hanging to be retrieved later for another birth ritual. My grandmother hands the baby back to her mother. Paida's grandmother emits a singsong, high-pitched, trilling ululation off her tongue as she welcomes her great-granddaughter into the world. After cleaning up and making sure Paida and the baby are doing well, we return home, exhausted and relieved. We have witnessed another difficult but successful birth.

I accompanied my grandmother on many such births, just as I accompanied her on many foraging expeditions where she taught me the power of herbs, berries, bark, and seeds. From a very young age, I knew the danger of birth and also its beauty. Now I am a grown woman who has birthed her own children, and who has been born anew many times already in my life. I have seen and heard the birth and awakening stories of many women from all over the world.

I know some of us have been malnourished, as Paida was, and I know some of us have birthed so many times in so many different ways that we do not know if we can make it through another delivery. I know some of us have groaned and cried and labored long into the night without being heard. I know there are seeds that have lain, long fallow, aching for fields in which to be planted.

But this I also know, my sisters: there is a Great Hunger within you, and you still have the strength to give it life. I am ready to help you ride through those waves of pain and fear. I know the recipes to sustain you through long periods of exhaustion. I know how to perform the celebratory rituals. I know how to prepare the soil. I hear the world waking up, my sisters, and so I collect my medicine bag and gather the seeds.

When I talk about sacred dreams, I am talking about a global movement that we can see and touch and hear with our own senses. For it is one that I see and hear everywhere I go, and it is one that I know so well from my own life journey. And I know that I can help you see and hear and touch it, too.

I want to be a midwife for this movement in you, as my grandmother was to hundreds of women, stirring you to name and recall and pursue your most sacred dreams, so that you are part of this global waking up. I want to do my duty as the granddaughter of a seed keeper to nourish you and to ease your transformation as you grow your sacred purpose.

Planting the Seeds for Change

Beloved sister, in order to give birth to what lies down in the depths of your being, you will need rootedness and groundedness—a ritual that centers you from all the chores, the soul wounds, and all the subtle and not so subtle silencing in the world. In my travels, I often tell people that if you feel depressed or angry inside, it's probably because you have yet to create a strong platform for your dreams. I know this because I buried my dreams under a rock. Literally. In doing so, I rooted my being.

After running away from Zuda, I was overwhelmed with my situation, a mother of three children with only a ninth-grade education. Even though I was home with my people, most of all with my mother, my grandmothers, and my aunts, fear of how I would survive without an income plagued me. Am I now settling for a poor rural life? How will I sustain my children? What will happen to my baby girls when they grow up? Will they follow the same pathway I did?

Weeks passed and I fell into an old familiar routine. Early in the mornings and into the evenings, I'd work long hours in the fields alongside my mother, arriving home late at night, feeling hungry and tired. At dawn, before the rooster from our village begins its first call, we'd plow the field and sow *rapoko*, sorghum, groundnuts, and maize. Soon, the crops began to emerge from the earth, competing with the weeds.

For six weeks after that, with only our hand hoes, we'd weed the fields until our backs couldn't take it anymore. When the weeding was done, we would rest and wait for the rains to end. On weekends, I would help tend my mother's vegetable gardens.

The reality of my situation was clearer than ever, and even as I fell into a rhythm of planting, weeding, and tending the fields and gardens, miles away from my abusive husband, I remained despondent.

For as long as I could remember, I dreamed of getting an education. There was not even opportunity for me to attend kindergarten. It never existed. Instead, like many children in the village, I spent my early childhood chasing birds and grasshoppers in my parents' fields. In addition to herding cattle, I worked the land and took care of my siblings, like many other girls of my acquaintance.

We girls would rather be in school, but what little education existed prior to and during the war was offered mainly to boys, since they are expected to become family wage earners. As future providers, boys are valued over girls, most of whom are married at a very young age. While I understood how important it was for boys to be educated to get good jobs, I wondered why girls could not also be educated to become future providers and community role models.

Growing up, I saw how poverty, war, and the absence of a reliable safety net affected everyone—but none more than poor women in rural areas with no access to education. They perform the grueling work of feeding and caring for their families. Even if they wish for a different kind of life, financial dependence forces many to remain in abusive and polygamous marriages. The prevalence of polygamy and the corresponding looser attitude toward male sexual promiscuity often means that women are made the scapegoats for every kind of problem. The situation felt hopeless to the women of my community who foresaw the same difficult path for their daughters and granddaughters.

Out in the fields, I daydreamed a lot about getting a formal education, as there was so much I wanted to know! My favorite part of herding was when the older herders would decide to pass time in the fields by teaching the young ones to read and write. My brother Tinashe taught me words that I practiced by sewing letters of the alphabet onto leaves. I enjoyed creating songs that helped me to remember the five vowels, especially when older herders reminded me that many of our words begin with vowels (a, e, i, o, u). For example:

> "a" for aaaha! *amai, ambuya!* (mother, grandmother)
> "e" for ehee! *enda, evo!* (go, yes)
> "i" for iii! *iwe, ini!* (you, me)
> "o" for ooo! *ona, ose!* (see, all)
> "u" for uuu! *uya, unogona!* (come, you can do it)

Because we did not have pens, pencils, or paper, we used charcoal, thorns from the *mubayamhondoro* tree (known as "elephant thorns"), plant pods, and leaves from a broad-leaved native tree called *muchakacha*. Thorns are also used as needles that help us string sheets of the *muchakacha* leaves together. *Muchakacha* leaves are so broad that they work just like the pages of a book. And with the thorns, we etched words onto the long, green pods. As they dried, the writing became more visible and permanent. Digging and weeding in my mother's gardens, I remembered the sweet smell of the *muchakacha*'s golden fruit, the way the leaves felt cool and thick in my hands, and the illuminating power they contained with words and letters on them.

My mind drifted back to another time, before I married Zuda, when my mother and I, along with many people in the community, attended a freedom fighters rally in the center of the village. Although some freedom fighters committed atrocities against civilians during the war, the words I heard that day from the impressive speaker stuck with me. "The colonial system denies us education so that it can oppress us more easily," the man said. He stood on an old anthill mound near a rock as a crowd gathered around him.

His stature was imposing, with his AK-47 tightly belted around his waist, his shiny green uniform fatigues almost a perfect match for his blackish-green beret, and a long cigar in his mouth. His thick voice boomed through the crowd. "To educate is to empower and to empower is to liberate and to liberate is to allow people to gain their dignity," his voice rang out into the otherwise silent night. "Can you imagine what would happen if all of you were educated and able to read and write?" he implored the crowd.

A round of "Amen"s rose from the men and the women ululated. I wanted to be like him: educated and an eloquent orator. That day I made the connection between education and my own freedom—freedom that enabled the empowerment and dignity of my very being.

I remembered, too, the American and British women who came to do research in my country after we won our independence. They wore glasses as they opened and closed notebooks full of information that was inaccessible to me. They talked casually about getting their master's degrees or their doctorates. I wanted those glasses so badly. I wanted the power and information that in my mind came with them.

When I mentioned these memories and the hunger they had long stirred in me to my mother as we sat preparing dinner later that night, she nodded with understanding. "We marry off our girls in exchange for cows as a form of bride price," my mother said knowingly. "And we have accepted the bride price because it's designed to nurture relationships and our culture. But it isn't working. Without education and their own sources of income, we subject our women to abuse. They rely heavily on men's income and never gain dignity, and the next generation of girls repeats the cycle." I let her words sink in as I added cold water to a pot of *sadza* (cornmeal) and stirred it over the kitchen fire.

I, too, would have repeated the cycle had I not met a stranger in my village a few weeks later. As though the stars were aligned, an American woman named Jo Luck arrived in my village, coinciding with a time when I was at my lowest point. This seemingly free-spirited and independent stranger exuded a kind of joy similar to what I felt on the day that Zimbabwe became a free country. During the early days of independence, a sense of hope was infectious between my people and strangers. Grandmothers, mothers, and daughters believed that the country was now on a path that would offer them many more opportunities.

The American found me and a dozen other women seated on the ground in a circle with only our Zambia cloths to protect us from insects and other crawly creatures and to preserve our already threadbare dresses. She asked to join the circle and, without hesitation, sat next to me as though she joined circles like ours every day. One woman placed an old reed mat under her. I had never before seen a white woman in such close proximity to black women, let alone in our poor, rural village.

The stranger began to speak. Before I could even hear what she was saying, I was hypnotized by her voice. It sounded like a lullaby, rising and falling as every vowel was enunciated (I later learned that this is how Southerners in the US speak). She told the group, "My organization works in many countries around the world. I have seen women who were once illiterate learn to read and write. They can feed, clothe, and educate their children. I have seen poor children who were previously denied education attend school. Some of the children even go on to higher education."

I was quiet. At twenty-two years of age, I could not believe what Jo Luck's translator was conveying to us. No one had ever spoken of the possibility of education for older women like me. I did not know what to make of the discussion. But I thought that maybe this was the opportunity I had been hoping for.

Women in the circle shared their worries about the lack of food and clothing and costs associated with their children's schools. They shared their hopes for a better life with more sources of income and food security as well as better education for their children. As is the tradition, we offered the stranger bambara nuts, which are derived from a common, but much appreciated plant that enriches the soil. However, when the nuts are cooked, the water turns a dirty shade of brown. I am transfixed as the woman dips her polished fingernails into the murky water to gather some nuts. I was amazed that she just sat on the ground with us in her pretty dress. Coming from a culture that pays attention to body language, I appreciated how at ease she seemed. And so the conversation flowed.

I didn't know if Jo Luck noticed how I looked at her, but at some point she turned to me and said, "You have been quiet, what are your dreams?" I hesitated because I was afraid that the translator might not convey my thoughts in a way that the woman could understand. I felt very shy. The women in my circle knew of my wish to be educated, but I did not even have a high school diploma. I could see the curiosity and concern in their eyes.

Looking down, I thought to myself, "I'm not going to talk about the poverty in my family, the abuse, or the lack of food. I want to talk about my own education." My mother's words echoed in my mind. "Someone needs to break the cycle," she had said. Could it be me? I allowed myself to wonder.

I said to Jo Luck: "My name is Tererai and I want to go to America to get an education. I want to get an undergraduate degree, a master's degree, and a PhD." This was the first time that I uttered aloud the dreams I harbored.

Silence followed my declaration. No one could believe that I spoke of obtaining an education, let alone going to America to obtain three degrees! While the women knew of my wish to be educated, they couldn't believe that I would say something seemingly impossible, given the fact that I did not have a high school diploma. Even I am not sure how I mustered the courage to speak, let alone to be so ambitious about where I wanted to get my education.

I suppose I knew that with only two major universities in my country, it was unlikely that I'd be able to earn a degree in Zimbabwe. Unlike me, with only high school correspondence certificates, many qualified people with formal classroom education have been denied a place in one of our colleges, and it was clear to me that the competition at home was incredibly tough. This meant that my true chance for higher education was in America.

My knowledge of America was relatively recent. As our country enjoyed its newly gained independence, radios, newspapers, and visitors from afar became carriers of the hidden world: they brought information that we had never been exposed to before. Finally, the world had opened its excitements, thrills, and anticipations to our ravaged, poverty-stricken villages. Place names such as America, Australia, New Zealand, China, et cetera, became part of our new vocabulary. Great Britain was an old song that we associated with our suffering, subordination, inferiority, and oppression. America was a new song and seemed to stand out as we learned more about the civil rights movement and the work of Martin Luther King Jr. and Rosa Parks, as well as musicians like BB King, Tracy Chapman, and Dolly Parton. America sounded to my evolving sense of the world like a place of possibility, and so I threw my dreams out in that direction.

This was a pivotal moment. I had no idea that speaking these words aloud would transform my life in the most remarkable ways. In the moment, I knew my friends were wondering "What about the kids?" and "What will your husband say?" Worries came flooding back almost as soon as I made my declaration.

I didn't know if the stranger understood my situation. When I finished talking, I was so overwhelmed that I began to doubt my sanity. But seeing my passion, she said, "If you desire and believe in your dreams, they are achievable." In my native language, the phrase "it's achievable" translates to *tinogona*. She continued, "Take mental notes of the things you want to achieve in life and you will achieve them." *Tinogona*. This became my rallying cry, my prayer. I later learned that Jo Luck was a director of international programs with Heifer International, a nonprofit based in Little Rock, Arkansas, that works to end hunger and poverty in the world. In late 1992, she became its president and CEO.

I shared the experience of meeting Jo Luck with my mother. Despite my fears, I reaffirmed my desire for an education. I told her, "The woman makes me believe that I can get an education and that my children can, too." You would think that my mother—like her mother before her—who had suffered through tremendous adversity and abuse, would be worn down by life. But not my mother! What I said was music to her ears! She told me to hold on to this dream as though my life depended on it.

She said, "If you believe in this dream of education and you achieve it, you are not only defining your future, but that of every life coming out of your womb, as well as those for generations to come. What you want to become will change how you see the world around you." My mother repeated this mantra often, which, to this day, keeps me grounded.

My excitement, however, was deeply vulnerable to the realities of my situation—poverty, an abusive husband, and my low self-esteem were ever-present to mock my excitement, to laugh at my dreams. My mother knew I needed to go back to my foundation to find my roots. And so she encouraged me to write down my dreams and bury them in the ground. She told me that Mother Earth would nourish them beneath the soil and help them to grow. To ease my doubts, she added, "*Vimba naNyadenga, nevadzimu vedu, zvaunoshuvira zvinobudirira*"—"Trust the universe to honor your dreams."

My mother trusted that burying my dreams would establish them deep within my psyche. My people are a farming people, and so we live by the spiritual and practical practice of sowing and tending the fields. She handed me two plastic bags and an old tin can that once held beef eaten by Rhodesian Independence soldiers. I carefully placed the scrap of paper holding my recorded dreams into the bag, which I then put into the can. When the can was wrapped with the second bag, I buried it to prevent rats, mice, and bad weather from destroying its precious contents.

I wrote my dreams in the Shona language: "*Ini Tererai, semunhu we mudzimai, ndaona kuti hupenyu ndisina dzidzo hwakaoma. Ndinofanira kuve nedzidzo. Ndasangana nemudzimai we ku Heifer International andishingisa kuti ndikavimba nezvandinoda kuzova pahupenyu hwangu, ndikashanda nesimba, ndinogona kubudirira ndikafundisawo vana vangu.*"

"I, Tererai, have decided that as a woman, a life without education will be a burden. So I must educate myself. I met a woman from Heifer International who encouraged me to believe that I could achieve my dream of educating my children and myself. Here are my dreams:

1. To go to America;
2. To get an undergraduate degree;
3. To get a master's degree; and
4. To get a PhD."

When I showed the paper to my mother, she said, "*Zvose zvaunoshuvira muhupenyu zvinobudiria kana zviinetarisiro youkukurudzira nzvimbo yaugere*"—"Every dream has greater meaning when tied to the betterment of the community. This is what creates a meaningful life." It is one thing to achieve a dream based upon individual needs and another to build upon the common good. Her words inspired me to add a fifth dream:

5. To give back to my community, especially to alleviate the plight of women and girls.

"The fifth dream is sacred," my mother told me, although I had no idea of the significance of this fifth goal at the time. In writing my dreams down, I felt like I had redesigned my life to reflect the future I wanted. My mother told me that this new narrative and the respect for the ritual of writing and burying would influence positive outcomes for my children and for generations to come.

On a bright sunny morning, with a timeworn garden hoe in hand, I headed to a place where I used to herd cattle as a child. I found the rock where I spent hours practicing my vowels and doing my brother's homework as a hopeful little girl. I remember vivid details from this day. In the background, two doves cooed and the savanna grass and the tree leaves rustled. I remember the feeling of the wind on my skin. I lifted the rock, dug a hole, and placed the aluminum can into the ground. I buried my dreams. Before leaving, I found a small, smooth, round rock to take with me as a keepsake.

As my mother would later explain, this act was more than just a symbol of respect to an ancient sacred practice of planting and harvesting. I had weaved the threads of my hurting soul, spirit, and mind together, enabling me to trust that I was more than my circumstances. Something bigger was taking place. No matter the forces that silenced my true potential, no matter my low self-esteem, the burying of my dreams reminded me that my desires now have a sacred connection to the earth below my feet. They had taken up space in the world. And I could take strength from the idea of my dreams growing. It felt good.

I developed a private ritual, in the months after meeting Jo Luck and burying my dreams, that kept me grounded. Early in the morning, I revisited the site of my buried dreams. I unearthed the can and reread them, savoring every word. As I held the scrap of paper, I imagined what life would be like if I achieved them. I could close my eyes, see myself in the new life, feel it and savor that life for an hour or so, knowing there was no turning back now. I called these times of reflection my "holy grail hours." The rock guarded my dreams as I envisioned the life and future I wanted and the work it would take to achieve all my dreams.

Becoming Symbolically Whole

Why is rootedness so important to reclaiming our sacred dreams? What was it that my mother helped me do when she instructed me to bury my dreams, and why was it so crucial to achieving my long-silenced and forgotten longings?

Study after study shows that women in most cultures are socialized to question their voices and to distrust their bodies.[1] What my mother helped me to do by encouraging me to write down my dreams and to bury them under a rock was to give me a solid foundation from which to grow. She helped me give my dreams weight—she emboldened me to let them take up space in the world, and as a result, they took up space in my mind and my life, in my words and my thoughts and my actions. We need to get comfortable taking up physical space and to claim the power of our voices, beloved sisters. And in order to do that we need to feel grounded and safe. We need to be symbolically whole.

You see, my sisters, burying dreams deep in the soil under a rock is a simple yet sacred act. While I am proud to have been born among the indigenous people of the Korekore, who believe in the energy of the universe and in our relationship to it, all people have an intuition and instinct to enact sacred rituals and connect with the universe in their own lives. When we are connected to a strong culture, we are connected to the elders who share these powerful traditions, who honor our connection to the living, breathing earth. It is when we are missing these traditions that we must form new ones, create our own, and share them with each other.

One tradition I like to share from my people is the burying of an umbilical cord at the place of one's birth. Many ancient cultures have a similar practice, and the common existence of this very old ritual is a testament to the sacred act of birth and transformation. In my village in Zimbabwe, a child's birth is not symbolically complete until a female elder carefully snips a piece of the umbilical cord, ties it with a piece of worn cloth from the mother's dress, and buries it deep in the ground near the mother's hut. My people believe that a child whose umbilical cord is buried in the ground will never forget their birthplace, literally and spiritually. Both my mother and grandmother strongly believed that once planted, the cord's gentle throbbing protects, sustains, and provides energy to the person it had once nourished in the womb. It is believed that a child whose umbilical cord is buried in the ground will never forget her family and from where she originated.

At an early age, I learned to appreciate that the soil connects us to birth and death in ways that defy simple explanation. After my own physical birth, my adopted maternal grandmother, Mbuya Mafukeni, birthed my spiritual being by snipping a piece of my umbilical cord, tying it with a piece of cloth from my mother's dress, and burying it deep into the ground near my mother's hut. At the birth of each of my six children, my mother and grandmother repeated this ancient practice, explaining that it connects the Shona people, irrevocably, to our spiritual and collective home. As part of the ritual, my grandmother sings a song, a kind of prayer for wholeness with the umbilical cord as its central image. She sings:

> Naked, vulnerable, you arrive in this world tied to a life support—I the umbilical cord / Tiny, vulnerable, you are welcomed in this world either with love or with regrets—I the umbilical cord remain the source of your life / Shriveled and tied in your mother's tattered and torn cloth, I am buried deep under the shade of the Musasa tree near your mother's hut. At the base of the tree, just where the roots are to bud, soon I become part of the root strengthening and nurturing all that is around. / I become the source and symbol of your dignity, and I remain to remind you of your identity / Wherever you go in the world, I hold your past, your future, and your dignity / Don't forget the roots, rhyme with the roots, time to the roots; it is the power within grounded deep down into the Mother Earth / When all is done and gone, I remain the only identity you have to your humanity / I remain to remind you of what's important—the power of your identity, the power of "we," the power of your roots / So ancient is the practice, and yet so powerful to your past, your present, your future, and your identity / I call you back home, to your groundedness, your foundation. I am the umbilical cord!

The singing of this song and the act of burying part of ourselves is a matriarchal tradition that ties us to our mothers and our mothers'

mothers and to Mother Earth. Ultimately, it ties us to a strong and fertile foundation of ourselves. This incantation implores us to dance with our roots, to organize our lives around our roots, to honor root time above all the many clocks of modern society, and to know ourselves as deeply, deeply planted. Whether we enter this world with joy or regrets, my grandmother sang, we are fed, we are rooted, and we are home in a very spiritual and earthly way.

Even when villagers go off to seek work in urban areas or journey even farther afield, they maintain a strong connection to home. Their umbilical cords remain behind, binding the travelers to their tribe and cementing his or her place in the larger universe. Its groundedness and sacredness cannot be overestimated. Even when threatened by an employer or landowner, my people say, *"Usandisembure, handina kupisa musha, ndinoziva kwandakabve, padzinde rangu, pamusha pandakasiya rukuvuhete rwangu"*—"Don't trouble me; I cannot take your insults anymore; I never burned my home; I know who I am and what grounds me in my identity. It is the place where my umbilical cord is buried."

Let's be expansive about what "home" means. I imagine it not just the physical location of my family's home, or even the geographic region where I'm from, although those ideas are very powerful to me. This groundedness also connects me to the broad, sprawling histories of the strong women who came before me, to so many wise ancestors, to sacred mysteries, and to the throbbing power of the earth's deepest and most transformative capacities. Burying the umbilical cord or your written dreams or some other item of significance is a physical manifestation of our connection to all: community, history, spirit, and earth. This act provides an endless source of strength and empowerment.

I buried my dreams under a rock as a reminder of the power of the earth and its connection to my umbilical cord, and of the power of a spiritual connection to something bigger than myself. Writing down these dreams preserved them, and also gave me strength to right the wrongs of my past, ultimately aiding me to find my own redemption.

We are alive, in flesh and blood and we have physical and spiritual weight and depth and power. In order to be whole we need to connect ourselves more fully to the ground, both literally and symbolically. Just like the ancient ways of burying a child's umbilical cord, bury and preserve your dreams in a safe place, a place of your choice, a place that centers your being.

Wherever you go in the world, the buried contents of your heart's desire will always stir your mind and soul—reminding you of the sacredness of your dreams, of your courage in naming them, of their rootedness in your being. You may have shelved your dreams or you may have not yet even realized the dreams within you. But they are there, waiting to be tended.

Dig deep into the private chambers of your heart, and build a foundation of strength and confidence on this path toward empowerment. You are embarking on a momentous journey to awaken your sacred dreams. You will need bravery and confidence and a strong center. You will need a sturdy root to hold on to when doubt and fear seep in. You will need to be symbolically whole.

It's easy for women to be uprooted in this world. So many of us put the needs of others before our own to the point we lose sight of what our own needs are. So many of us shrink back during moments of decision-making, or are afraid to make demands of those around us for fear they won't like us or they'll leave.

Dear sisters, if we consciously or unconsciously understand that the world prefers our smallness, our silences, our uncertainties, or our weightlessness, then in order to reclaim our whole selves we have to get bigger and *more* substantial. We have to ground ourselves, to come home to ourselves, our bodies, our histories, and the physical world around us. It's time we take up more space, from our roots to our branches and leaves. Make your desires and your dreams concrete and link them to the material world around you.

This rooting and grounding is an important first step to recovering lost parts of yourself, or achieving seemingly impossible dreams. I know this not only from my own experiences, but also from the stories I hear from the many women I meet in my travels.

I met Michelle Stronz, chairperson of Women's Leadership Council, United Way, in 2014 in Hartford, Connecticut, at the United Way's Power of the Purse conference. Inspired by the encouragement to bury her dreams, Michelle went home and buried her dream in her garden. She was just beginning the process of ending her twenty-year marriage and launching a new business.

Michelle wrote to me later to thank me—her dream had already begun bearing fruit. I asked Michelle why she thought getting rooted in the earth was successful for her; she said it's because writing down and burying our dreams gives us pride in the knowledge that we are creating something truer and bigger than who we are.[2]

I have seen it happen time and time again: when you bury your dreams you plant seeds. Now you have something to tend, something to water, and something to watch grow. This very physical and spiritual practice shows you the power that is in your hands, the power you alone have to birth your dream into existence.

SACRED RITUAL FOR PLANTING YOUR DREAMS

I offer you a practice for rootedness and planting your sacred dream seeds with the intention of grounding you in the face of busyness, adversity, fear, and the common chaos in our modern lives, of inspiring you to remain on a clear path toward your true purpose. I invite you to read it more than once, to spend some time thinking about it without any specific goal in mind (just let your creativity free flow—daydream about it). So clear some time for yourself, sit down in a quiet space, and do the meditation and writing practice.

This prayer offers much to you, but it also asks a lot of you: it asks you to spend some time in purposeful reflection on what needs to be healed and what longs to be manifested. I know this can be an intense experience. But consider this my plea for you to do this important work to awaken your beautiful soul and nourish the sacred dream that lies in your heart; feel it stirring, feel its significance to you, write it down, and like a child's umbilical cord, bury it deep in the ground.

Find a quiet place, your *masowe*, where you can relax into the moment. If you have a meditation cushion, go ahead and use it. Choose whatever position is most comfortable. Read the following words, take a few deep breaths, close your eyes, and begin.

Dig Deep into the Visceral

I ask you to dig into the chambers of your heart, into the viscera and the depths of your being. Search inside yourself for the place beyond fear where your dreams remain untapped. Dig and get to the core, glimpse into the solitary space of your own soul.

Return to your responses about what breaks your heart and how it aligns with the greater good. Ululate to grow in confidence of your voice. Then ask yourself: *How can I make this Great Hunger of mine a ritual for healing myself and the world?*

I invite you to speak the words that have surfaced in your body. These are the raw materials of your sacred dreams. Your hunger and your heartache have guided you here. Your voice is ready to proclaim your dreams; you believe you have that right. Name how you will act on your desires. Perhaps, like myself, your dream is an education for the purpose of lifting up others. Perhaps, like my friend, your dream is to support and befriend refugees struggling from global unrest. A whole world of possibilities is open to you.

Pause for a few moments, roll the shape of the dreams around in your mind, perhaps sway your body side to side, feel your hips rooted to the ground while your lips enunciate the shape of your dreams.

Like a basket weaver thread the strands into a goal, a plan. It gets stronger and stronger as your mind imprints them on your body, as your hands become more adept at weaving.

How will you turn the hunger in your heart into a practice for personal and communal recovery?

Sacred Writing

Now I encourage you to practice what I call "sacred writing." Sacred writing is writing from the depth of your feminine energy. As though you are about to give birth, call into the power of your creativity.

While asking the questions allows us to tune into our intuitive self and for our forgotten dreams to resurface, sacred writing wills us to sift what has been dug up and put it to paper. Sacred writing is soulful; it opens your eyes to what your soul has been searching for all these years. I say sacred writing because you are about to name your sacred dreams.

Before I do my soul writing, I clean the space and make sure there is no clutter around me. When I'm in this mood, I love to take a shower and wear a nice dress that makes me feel like a goddess. I call to my ancestors and give a prayer to the powerful universe—which is my name for God. Now the world belongs to me and the pen gives me the power to invoke what's within. If this ritual resonates with you, take the time to prepare the space and yourself.

Now you are ready to write your sacred dreams, the answer to how you will turn the hunger in your heart into a practice for personal and communal healing. As Mary Oliver asks, "Tell me, what is it you plan to do / with your one wild and precious life?"

What is it you plan to do to feed that Great Hunger in you?

Be wise with the words that you choose to name your vision, as those words give shape and definition to your sacred dreams. I wrote my dreams in a list; others write theirs as one goal: "to help women heal from abuse," for example, or "to protect clean water in my community." Sometimes it's more of a feeling: "to nurture connection" perhaps, or "to make creative pursuits more central in my life and my community." Remember to include the sacred with the personal, for it is an honor to be of service to the greater good. As my mother would say, "The focus should not be about our greatness; rather, it should be about serving others." This is what defines our success. This is what makes our individual dreams sacred.

You are preparing the fertile ground for the manifestation of your dreams. Let the power of your thoughts become a sacred space to experience possibilities because your imagination is boundless.

Planting Your Dreams

Once satisfied with your written dreams, find a place to bury them. Perhaps your garden, or a flower bed that hangs on your balcony, or in a favorite park. Find a hoe or any garden tool sharp enough to prod the earth. Dig in the soil. Dig with the confidence of a farmer about to sow a harvestable seed, believing rain and sunshine will come and nurture the seed.

Armed with the "farmer's conviction," make sure the hole is good enough to support your dreams. Pause. Reflect. Listen to the sounds around you; the resonances of birdsong, the creaking of tree branches, the rustling of the grass, and the sound of the wind and its breeze as it passes your skin. Feel the warmth of the sun or the bite of the air on a cold day. Send a prayer to the universe. Bury your sacred dreams. Envision them growing until they are manifest.

Dear sisters, hold on to that vision until it engrosses you and it becomes you. Visit the place where you buried your dreams as often as you can, as often as you need to. Think of your dreams throughout your day. Imagine them taking root; imagine their resilience in the bleak times of cold or snow and their fecundity in the growing season. Let the vision of those dreams engross you.

Become one with them. Feel the cathartic *oomph* of their presence in the world, giving you an electrical charge that remains with you as the vision takes over your life. For me, it was this very electrical energy that sustained me, charging me to see and experience the tangibility and achievability of the vision for my sacred dreams.

Others will begin to see the change in you, the transformation for greatness, like an iron rod being polished for great things to come, dear sister, you will shine with confidence. This intentional rootedness will give you the strength to remember your lost dreams, and to awaken your whole self. What is written and preserved with intent becomes ingrained in your thoughts. An ingrained thought becomes a deep-rooted belief. Strongly held beliefs can ground you and help you to achieve your dreams.

4

BE YOUR OWN STORYTELLER: CREATING NEW PATHWAYS

> *Until the lionesses have their own historians,*
> *the history of the hunt will always glorify the hunter.*
>
> —AFRICAN PROVERB, AS REIMAGINED
> BY TERERAI TRENT

In my culture we say, "If you are indifferent at the meat-sharing gathering, you end up with dry bones." Well, women have borne the brunt of history's indifference because most history books were written by men from the male perspective and often ignore the presence of women or position them as minor players or invisible objects. More often than not, women have ended up with dry bones.

Even today, the world tells many stories about women, both in narrative form (as in, "women can be either successful or happy," or "women can be either beautiful or strong") and in the form of quantitative data, where a slew of studies reveal women's absence in much of today's public culture in the United States. While women make up 51 percent of the US population, for example, they comprise only about 18.5 percent of congressional seats and 20 percent of US senators, a number that has been almost stagnant since the 1990s.[1]

Women are unrepresented in business, where they occupy merely 9 percent of top management positions,[2] and in journalism and popular culture as well. As Julie Burton writes in the foreword to "The Status of Women in the U.S. Media 2015," a report from the Women's Media Center, women "are assigned to report stories at a substantially lower rate than men. In evening broadcast news, women are on-camera 32 percent of the time; in print news, women report 37 percent of the stories; on the Internet, women write 42 percent of the news; and on the wires, women garner only 38 percent of the bylines."[3]

The status of women in film and television, according to the Women's Media Center, might best be summed up as dismal but with potential: "White men hold the power, [says] Darnell Hunt, director of UCLA's Ralph J. Bunche Center for African American Studies." At the same time, "We are seeing the beginnings of great change" in the industry, adding that, "Power doesn't voluntarily give itself up."[4] Stacy L. Smith agrees. "The numbers are not changing," she says of gender and racial parity both before and behind the camera. "However, awareness is at an all-time high."[5]

Taking a good hard look at these social and statistical narratives is informative, but we cannot stop there, for they tell only one side of the story. When we remain frozen in statistics or stuck as supporting characters in someone else's story, we remain silent and forgotten. In this we risk being forever kept in a secondary role—we risk seeing the problem and not the potential. If power isn't willingly given up, then we must claim it in words and deeds.

Let me tell you this: there is much to be gained from becoming the heroines of our own stories. When we collectively tell our stories, we reveal the richness in that diversity and we create a beautiful cross-pollination of lessons to teach and strengthen each other. Our stories need to be told, by us, so that we can heal any residual pain from our past and create our bold new future—individually for ourselves and together as a human village.

Many great writers and poets have written about the power of storytelling: "There is no greater agony than bearing an untold story,"[6] wrote author, folklorist, and anthropologist Zora Neale Hurston. Author, conservationist, and activist Terry Tempest Williams writes about learning from the Diné, or Navajo, that "voice finds its greatest amplification through story."[7] "[M]any more in number are those stories which are not written on paper, but are written on the bodies and minds of women,"[8] wrote poet Amrita Pritam. These and so many other great thinkers speak a profound truth: we need to tell our stories for our own health and well-being. We need to tell stories, so that we harness the power of our voices, and we need our bodies and our minds to demand an audience in the world. Because whether it knows it or not, the world needs our stories for healing and creating, as much as we need the world to hear us.

Recording your sacred dreams is powerful and liberating. It allows you to tell *your* story about your life, empowering you to reach out and touch a future of your own making.

A world of possibilities emerged once I clarified and visualized what I wanted my life to be. Like an architect, I redesigned my life to reflect the future I wanted, and I believed that my dreams were doable in large part because I no longer suffered the agony of carrying an untold story within. My new narrative influenced my life profoundly, and it also influenced my children and generations still to come.

But the act of burying my dreams alone would not have been enough to sustain me. I needed also to keep speaking them. And I spoke them constantly. My mother would tell me that whenever I talked about my dreams, I sounded like a woman possessed. We'd both laugh, but we knew the truth of her statement: the ongoing act of speaking and writing my dreams was a promise I continued to make—to end the cycle of hardship in my family. I spoke my dreams with pride because I knew that with my words I created someone bigger than who I was in the moment. This is the power of naming your truth: you set an intention, you make a promise, and you make your dreams start to take shape in the world.

I come from a long line of storytellers, and so do you, even if that part of your history has been forgotten or hidden—after all, it was the hunters and not the lionesses who wrote so much of human history. But I have witnessed the heart and soul of an oft-forgotten oral tradition in which many women told stories that wove communities together, reverberated beyond the walls of the room in which they told them, and illuminated unforgettable and actionable global healing. Let me share my heritage of storytellers so that you might remember, seek out, or imagine your own.

Cross-legged and barefoot around the fire, I heard stories that had been passed from my great-grandmother Sekai to my grandmother Rufu to my mother Shamiso: stories of how they had survived in poverty, stories of enduring a world ruled by men, stories of their strengths and healing. At times sad, these were stories of women trying to narrate and redefine their lives, women refusing to be victims and declaring themselves part of the solution. These women were not only storytellers, they were also medicine healers, traditional midwives, and village psychologists.

One story of my grandmother's remains particularly vivid in my mind. After a long day away from home, my grandmother arrived late in the evening after supper and found the village women sitting around the fire. We knew she had tended a hard labor. In the weeks before delivery, the pregnant woman was very thin and sickly, though her stomach was huge. Without knowing how big the child she carried was, no one knew what to expect. My grandmother predicted it was going to be a long labor. We waited to hear news of the delivery.

Limping slowly toward the open fire, my grandmother looked tired and resigned. We knew something terrible must have happened, because her walk was familiar: either my grandmother lost a baby or the mother—or both. "Then why didn't we hear the mourning call?" we murmured quietly among the group. My grandmother heaved her weight down as she joined the circle of women.

The silence was palpable. My grandmother sighed twice before someone offered her water. "*Aiwa, ndipei mukombe wechingoto kana pane chakasara, nditonhedze pfungwa"*—"No, please give me the leftover beer to cool off my soul!" No one dared ask what had happened. This story was hers to tell when she was ready to tell it. My mother hurriedly went inside the hut and brought the beer in a *mukombe*—a gourd. Taking one big gulp, she wiped her mouth, and then settled into her body. My grandmother hardly drank and when she did, we all knew she was troubled. We could see my grandmother was visibly shaken and worse, as she was growing old, her eyes started to fail her and her hands would shake uncontrollably.

All eyes were on my grandmother, but her eyes were set on the red embers of the fire, her body now completely still. "I have lost the twins," she declared. "This should not have happened. The mother was frail and Nyadenga—the Creator—saved her, otherwise, I would be telling a different story here." Her words were met with silence.

"The mother labored long and hard, but both babies were stillborn," she continued. "There was nothing I could do except to perform the burial ritual." As was the custom, my grandmother, the midwife, and the female elders of the village buried the two infants by the watershed near the river. Even though my grandmother was old, she walked everybody through the birth process like a master preparing her students: how she had prepared the herbs to ease the birthing woman's pain, massaged her belly to aid in the afterbirth, and consoled the family at the birth of not one but two profound losses.

When she finished speaking, she paused and then spread her hands out for all to see. "These hands have delivered so many babies in my life and no birth has affected me like that of the stillborn." The women's eyes scanned my grandmother's wrists and fingers, taking in every wrinkle on her well-worn hands that had touched so much life and death. "The poor woman was too old to carry the pregnancy," she says. "Women, oh, women, but why . . ." She trails off. Her unfinished sentence haunts me to this day. For a long time I wanted to fill in that gap of her silence and didn't know how.

But then she continued with a hint of laughter, "And these eyes have seen so many private parts that it's no wonder I'm blind, but my mind is sharp." In that moment, her frailty and pain was shared with a healing laugh; we in the circle laughed and she joined in, laughing so hard she exposed her one remaining tooth, allowing us to see the beauty of her vulnerability, and hear her wisdom beyond age and poverty.

In this, my grandmother became the author of her life story— she is not an illiterate, subordinate, oppressed weak old woman, but instead an experienced and compassionate healer, a humanitarian, a leader. That is how we remember her.

Her story awakens many questions within us: What if my grandmother had been given an opportunity for an education? What if this mother had not been impoverished, had been educated, had reproductive autonomy? My grandmother's story arouses a deep hunger in us, a desire to carry forward the work of this great woman. And so by telling this story with the incidence of the stillborn babies, she was also telling her life story. My grandmother gave voice to women's desolation, her own sadness, her losses, her longings, and she also gained confidence through celebrating herself and having herself witnessed by others. This had a profound effect on the listeners.

Once my grandmother had spoken, once she had opened the door to us in the circle, we could talk about the longing in our own stories. Now we listeners could work our way toward solutions— dreams of education, independence, and healing—to dive down deep into our own forgotten dreams, finding solidarity and encouragement there.

As a child, while these stories framed and shaped my perspective in my limited village world, unknowingly, these stories strengthened and became part of my tenacity, my source of inspiration, and ultimately my healing because I knew I could also be a creator, a maker of my life no matter the circumstances. We *all* have the power to seek communities—friendships, poetry readings, book clubs, even social media groups—where imagination merges with voice to create a fertile soil for new possibilities to emerge.

Creativity and Creation

The world would have told a very different version of my grandmother's story if she had not told it to us herself: to outsiders and foreigners who did not understand her way of life and her deep hunger, she was often seen as little more than a poor, illiterate woman, an uninformed "bush" healer, victim of a patriarchal social system. This is not the whole truth about my grandmother. It is a partial truth.

If the story of her life continued to be told that way, her oppression would dominate and overshadow her power: my grandmother was a heroine to her community. She was not just a victim of a patriarchal and colonial environment, she was also a woman who thrived, a respected woman who transcended her circumstances, a wise woman full of grace and dignity.

Like my grandmother, we do have the power to tell alternate stories, to tell authentic stories, to tell complex and messy stories, and to tell our own stories. Sacred sisters, this is about taking responsibility for who we are, engaging our minds and hearts in creativity and storytelling that builds the very core of ourselves to our fullest potential, and to speak to our future selves the once painful aspects from which we've healed.

Unlike the usual, linear way we set our life goals—school, then career, then marriage, then children, as one example—storytelling enables us to be imaginative and inspirational in our goals. It allows for revisions and make-believe, for unhindered creativity and mystery. When told in supportive outlets, such as with friends and mentors, or through blogging or writing, it allows others to revisit their own stories, to creatively craft a new self. Like our buried dreams, stories are little seeds we plant: who knows what will heal or grow once they begin to germinate?

I once spoke with a woman named Ana who shared with me how

storytelling helped her through a difficult time in her life. In her late thirties, Ana suddenly realized that she was actually a terrible fit for the profession she had spent so much time and energy seeking. She was unhappy, unfulfilled, and stuck. This young woman had spent many years training to be a psychologist. It had been her life's goal since she was very young, and so right from college Ana went to graduate school, working very hard to be academically successful, taking on loans to make this goal possible, and even sacrificing her personal life for her studies. Yet she was confident and comforted in the knowledge that she was pursuing her dreams.

Ana celebrated a joyful graduation day, but a few years later she knew by the terrible feeling in her chest that she was burned out, miserable, and that she needed a professional rebirth. A good amount of shame and fear accompanied this feeling: She had school debt! She had no idea where to go next! She was supposed to be responsible and settled by now! She had wasted so much time! She had been so confident that she was on the right path, how could she trust her intuition again?

Ana didn't realize it at the time, she told me, but it was storytelling that helped her begin to move from a wilted old dream into the budding seed of another. "I was feverishly imagining other ways my life might look. I told people, 'I love to bake. I'm going to open a bakery.' I'd announce on social media that I was thinking about opening a day care with all the most recent child psychology research in mind. When strangers would ask what I do for a living, I'd try out my newest idea. 'I am applying for jobs at nonprofit domestic violence shelters'; 'I'm going to do a yoga teacher training'; 'I'm a writer.'"

Ana confided in me that she often felt embarrassed that she'd told people she was going to do something that never came to fruition. More often, however, the stories she told about her future helped her imagine herself beyond the pain and fear she felt at making this change. If Ana could imagine her life differently, she said, then she could live her life differently, too. "I had to inhabit a new life a little bit first. It was like trying on new clothes to see myself in that way, like when I was little playing dress up." And that's how she worked her way out of a dark and confusing time of personal upheaval; through imagination and play, one of those alternate dream paths became her new reality.

Playing and imagination are both central to storytelling. I'm not talking about freewriting as a form of therapy, where you just pour everything out onto paper in a stream of consciousness (although that can be great, too!). I'm talking about telling stories as an act of creativity and creation. I'm talking about a mixture of knowing and mystery. As author and activist Parker J. Palmer writes, "The facts can never be understood except in communion with the imagination."[9] Don't feel limited by your current reality. If we are to get in touch with our sacred purpose then we must be willing to dive into the not-yet, and dance around for a while in the endless possibilities open to us. You've written your dreams down and rooted yourself to the earth, now air them out a little. Stretch the boundaries. Through language we can rewrite our stories, we can tell our stories with ourselves as the protagonists, and we can tell the truth; otherwise, someone else is measuring our lives.

Don't be fooled by the idea of your life as one linear timeline—from birth to death—as if a neat, orderly narrative is the organizing structure of your existence. The power to craft and create through your creativity and nonlinear imagination: this is your birthright. It has been passed down to you from many generations of storytellers back to the origins of humanity. It will probably be messy. All great works of art require rough drafts. You might feel you are too old to engage in such seemingly frivolous creative pursuits—only children get to play dress up, you might think, or only children get to play make believe. But I'm here to tell you that through imagination and play you are creating a great work of art. It's an ongoing project of revision and reimagining that has no clear beginning or end, and is a project worth doing at any age.

I once attended a book club discussion of Elizabeth Gilbert's *Big Magic* led by a woman who began the meeting by asking everyone to introduce themselves with their names and their favorite creative pursuit. One woman responded, "My name is Tracy and I'm a singer," another said, "I'm Noelle and I'm a writer." And so I met a singer and a writer. As the discussion proceeded, however, we learned that these women were not writers or singers—at least not yet! These were their dreams for themselves; they wanted to sing and write and they had recently begun to do it in their spare time. We in the group did not judge; we met these women as they were, on a journey toward a new—yet original—self.

Poet, psychoanalyst, and post-trauma specialist Clarissa Pinkola Estés celebrates the power of working with stories so that they don't just define us, but that we speak back to them and make something from them. "I hope you will go out and let stories, that is, life, happen to you," Estés writes, "and that you will work with these stories . . . water them with your blood and tears and your laughter till they bloom, till you yourself burst into bloom."[10] My soul sings stories in this way. This is the creative potential of storytelling: a full-bodied experience, like kneading dough or dancing in the rain, in which we give birth to new versions of ourselves.

Story as Medicine

The power of storytelling is indeed full-bodied. It not only nurtures our souls, it also heals the body: many health professionals proclaim the health benefits of telling, and listening to, stories. "Telling your story—while being witnessed with loving attention by others who care—may be the most powerful medicine on earth," says doctor and bestselling author Lissa Rankin.[11] "Each of us is a constantly unfolding narrative," she continues, "a hero in a novel no one else can write. And yet so many of us leave our stories untold, our songs unsung—and when this happens, we wind up feeling lonely, listless, out of touch with our life's purpose, plagued with a chronic sense that something is out of alignment. We may even wind up feeling unworthy, unloved, or sick."[12] Storytelling can be a mighty salve for our bodies, minds, and spirits. If we are brave enough to dive into creativity and voice, we can heal.

Telling our stories is an antidote to the chronic misalignment, or sickness, that we experience in a world full of silences. When we fill those silences with our voices and speak our fullness, we heal body and soul. As Rankin puts it:

> Every time you tell your story and someone else who cares bears witness to it, you turn off the body's stress responses, flipping off toxic stress hormones like cortisol and epinephrine and flipping on relaxation responses that release healing hormones like oxytocin, dopamine, nitric oxide, and endorphins. Not only does this turn on the body's innate self-repair mechanisms and function as preventative medicine—or treatment if you're sick. It also relaxes your nervous system and helps heal your mind of depression, anxiety, fear, anger, and feelings of disconnection.[13]

Our lives are measured by the stories we tell; we need to be witnessed and embraced, not through our silences, but through making ourselves heard. When this happens, the soul sings and the body flows in harmony, free from strain and defensiveness.

Research supports this notion that telling stories is good for your health. A study reported in the January 2011 issue of the *Annals of Internal Medicine* found that "storytelling is emerging as a powerful tool for health promotion," especially in populations that are considered vulnerable. In one study, researchers monitored the blood pressure of nearly three hundred individuals who lived in urban areas and were known to have hypertension. The patients were divided into two groups; the first group was given videos to watch of patients telling stories about their own experiences with blood pressure, while the second group viewed videos of more generic and impersonal health issues on topics like dealing with stress. The results were impressive: the study indicated that all the patients listening to the personal stories had a reduction in their blood pressure readings and were better able to manage the condition without medication. The researchers concluded that "storytelling intervention produced substantial and significant improvements."[14]

In fact, the US medical system is on the verge of quite a transformational period, with storytelling as the catalyst for change. Patients are often understood as a collection of data about our physical states, and doctors learn our "stories" through answers we fill out on an intake form and information they take from us: our blood pressure and our lab samples, for example. Some physicians are starting to harness the power of storytelling to cultivate stronger relationships between themselves and their patients, and what they are finding helps us understand how powerful storytelling can be in our lives.

"Telling and listening to stories is the way we make sense of our lives," writes Dr. Thomas K. Houston, lead author of another study on the power of storytelling on health. According to Dr. Houston, storytelling could be an effective way to improve health outcomes without the side effects of medication.

Focusing on narratives in addition to physical health data would also connect and forge better relationships between doctors and patients, because telling and listening to stories allows better trust in the doctor-patient relationship. "We would never graduate someone from medical school who didn't know their pharmacology," writes Dr. Sayantani DasGupta.[15] "We also shouldn't graduate someone who doesn't know how to listen to a story."[16] Dr. DasGupta talks about "transforming medicine into the kind of collaborative endeavor" wherein doctors learn to listen to patients better, and are taught that medicine is less quantitative than was once believed.[17] Indeed, measurable bodily data is in a dynamic relationship with patients' narratives about their experiences—and both are more fluid than static. What doctors need to learn is to see patients as active agents in their own lives, not just as victims to their bodily circumstances.

She writes: "Stories are the way that we all understand the world and the way all of our professions operate and thrive. They keep us self-critical, engaged. We're all trying to figure out what it means to be present for stories, to receive them in meaningful ways, to co-create the stories of our lives and our world together."[18]

Storytelling, then, is a powerful source of "lived evidence." There's your GPA, there's your annual income, there's your height and weight. But that's not who you are; in fact, you can't really quantify the fullness of who you are. That's where telling stories comes in. The medical field is increasingly becoming aware of the healing power of storytelling on the body and on relationships between the teller and witness.

Storytelling is good for your health, because as social beings we need to make meaning for our lives through narrative. We need to be heard. And to do so in a culture that often prefers our silences means being bold enough to speak our stories, and vulnerable enough to ask others to witness them. This is a pathway to wholeness and healing.

Be the Heroine of Your Own Story

When Black feminist lesbian mother poet warrior Audre Lorde (this is how she prefers to name herself, so who am I to silence or edit her?) was first faced with a tumor on her breast, she had an intense wakeup call. She writes, "In becoming forcibly and essentially aware of my mortality, and of what I wished and wanted for my life, however short it might be, priorities and omissions became strongly etched in a merciless light, and what I most regretted were my silences."[19]

Thus begins a gorgeous meditation on the weight of our silences and the power of transforming silence into language and action. Lorde even invented her own *kind* of writing in order to tell her story in *Zami: A New Spelling of My Name*: she called it "biomythography."

A biomythography is a kind of melding of myth, history, and biography: a way of writing one's life that intertwines myth and history and self. It uses imaginative thinking to write the self not so much by chronological life events, but by theme, sound, and image, allowing the writer to define the self on her own terms rather than by strict historical facts. In other words, it plays with that often thin line between fact and fiction, emphasizing perception and lived experience as well as personal empowerment and self-definition.

In fact, Lorde was joining a long line of women who have invented their own forms of self-expression when the social narratives available to women were less than ideal. Women in China who used a script called *nushu*, or female writing, are also part of this lineage.[20] Denied an education for centuries in China, women of the Jiangyong Prefecture in the southern Hunan Province created and used this script to share fears and anxieties about arranged marriages, to record songs and poems, and to share love and intimacy with one another. Forbidden to use this language, the women would embroider it on handkerchiefs and write it on fans.

As Douglas Martin reports in his 2004 *New York Times* article on the death of Yang Huanyi, the last woman to communicate with other women in *nushu* under this oath of secrecy: "popular writers have called *nushu* 'the witch's script' and the 'first language of women's liberation.'"[21] I confess that I adore both phrases, as they reflect the rebellious nature of women who dared to speak and to the liberating potential of such speech acts.

My grandmother and mother are also part of this lineage, for they also spoke in the language of women's liberation, because in their storytelling they told the fullness of their lives, claimed their wisdom and intelligence, and asserted their value. They were *sarungano*,[22] "owners of the stories," highly imaginative female artists, masters of imagery, wisdom, and creation. Their bodies swayed, interpreted, and personified humans and animals alike as they imparted worlds of possibility and information to us.

I call upon this matrilineage to inspire you to become the heroine of your own story. Write on napkins. Sing in the shower. Organize a poetry reading. Reconnect with a friend and listen to old stories and make up new ones. If there is no name for the kind of storytelling you want to do; if no outlets, no languages, allow you to speak the fullness of yourself, then invent one. Know that you do so not in isolation, but in a rich and far-reaching ancestry of women storytellers who have done the same: women who spoke—in secret handwriting, in deserts, with fearful diagnoses, on handkerchiefs, over campfires, with fear and delight and a little wildness in their voices—they spoke. And so can you.

Speak the Self, Heal Nations

Our stories have magic—they give shape and purpose to communities and even nations. Storytelling has depth that brings collective empathy, reminding us of the essence of our humanity, the *ubuntu*, the humanness, that makes us human beings. When I heard my grandmother tell of her pain as well as her expertise, she showed me that a woman can be vulnerable and strong. I saw her humor and her sadness, her frustration at the cultural limits for women and her longing for something more, feelings that were both personal and cultural. I intuitively understood myself as capable of asking those same questions and seeking to fill in the blanks her story created. When a mother in the US hears in a Syrian mother's own voice how she carried her two-year-old on her back, drugged so he would not cry and alert the heavily armed border patrol, across hundreds of miles in the damp and rain to a refugee camp, the distance between these women collapses—as do geographical, political, and cultural borders that may divide them. Our stories have power because through them we embrace our collective vulnerability and worthiness—when you share your pain and resilience, and I share mine, we become one.

We might say that the world oppresses women by silencing our voices, but the inverse is also true: the world suffers (in many cases without knowing or acknowledging it) without women's voices. Sacred sisters, that is the power we have—to tell stories that deepen and extend human consciousness, that heal our souls, and that can bring a global spiritual and physical healing. When we tell our stories, when we embrace creativity and imagination to not only tell ourselves as we really are but also to imagine ourselves beyond our current realities, that act echoes beyond the self in powerful ways.

Our stories need to be told, and there is richness in our diversity because we are not monolithic; rather, it is the beauty of our differences that will bring a cross-pollination of great lessons to be learned that will strengthen not just ourselves but also the world around us. Let us not forget that we have the power in our hands to tell our stories, stories that heal not only our sisterhood, but nations as well.

SACRED RITUAL TO AWAKEN AND INSPIRE YOUR STORYTELLING

Beloved sisters, my hope for you is that you will hear the call of the ancients and the women who've gone before you, and know that they were storytellers. They told stories not only to survive but to flourish. They told stories to find each other, even when the words were forbidden for them to speak or write. They told stories to claim the truth of their lives, to share their hurt and joy, to know themselves through the mirror of the listeners.

They told each other stories in order to *create* themselves. They told stories to imagine themselves differently, even when they were afraid of past mistakes, or that they would be mocked for desiring something more. They are asking you to add your voice to the telling, to be part of the continuum of storytelling that has no beginning and no end. Will you answer their call?

We have been doing a lot of writing and reflection. Now it is time to go public with your dreams. After all, a storyteller is nothing without the ability to incite the listener to embody the experience of the tale and to invoke action. With the vision of your planted dreams firmly in your mind, practice being a storyteller.

First, practice telling yourself the story of your own dreams with confidence. Then set an intention that this week you will be bold enough to tell it to someone else. Identify a safe person or group to whom you can share your story. Perhaps, like Ana, you feel most comfortable telling someone you don't know at the start, because the interpersonal distance is comforting. Or you may want to tell a therapist, coach, or mentor. Protect yourself and your dreams by avoiding telling family members or friends who may have their own reasons for doubting you.

You may find though that what you thought was a supportive environment or person turns out to be judgmental or critical. If someone reacts negatively to your story, I encourage you to take this opportunity to cultivate your *tinogona*—it is achievable!—spirit. *Tinogona* spirit is your inner spirit of resilience driven by determination in a graceful and compassionate manner, knowing you can achieve anything. You strengthen it by remembering your buried dreams.

Your groundedness is strong enough to transcend the unpredictable and changing world without pushing you off course. Say to yourself: "I am not telling my story, my dreams, in order to elicit a particular response from a listener. I cannot make someone respond the way I hope they will. I tell my story because I need to speak it; I need to feel the words take shape in my mouth and hang in the air. I tell it to exercise my creativity and imagination. I tell it because it is my Great Hunger that must be expressed."

Once you have prepared the ideas and your audience, you are ready to tell your story. Tell a story of your inner self that doesn't necessarily fit the narrative others have about you. A story that has been buried inside you, and yet, its revelation adds power to your sacred dreams—the buried dreams.

Talk about your buried dreams. Discuss what's at the heart of your dreams. What awakens you when you think about your dreams, what overwhelms you? What will inspire others about your buried dreams? Start small, but be deliberate: speaking of your dreams strengthens your connection to them.

Once you have done this, set a new intention to tell a make-believe story about yourself, to the same audience or to a new one, full of something that does not yet exist. Talk about the dreams you've written down and buried so that you can hold them and give them shape. Tell how things will be when you get there, even if it seems silly (*especially* if it seems silly). Be bold and brave in your imaginings.

In your journal, reflect on how it felt to speak your dreams to others. Were you afraid? Inspired? Impassioned? Did the telling make your dreams more real to you? Keep going. Tell the story of why your dreams have surfaced for you and imagine achieving them over and over to anyone who will listen.

Celebrate your creativity and your fullness, even if you feel full of contradictions at this pivotal moment of verbally manifesting your dreams. As poet Walt Whitman would say: "Very well then . . . I contradict myself; / I am large . . . I contain multitudes."[23] Respond by claiming your contradictions, all the multitudes you contain, and speak them!

Who knows what will happen? Your creative storytelling is just planting seeds. Some won't grow. But oh, my beloved sisters, some will.

5

VALIDATE YOUR BODY'S KNOWING: HARNESSING YOUR SENSUALITY

> *What is erotic? The acrobatic play of the imagination. The sea of memories in which we bathe. The way we caress and worship with our eyes. Our willingness to be stirred by the sight of the voluptuous. What is erotic is our passion for the liveliness of life.*
>
> —DIANE ACKERMAN, *A NATURAL HISTORY OF LOVE*

In October 2015, I attended the First African Girls' Summit on Ending Child Marriage in Lusaka, Zambia, where I spoke about the importance of eliminating the scourge of child marriage in the world. It was an informative and emotional event, where I heard many stories and met many women who had experienced sexual trauma.

During a break between sessions, a tall woman with smooth olive skin sat down next to me and introduced herself as Seynabou Tall. Tall was a perfect name for a woman of her stature and presence. It wasn't until I looked at her business card that I learned she was the regional adviser with an international organization whose mission is to ensure universal access to reproductive health, including family planning and sexual health to all couples and individuals. I can tell that, like me, she had been reflecting on her personal and professional experiences in this area and she had a story to tell.

She scooted her chair so we were much closer. "I grew up in Dakar, Senegal," Seynabou began.[1] "I was one of six aunts whose advice was always sought out by the younger women and especially cousins and nieces." Other women in the conference joined us and soon we formed our own circle, all eyes on Seynabou.

"One of my younger cousins was forced into a marriage at the age of thirteen to an older man, and before long, she bore him many children. It was before I could find my own voice and so I stood by and watched my cousin struggle at the hands of this man. He was jealous and domineering; he kept her pregnant back to back as a way to control her. Where would she go with all those children? As was the custom in cities and rural areas like ours, my cousin's parents believed that marrying their daughters off early was the right thing to do. It was their way of keeping them away from early pregnancy outside of the protection of marriage.

"Thank goodness, soon, the husband died of old age," Seynabou said with a serious expression and a hint of laughter. I heard suppressed giggles among the women as they cheered the cousin's freedom. "By now, my cousin was hardly in her forties, too young to be alone in the eyes of the elders. As per the tradition, the late husband's family was ready for her to be inherited by one of the men in the family. My cousin didn't want any part of it. Another marriage!

"No, she complained bitterly to us aunts. But what could we do?" asked Seynabou. "Thank God, my cousin's sons were now older and they sided with their mother. They threatened their father's family that if any men attempted to come near their home they would regret it." Everyone in the group sighed with relief. "Good for her! Good for her! Oh, what amazing sons! We need more sons like that!"

"One day, without asking for her consent, the elders met with and married her off to a cousin of hers, a forty-year-old man named

Samba, also a widow. My cousin was very upset. She went around and complained to each of the elders, asking them to cancel the marriage. They refused.

"Out of desperation and with no support, she decided that the marriage would be a companionship: Samba would visit once a week in the afternoon, but would never sleep with her. Samba accepted the deal. In time they became friends. Samba was patient and respectful of the terms and conditions of their relationship, and in turn, he was accepted into her home, helping with the bills, offering gifts, and advising the children in their studies and personal lives.

"One hot afternoon, Samba visited my cousin looking for medication to alleviate a pounding headache. She had none, so Samba asked if she would have her sons rush to a nearby store to buy some pain-relief medication. My cousin is a very compassionate woman. Samba was now resting on the dirt floor outside and he seemed to be in much pain. My cousin did not have much room in her house, but she could not just watch a man in such pain.

"She asked Samba to rest in a small crafts room adjacent to her bedroom. After making sure that Samba was settled, my cousin tiptoed out and left Samba while she looked out to the road to see if the boys were anywhere nearby. Soon, in a strained voice, Samba was calling for water. My cousin entered that room with a gourd of water and did not come out until the boys arrived.

"Soon the boys returned and found the small room locked. The older son found it very strange and asked his mother if she was okay. My cousin came out of the room with such sadness in her eyes; she seemed to be on the verge of tears. Did he harm you? the son asked his mother, and my cousin remained silent. By then Samba was out of the room and about to leave. The son turned to Samba and asked if he had harmed his mother. Samba kept walking, and the son warned Samba that if he ever stepped his foot in their yard again, he was going to kill him. Samba took his bag and quietly left.

"Days pass and all ears are kept to the ground. We wanted to know what Samba did to our cousin, but no one was talking. We knew that nothing in the village ever stays hidden, and so we waited. We knew that whatever happened would come out eventually," continued Seynabou.

"Soon it came time for a family gathering where everyone was present. These gatherings bring women together: they congregate to mourn losses and celebrate blessings, and to catch up with each other. Old stories are revisited, some with a little bit of exaggeration, and new ones are told in such vivid detail that they burn into your mind forever. As aunts of the village, we collected in our own room, where we sat and visited, inquiring about each other's families and exchanging the latest news.

"We all looked for our cousin. We asked after her, but she was nowhere to be found. Yet all her children were present. We continued with our conversations as normal, but I knew that each of us had burning questions that needed to be answered.

"The following morning, we were all surprised to see our cousin approaching. This was not the shy beloved cousin we knew and expected. Dhi... dhii... dhii... we heard the sound of her feet as they hit the ground. She walked like a woman on a mission. In silence, we watched. She wore her usual attire, a red cloth tightly worn over her skirt, old sneakers torn at the corners and showing holes where each pinkie protrudes from the shoes. She entered the yard with deliberation. We looked at each other with amazement.

"Culturally, young women are expected to kneel down as they greet their elders. This time, however, our beloved cousin spared no time for greetings or any small talk. She remained standing, looming over all her aunts and cousins of the same age like a soldier about to give instructions. She wagged her finger at us, one aunt at a time. It felt like a lashing on our skin.

"'You old witches,' she said, and before we can recover from the initial shock, our cousin rests one hand on her hip and puts the other hand to her lips, signaling to us that we dare not speak. All we could do was gasp. 'All these years you were enjoying this thing'—now pointing to her vagina—'while you watched me suffer? I had no idea how sweet it is to be aroused by a man and left intoxicated while I feel the explosion of my clitoris!'

"Now we were in shock. We had no idea how to respond, but we didn't have the chance anyway, because our cousin went right on testifying to her pleasure. 'Samba took me to a level I had never been before. He aroused me with a desire that leaves me demanding more. My whole body erupted like a volcano when he stroked my clitoris and I experienced parts of my body that I never knew existed. Forty years ... forty dead years of being denied what's rightfully mine. How dare you for never saying anything?'

"Stunned and silent, we watched our cousin as the weight of her words penetrate our ears. 'Is this what you have been enjoying all along in your marriages ... and did you ever think of me and that old man? How could you?' With tears streaming down her cheeks, our cousin stormed out. Just at the door of the room, she looked back, took two steps toward us, and said, 'One last thing, tell my son never to threaten Samba. I will kick anyone who interferes with my Samba.'

"She swung her head, tightened the loose fringes from the colorful cloth that had loosened in her powerful speech, and headed back home, where we can only assume Samba waited in bed. We all remained speechless for a few moments, until the eldest of the aunts let out a high-pitched ululation loud enough to be heard in the corners of our small hut. My cousin had found herself."

Seynabou paused to let the full effect of her words settle on each woman in the circle. "My sisters, the eruption of orgasms is beautiful, and yet we seem not to think about it as we discuss the stories of our sisters and daughters forced into early and child marriages. Why can we dedicate whole conferences to discussing our pain, but never our pleasure? In all of the work we do, our inner work and our community work, our goal is not simply to eradicate suffering and injustice, is it? We also want to create a world with more harmony and wholeness. If this is so, then I believe that we cannot make the same mistake the other aunts and I made with our cousin. We must also testify to our pleasure."

I was stunned. I had never heard anyone speak openly about our erotic power. Because I was married very young and sex became an obligation, it was never a topic about which to talk. Therefore, I had no idea of an orgasm and never knew it existed. As I reflected on this story, I found myself thinking of the first time I had sex with my current husband, Mark. I thought I was having a heart attack and even asked him to stop. The poor man was shocked, as he had no idea why I would push him away. Later I realized I was having the first big O of my life! Like Seynabou's cousin, no one had told me about the power of sex and its liberating effect.

I looked around, seeing my shock mirrored on the faces of the women in the circle. I knew that, like me, for most of the women who listened to Seynabou's story, this was the first time that they also heard anyone publicly speaking about sensuality, the first time anyone had encouraged us to embrace our deepest desires and be openly connected to our own bodies and sexuality.

Sex for some of us and for many of the women who came before us—our great-grandmothers, our grandmothers, our mothers—had always been for procreation, a marital duty for women, and never for its pleasures. And for many it has been a source of shame and fear.

The moment of the cousin's declaration of her sensual arousal, how she was taken to deeper places in her body that she never knew existed, left many of us tangled and scrambling for something to which we could not put words. This dirty, off-limits, forbidden thing—might it be central to our awakening as women, to walking the path of our sacred dreams?

What We Have Lost

I know I am one of more than 700 million women and girls worldwide today, girls like Seynabou's cousin, who had babies or were married before their eighteenth birthday.[2] Seynabou's story brought home the realization that 125 million of those girls live in Africa, and that I count myself in those statistics. I am also counted among the more than one in three women who were married or in union before the age of fifteen.[3]

At one point during the conference, two women approached me so they could introduce Sarah, a fourteen-year-old girl they had rescued from a horrible marriage. Sarah had been married to a man old enough to be her father, and she was his fifth wife. Shy, using her front teeth to chip away at her fingernails, Sarah hardly looked at me as she shared a harrowing story of abuse at the hands of this man and his wives.

We soon split off so that Sarah could nurse her nine-month-old baby, while I literally dragged my way to find any open breakout session. I didn't care what topic or what expert panel; I just wanted to be in some corner with my thoughts. I couldn't take my mind off Sarah and the many young girls I had seen. Here I was, in my mid-fifties, crying for my own lost childhood. It's hard to be a child when you are married at the onset of puberty and made to have children right away. Having a child at the age of fourteen, what did I know? Innocence, pain, misery, shame, and blame all mixed in equal doses like some recipe for a stew that no one wants to eat, and the world goes on as if nothing is wrong. I saw myself in Sarah.

My thoughts traveled back home and I remembered a young girl named Marita. Marita was married at a tender young age to a man named Bob. As is the custom, Bob's family wanted proof of Marita's virginity when he married. On the night of the wedding, the couple is instructed to have sex on a plain white cloth. In the morning, Bob's aunts check the cloth for blood. If there is no blood, the aunts will poke a hole in the middle of the cloth, exposing a nonvirgin. With blood, a different cloth with no hole is presented to the family. Silence prevails until the aunts present a folded cloth to Bob's family and the elders. Fortunately, the cloth has no hole and both families are happy to know that Marita is "pure and untouched," especially her father, who is given a substantial bride price. A different outcome would have embarrassed the family and Marita's character would have been forever tainted.

Bob was proud to be marrying a virgin. He let it be known that he paid *mombe yechimanda*, a "virginity cow," as part of the bride price. To provide for his growing family, he moved to the city. Eventually, though, he wrote home to say that he contracted a strange illness. No one knows what ails him, and he soon loses his job as a "garden boy" (a term used by white masters during the colonial era that is still used today; white settlers would call the Black men who served as gardeners "boy" regardless of age). He returns home to Marita and their two young children in defeat. It is believed that Bob had another wife in the city and that she left him when he fell ill, but no one is talking details.

Still quite young, Marita is a very quiet woman who treats her husband and father-in-law with humble servitude. Bob dies not long after he returns to the village. He was only in his thirties. As custom dictates, Bob's younger brother Vashe inherits his brother's wife and children, and so Vashe moves in with Marita to assume the role of husband and father. Vashe is a good man, who understands the connection between many wives and poverty. Vashe had hoped to get an education, but he was forced to drop out of school at age thirteen because his father, a polygamous man, could not afford tuition—indeed, his father could barely afford to feed his forty-plus children, and this desperate situation forced some of his wives to return to their families of origin. Despite this hard upbringing, or perhaps because of it, Vashe is proud to be known as a responsible man. He promises me that he will do whatever it takes to provide for his new family, Marita and his brother's children.

I had returned home on a short visit from the United States when Vashe showed me a rash on his arm that is not responding to medication. Do I know of a strong American drug that can cure him, he asks? It feels as though a knife pierces my heart when I realize what might be happening. With no HIV medication available, it does not take long for Vashe to succumb to his brother's disease.

Vashe's widow, Marita, packs her bags and children to return to her birth family in disgrace. This once-hopeful young woman will forevermore be referred to as "the one who killed two husbands." How infuriating, I reflect. Her virginal purity was demanded for her marriage and yet she is the one who is blamed for contracting sexual diseases. The system was designed so that there was almost no situation in which she could prosper: her worthiness was measured by her virginity and ability to produce children; sexual stigma was always going to be closely tied to her value and her identity.

I wonder, if Marita, Sarah, and all the young women I have met, as well as all those millions of women and girls in many countries around the world who still practice child marriages, wife inheritance, and value virginity, had the power to define their own sexuality, how different would their stories be?

Now that I've spent many years living, studying, and speaking outside of my village, I know that the problem of women's sexuality is not limited to the issue of child marriage, nor is it only a problem in Africa. In fact, every day in the US, I see evidence of the many ways women's sexuality is distorted and limited, from the hypersexualization of young transgender girls (our cultural obsession with their genitalia or where they use the bathroom) to the widespread practice of men catcalling women on the street (and often threatening women if they decline to smile or respond), to the fact that we elected a president who, in 2005, bragged about kissing women without their consent and grabbing them "by the pussy."[4]

Research has shown, for example, that American women have one orgasm for every three a man experiences—this is what we call the "orgasm gap."[5] There are several cultural norms that might explain this: it is more socially acceptable for men than it is for women to express their sexual desires; women's sexuality is considered mysterious and more challenging than men's; women may be more likely to be concerned about how they look rather than how they feel; men's pleasure is prioritized in the media and in patriarchal cultures. Whatever the reason, the effect is that in our most intimate of encounters, statistically speaking, men have been shown to receive more fulfillment than women.

My research on HIV and sexuality brought me some additional information, which is supported by recent studies of American women: women in intimate relationships with other women have more orgasms than do heterosexual women.[6] I have to wonder at studies like these, if we are fully harnessing our sexual power and pleasure.

My grandmother had a way of describing the clitoris: "*Ndi chikarakadzi anopedza nyota yekadzi*"—"The feminine goddess that quenches a woman's inner thirst." Never a proponent of a practice among my people known as *kudhonza matinji*—the pulling of the inner labia minora of the vagina, which is said to sexually satisfy men and also make birthing easier, but is in fact a painful distortion of the body—my grandmother belonged to a secret society of women who discouraged this practice because they believed in the power of women's pleasure.

I never knew who these women were or when they met, but as a *nyamukuta* (midwife), my grandmother could see that elongated labia hindered rather than helped the birthing process. "I have to keep flipping those chunks of meat down there that look like the ears of an elephant while taking away my time from delivering the baby," she once told me, an explanation I knew would have my mother in stitches with so much laughter.

I recently shared with an American conference group a statistic that I found interesting: 30 percent of women and 25 percent of men don't know where the clitoris is located. Right away a man in the group expressed astonishment that more women than men are confused about female anatomy. But this is not so surprising when you really think about it. Women, even in so-called developed countries, are often taught from a very early age that their bodies are a source of danger or shame—even in notoriously inadequate American sexual education classes, for example, or well-meaning rape prevention campaigns, which put the emphasis on teaching girls to say "no" so much that we effectively discourage them from saying "yes" to their own desires.[7] Like the pulling of the inner labia minora of the vagina, there are many different ways human cultures distort "the goddess that quenches a woman's inner thirst," as my grandmother would say, and disconnect girls and women from their bodies.

At its most extreme, some cultures, primarily in sub-Saharan Africa and the Arab states but also in some Western cultures, completely mutilate female sex organs, from female circumcision to expensive cosmetic surgeries that "improve" the appearance, size, and shape of the clitoris, and the practice is increasingly gaining in popularity. More than five thousand labiaplasties were performed in the United States in 2013, a 44 percent increase from the year before. Even bigger surges in the procedure were reported in the UK and Australia.[8] The secret society of women my grandmother belonged to knew better, and yet they were too afraid to openly oppose it. Unfortunately, sex is a taboo subject in my culture, and as children we would hear about it only when my grandmother was not happy about something concerning women and their sexuality.

Cultural norms and practices that deny women's sexuality by devaluing female orgasm, or at the most extreme mutilating their sexual organs, robs us of our erotic power, our bodily knowing. Harnessing the power of our deepest, most sacred sexualities is an essential part of creating a more harmonious, balanced world.

The sexual revolution of the 1960s and 1970s was widespread in the US yet the orgasm gap persists, and more than six hundred American women are victims of sexual violence each day.[9] The sexual revolution will not be complete as long as some cultures prize profit over emotion, wealth accumulation and hierarchical power over embodied joy. Women must continue to rise. For how can we have the confidence to follow our inner compass and seek the fulfillment of our sacred dreams without also cultivating a sexual revolution from within?

A woman with awakened sexuality has cultivated love and respect for her body and the bodies of all living beings. She celebrates the power of her femininity and her ability to forge sacred connections and generative creativity. She embraces joy and pleasure, expands rather than shrinks into her environment. She has recovered what has been kept from her, the knowledge of her own corporeal self and its powerful potentials. She holds the key to love and community in the sacred shapes of her physical incarnation.

I Am Deliberate

I often find that my favorite moment in books, poems, and the stories women tell me is that point when a woman stops asking for permission and gets in touch with her power in the world—when she realizes the strength of her own shape and feels herself tangibly in her environment; when she lets go of shame and fear and awakens her sensual, physical being. When Cheryl Strayed reflects in her memoir *Wild*: "Of all the things I'd been skeptical about, I didn't feel skeptical about this: the wilderness had a clarity that included me."[10] Or when Zora Neale Hurston's character Janie in *Their Eyes Were Watching God* learns what love is by watching spring unfold:

> She saw a dust-bearing bee sink into the sanctum of a bloom; the thousand sister-calyxes arch to meet the love embrace and the ecstatic shiver of the tree from root to tiniest branch creaming in every blossom and frothing with delight. So this was a marriage![11]

My body sways and sings in admiration and recognition of these moments. I feel a giant "Yes!" ringing in me like a gong. This is the moment when a woman stops asking for permission and starts charting her own course. Why? Because she feels herself connected to something greater than herself, and she also feels that greatness dwelling within her very being.

Give your body freedom to let loose, be true, embracing all its softness, curves, and pulsating energy. Let your body express its desires, hopes, and dreams to and through you—let your feet, legs, hips, stomach, hands, arms, and neck do the talking. Feel in the sacred body of the wild forest—the crisp clean air, the strong sturdy trunks and branches, the soft wispy unkempt undergrowth—the contours of your own sacred body; taste the syrupy sweet nectar of the world just as the bees and the birds do. These fleshy pleasures include you. Go on this nonlinear, daring journey toward your sacred purpose with all parts of you—body, mind, and soul.

It is so hard to do, I know. There are many forces discouraging us from loving and trusting our bodies, many voices drowning out the sound of our bodies' expression. This is why my body and soul thrill at every moment when authors like Cheryl Strayed or Zora Neale Hurston refuse that shame and voice the freedom to love one's self—because in spite of how difficult it is to do, we have the opportunity to do it anyway, in every moment of every day. "You only have to let the soft animal of your body / love what it loves," writes poet Mary Oliver.[12] I am here to tell you that you are enough. I am here to tell you that you are, in fact, abundant. You will come to know and believe this if only you are brave enough to awaken your sensual body.

Harness Your Sacred Sensual Power

Seynabou's story brings awareness of the deep wounds that so often accompany the development of women's sexual selves. For some women the wounding comes from child marriage, for others it comes from sexual abuse, others grow up being told to cross their legs and cover up as adult men gawk at them, and on and on. We are indeed in crisis in this area. I am also moved by Seynabou's story, however, because in it she provides a potent example of a woman who harnessed her sensuality despite her culture and society. Inspired by Seynabou's guidance, we must meditate on, find solutions for, and celebrate our deepest sexual desires.

Seynabou's story is not just about the day her cousin found out about orgasm and the generational silence around such pleasure that the aunts displayed; it is also a story about a woman getting in touch with her erotic power, claiming and voicing it as her inherent right. We all have that same right to embrace and radiate our feminine sensuality as whole women, and by doing so, there is a ripple effect of healing connection with others.

My beloved poet warrior Audre Lorde wrote that the erotic is a source of great power and information, a source that lives in a sacred, feminine dimension. She defines the erotic as "a measure between the beginnings of our sense of self and the chaos of our strongest feelings."[13] We can know it by the feeling of internal satisfaction that it brings. Once we know this feeling, we will most certainly measure every other thing against it, "for having the fullness of this depth of feeling and recognizing its power, in honor and self-respect we can require no less of ourselves."[14] It is like finding the source of life. We are liberated, happier, and can work on our dreams with confidence and gusto. How can we care for something outside of us when the erotic within us is silenced?

Lorde insists that the erotic is "the personification of love in all its aspects";[15] it is creativity and harmony embodied, it is "creative energy empowered."[16] Tapping in to this resource is revolutionary because we live in societies that rob us of our erotic potential by privileging profit and individual gain over emotion. The erotic is another kind of power altogether, not one that exploits, but one that empowers and loves. Perhaps we experience the erotic during sex, but we are just as likely to experience it through reading, through singing, through dance—or whatever else explodes your inner self with a sense of fullness and bliss.

I remember feeling this connection to my body and my joy when I was small and spent my days working in the fields. The other herders, all boys, would often make terrible fun of me when they caught me talking to lizards, cow dung beetles, and chameleons as if these creatures could hear me, and they hated that I was faster and stronger than they were as we climbed trees or raced through the fields. But to me, playing out in the trees, grasses, and clay soil with these creatures, and the combination of using my imagination and my body, was an experience of the erotic, creative energy empowered.

I loved to watch big black ants, known as *mashingishingi*, form a long winding line to build their mounds. Sometimes I would get distracted trying to rescue drowning ants and fishing worms from water puddles. I followed along as big black ants led me to their final destination, a feeling of amazement at how they stored water to build their beautiful home running up and down my spine. I followed the slimy trail of snails until I found their home, too, cheering them on for walking such long distances. I knew better than to touch them or distract them in their journey, because my mother said they were in a hurry to feed their young ones. During the rainy season, I dug the red clay soil from the dead anthill, shaping it into all kinds of animals, including dogs, zebras, and elephants.

I loved climbing wild fruit trees, too, and was proud of my speed and agility, which helped me to reach the highest hanging fruit. I remember one day, a neighbor's son, called Kunesu, complained that my tree climbing was unladylike. He decided to show the other cattle herders where I belong—in the kitchen—by challenging me to a climbing contest. I agree, and beat him to the fruit! While others laugh, Kunesu seethes with anger. I knew that this was not the end, that there would be a fight. When this happens, I cannot win because Kunesu is physically stronger than I am. My brother and his friends warn me to stay away from him because they, too, fear him.

One day, Kunesu insisted that I fetch a stray cow. Refusing, I walk away, muttering insults as I go. In punishment for my insolence, he scoops soil into two small rounded mounds, draws a straight line in the soil between the mounds, and tells me that each represents a breast, one of his mother's and one of my mother's. This kind of talk excites every adolescent cattle herder because it is taboo. In my culture, a mother's breast is not something with which you play around! Mothers are well respected and their reproductive parts are generally not discussed.

Kunesu dares me to "destroy" his mother's breast. By this time, we are surrounded by herders who are itching for us to fight. Kunesu and I face off like two bulls and I stare him down. He crosses the line and stomps on my mother's so-called breast with his foot. Oh, I am angry—my blood is boiling and I want revenge. Punching him in the face, I scream, "How dare you have no respect for my mother's breast!" In the background, I hear cheering. The crowd is getting rowdy and many probably expect boys related to my mother to come to my rescue. No one does because Kunesu is a very strong boy and no one is willing to cross him.

Those watching laughingly call him a coward for taking a punch from a girl. Kunesu slowly wipes off the part of his face that I've hit as though he is cleaning off my filth. As he looks me up and down, it is clear that he plans to show me where I belong. Silence fills the humid air except for the soft rustling of savanna grass and the singing birds. With one quick movement, Kunesu punches my nose so hard that blood splatters everywhere. Bleeding but determined, I hold my ground. Biting my lower lip to hold back tears, I see from the corner of my eye the cattle herders scatter. The noise has attracted Kunesu's father, who grabs his son by the ear and drags him home, yelling at him for letting a girl challenge him and then beating her up.

There will always be bullies like Kunesu who want to denigrate our power, to mock our mother's breasts, or to stomp the feminine body. There will always be harmful forces who would rather keep us out of the trees, tucked away controlled and disembodied, far from the fruit for which we long. And so you have to be willing to fight for it, as my younger self did without knowing it; you have to make a practice of honoring the erotic within you, and embracing your tender, feminine parts.

This younger me found a source of the erotic in the strength of my arms and legs as I climbed fruit trees, in the miraculous movements of insects and animals, and in forming creatures out of clay with my hands. I found it instinctively and without questioning. I found it without shame. There is something instinctive in you, too, which longs to slough off embarrassment and control in pursuit of touching and tasting the wild fruit hanging from the highest branch.

We can only tap into the fullness of our beings and our strength if we liberate our sensual, erotic power. Otherwise, we remain incomplete, stuck in our heads, pursuing our sacred dreams only from the "neck up." From the moment I experienced my own sexuality with my current husband, Mark, without shame, I began to experience true joy and an inner peace. I was a fulfilled woman, a goddess on a mission. Connection to my sexuality and my sensuality meant I was in a relationship with myself. I valued and practiced self-love and care. Embarrassment and fear had no more power over me. Instead, I was using my energy in pursuit of my sacred dreams, able to give back to others from a place of wholeness.

In October of 2015, I was invited to speak at the Emerging Women Conference where I shared a speaking platform with Esther Perel. Esther is a native of Belgium and a practicing psychotherapist who spent most of her time consulting with Fortune 500 companies. Her 2013 TED talk, "The Secret to Desire in a Long-Term Relationship," attracted more than a million views in the first month after its release. Esther's topic at the conference was "The Fluidity of Sexual Desire," which left the audience in awe.[17] She described how women can easily lose connections to their arousal, to their sense of excitement, to their playfulness, and yet, this loss is also connected to their aliveness.

Esther's talk brought some truth home when she talked about how our passion and connection to our work and for things in life can have deeper meaning when we are connected to an inner source of excitement—awakened to our own desires, our own erotic vitality. These self-connections make us feel alive and from that place of aliveness with the erotic self, then it's much easier for us to connect to our work, our relationships, and our dreams.

Sacred sisters, claim your sensuality, the erotic power of your body uniting with your spiritual and emotional self—it heals you. Accept the exploration of your own long-denied erotic needs; find that fullness not only in your body but in your work, your relationships, and your spirit. That is the opportunity that talking about this often-taboo subject of sexuality offers us.

You are more than an object for someone else's pleasure—you can be your own source of pleasure and joy. You contain deep wells of feeling within you. Share your stories of erotic fullness with others, for the time has come for us to help one another tap into our authentic true selves so that we all shine as the uniquely impactful global sisters we are meant to be. Love yourself before you love your work, your dreams, or someone else. Celebrate your body's and your soul's desires: you deserve your pleasure and your joy, for you are creative energy embodied.

SACRED RITUAL TO VALIDATE YOUR BODY'S KNOWING

Express your deeper knowing to everything that is true to your soul with movement and awareness in your body. As my grandmother would say, "When the truth hits you at the center of your knowing, every fiber of your being responds in agreement. A deep joy rises and an uncontrollable, deep ululation erupts, surprising even you, and you know in your bones that Nyadenga, the Great Spirit, has heard your truth." Your body will speak when you are in tune with your inner knowing.

In celebrating my authentic "yes," the moment when I feel my soul awaken within, I dance as I ululate to my *chinyamusasure* dance, the dance of my people. Slowly, in my dance, I make a circle as both my feet and hips respond to my favorite music. As the rhythm of the music picks up, my steps increase. I move with such fluidity, feeling no separation between the physical space around me and my body.

I find my feet consciously remembering the sacred circle marking a pathway created to cement my ritual dance. I respond to my "yes" with this ancient dance and music that fills my body as I raise my hips in response to my feet. This dance pulses healing energy through my physical body as the movements I make respond to the calling of my cellular soul truth. In this moment, I am powerful, and I know my "yes" is a profound affirmation that who I am and what I bring to the world is important.

As I move, I know Nyadenga, or the Creator, has a clarity and a purpose that includes me, that celebrates and loves me. It loves the curves of my soft flesh, the strength of my muscles, and the firmness of my bones. It revels in my laugh lines and my thinking lines equally, it rejoices in the stretch of my skin, and the sound of my bare feet hitting the floor. In body and soul, I rise to meet this love and this sacred purpose.

Chinyamusasure is an erotic dance in the spirit of Lorde's definition of the erotic. It is a physical expression of storytelling, a practice of learning to listen to your body. It is an expression of joy, fullness, and feminine wisdom. In *chinyamusasure*, you let your body speak. As you dance, your body tells a story, perhaps of your past or your future. Give your body permission to express what it yearns for. Make a circle with your movements, as wide and big or small and compact as feels right to you. Know that the circle is a safe space, a sacred enclosure with no beginning and no end. In that space, honor what your body hungers for through movement, as spirit and body become one.

Choose any music that makes you happy, and let your physical body meet the joy of your soul. Feel the wild woman in you. As you dance, notice in what part of your body your definite "yes" resides. Now change the rhythm of your dance, moving more slowly. Where in your body do you feel your definite "no"?

As the music comes to an end, can you determine your true "yes" about yourself, your dreams, or your life beyond what you may have been taught and conditioned to believe? Reflect on the source of this conditioning. Practice developing your "yes" and your "no" so that you are clear how to express what is true for you. Notice when your head is blocking your heart or when you are overthinking your "yes." How is that different from when you are feeling your "yes" deep inside?

When your body tires, pleasantly spent from the beautiful exertion of your dance, take a few moments to reflect in your journal. Before you begin writing, hold your hand over your heart, which may be beating quite fast. As your heart slows back down to its normal resting beat, hold that energy in your hand, bringing it with you as you prepare to write.

First, describe what felt good about dancing. Where did you feel positive energy most flowing? Be detailed: What felt good? Where in your body did you feel loving energy? What color was that energy? What words would you associate with it? Take a few moments to sit in the pleasure that these reflections bring you.

Now let us fill those more challenging parts of the body with self-love. Spend some time reflecting on any insecurity that may have come up in your dance. Where in your body did you feel pain or shame if you did feel some? Where did you feel fear or uncertainty? Name those places and those feelings in your journal if you experienced them.

Take a few deep, cleansing breaths. Close your eyes and imagine a brightly colored pattern on a stunning white background, with bold greens, crisp blues, and deep reds in geometric shapes that feel warm and loving to you. Move this pattern from your mind's eye down into your heart. Breathe as you imagine these bright colors and this joyful pattern expanding in your heart.

When your heart feels full, send this image into those parts of your body that might have felt some hurt, pain, or uncertainty during your dance. Any part you do not particularly like or anywhere that is a source of struggle for you. As you continue deeply breathing, fill those perceived "challenging" parts of your body with the bright, healing colors of your heart pattern, sending love and warm energy there. You may feel your nervous system calm down and a sense of self-acceptance soothing you.

Before you leave this space, let out an ululation. Let the world within you know that you have been in touch with the sacredness of your femininity. Then say to yourself, "I fill my body with love and dignity. I honor and respect the sacred depths of my being, the place in me where my soul's desires meet the curves of my body. I celebrate and embrace my body and its intuition."

6

LET YOUR SPIRIT TAKE ROOT: BELIEVING IN YOUR DREAMS

There is only one history of any importance, and it is the history of what you once believed in, and the history of what you came to believe in.

—KAY BOYLE, "WHITE AS SNOW"

For all the many reasons we may have forgotten our dreams, we share one similarity: we stopped *believing* in them. Yet the power of redefining and re-creating a new narrative is grounded in our belief of who we can be, and that power is in our hands. It's our heartfelt desire grounded in a belief—a mental state of knowing with strong conviction and certainty that we are connected to something greater than self, something sacred, something that heals the past, present, and future generations—that makes achieving our dreams possible.

As my mother would say, "Sometimes our life is like a hut that needs to be built and perfected until it resembles the home we want to leave behind for future generations." Before we children and young mothers could wrap our minds around her meaning, she would ask, "Is the foundation strong enough to stand the many *chinyamusasure* dances, the tears of joy and sorrow, and the healing that needs to take place for the hut to be a home? Does this hut have what it takes to pass on these rituals and your healing?" Remember the *chinyamusasure* is an erotic dance, and for my people it chronicles important historic and cultural events as well as personal milestones. Hence the floors of one's hut, which is made of clay soils that are compacted and then polished with cow dung to give a smooth and shiny look, must be strong enough to accommodate not only the slow swirling dance that follows the rhythm of the drums, but also the impact of our bare feet as we stomp the ground.

Thus my mother imparted to us that we are the architects of our lives. The power to change the status quo is in our grasp; how we work and believe in our efforts should be grounded in the inner knowing that we are forever on a journey to right the wrongs of the past and pave the way for future generations. My sacred sister, to right the wrongs, to heal the past, to become who we truly are, requires not only courage but also belief that our dreams are achievable in our lifetime—*tinogona*.

Forgetting our greatest dreams means that we have lost our faith in them, which in turn continues to create a division between who we are and who we once dreamed we could be. We then may become indifferent, no longer seeing our purpose here on earth, or how we are connected to something bigger than ourselves. Our loss of conviction can then make our dreams quieter and quieter until we hear their sacred calling no more. Our dreams are not fund dependent, age dependent, or even skill dependent. Rather, our dreams are built on what we believe about ourselves, and the part we play in the great universal consciousness.

Believing in our dreams is equally about the past, present, and the future. We live in a world with so many injustices for women, and yet, we also live in a historical moment that is better for women than it has ever been. We owe a debt of gratitude to those who have gone before who have helped us get to this point, and we can also gather strength from those women of the past who have transformed their belief into a better world for us today. And belief is also about honoring that legacy in our present time so generations to come will have a better future. Without belief, how is it possible to be inspired and be able to inspire the next generation? A richer relationship between those two poles gives us hope and strength in the present, for they show us our connectedness to the greater whole.

We all have a belief system, whether intentional or not. We may believe stories of our own inferiority or of our power. The question is, Are our beliefs worth passing on to the next generation? Are our beliefs a source of pride to those spirits from the past? Are our beliefs serving our souls in the present?

Trusting in our dreams should make us hopeful and confident; strengthening the continuity of an unbroken thread of conviction that has been passed down to us and lays a strong foundation for future generations. In other words, belief instills confidence and a higher expectation to change the course of our lives for the better. Without that expectation we have no hope, and without hope we are useless to ourselves and to the next generation.

I came to America irrevocably grounded in knowing I was to achieve my dreams. I knew without a shadow of doubt that I was on a journey to heal not only my past, but also my future, because my children were connected to my success. It was important to believe in my dreams so that I was connected to something bigger than myself. I trusted in the significance of that connection always. I was downright stubborn about it. My stubborn belief did not emerge from my ego: it strengthened not the small me but the sacred me, my spirit, my connectedness to the universal life force. This belief served me through many difficult times. The power you see, sacred sister, is not in the world's belief about you but in your own. By claiming and *believing* stubbornly in your dream, you re-create the world. This power you have within you has the power to heal and change our world for the better, for other sacred sisters, for daughters, nieces, mothers, sisters, aunts and even sons, husbands, fathers, brothers, nephews, and uncles.

I remember I was incredibly nervous when I took my doctoral

exams, and I felt my dreams of the future weighing heavily on my shoulders. By that time I had, with great determination, hard work, and support from my mother and my community, achieved my goals of a high school diploma in Zimbabwe, and a bachelor's degree and a master's degree in America. I worried: What if I fail now when I am so close to my fourth dream?

I could not afford to fail. I had buried my dreams under a rock as a reminder of their connection to my history and essence. I felt achieving my PhD, the highest level of education, was not only part of fulfilling that connection, but also part of claiming my power and the freedom to stand in my own skin with a strength to right the wrongs of my past. If I failed now, then how would I be able to go back to my village to educate young girls and create spaces for women to empower themselves, my sacred purpose? How would I bear fruit to all the things that my grandmother and mother believed in—the fight for women's dignity?

I visualized my maternal and paternal grandparents as well as my mother standing in each corner of the room, whispering to me, ululating, and supporting me. I grasped and squeezed the small rock in my pocket that I've carried since burying my dreams. I felt protected and present. Confident. Trusting. Fortified with a strong rootedness (the rock in my hand), and visualizing the life I wanted for myself, my children, and my community, I could then take the leap into the unknown direction of my dreams to send my voice, my stories, out into the world.

My sisters, the choices we make to honor our belief in ourselves is a sacred thread that ties us to the most profound aspect of humanity: to a connected oneness that heals the wrongs of the world. We only thrive as a species through this belief. Belief strengthens one's resilience and leverages the power to improve our condition, no matter where we are born and under what circumstances.

I know that belief can be a tricky subject, especially for women, because many of us associate belief with institutionalized religion, where messages of women's inferiority vibrate intensely—either leaving many women at odds with the dogma or making them internalize their own silencing, normalizing it like a belt securely tied to shape a waistline. To those who have no relationship with institutionalized faith practices, belief can seem like it only belongs to those who have religious affiliation, as if our belief must be filtered through an institution to be valid.

Another reason that consistent belief in our dreams can feel so challenging is because most of us were raised in cultures that taught us to seek external validation over trusting our inner voices. We have come to accept the voices of doubt within us as the voice of reason or authority. These voices tell us that in order to be loved we must be "good," that we must be perfect before we can even begin pursuing our dreams, that failure is a source of shame rather than simply information or a chance to learn, that speaking up for ourselves and our dreams makes us bossy or bitchy, unladylike, that we must do the "right" and "sensible" thing or risk everything.[1]

From very early on, in most parts of the world, girls are raised to believe they must seek permission and authority from external sources. This has major consequences. "Our culture is teaching girls to embrace a version of selfhood that sharply curtails their power and potential," writes author and educator Rachel Simmons. "In particular, the pressure to be 'good'—unerringly nice, polite, modest, and selfless—diminishes girls' authenticity and personal authority."[2] Thus we become adult women with a lifetime of experience diminishing our own inner authority, perhaps even shaming and judging other women who have somehow managed to hold on to theirs.

In so many ways, we women find ourselves stepping over our inner authority and asking for permission outside of ourselves—and this need for external validation, whether it be for survival, love, fitting in, professional success, economic security, or whatever you most fear, can cut us off from our sacred calling.

I am not going to say to you that the problem is women's lack of confidence, although many of us struggle with insecurities. I'm also not going to tell you to "lean in," as Sheryl Sandburg advises, although I encourage you to take that recommendation whenever possible. I won't tell you these things because I know that even the most confident and charismatic person struggles to achieve their dreams in an unjust world. There are many obstacles beyond our control. Just having more confidence or speaking more in meetings is not a long-term solution to the problems we face. Instead, I want to help you see that giving *yourself* permission to seek your purpose in this world is a sacred, social act. This is my refrain: *When you link yourself to something bigger than your individual gain, you no longer have to ask for permission, demurely waiting for someone to give you the green light. When you are tapped into a spiritual force for good you have all the permission you need to follow that path.*

We must come to know and trust an empowering belief that we can achieve our dreams, and to do this, we need to be liberated from toxic beliefs about ourselves and our potential, we need to transcend any devaluing messages that media, religious customs, or social traditions may encourage. We must learn to believe from a place of unfettered freedom and strength. My dear sisters, we must reclaim and proclaim our faith in ourselves.

Losing My Religion, Holding My Spirituality

Even after I buried my dreams, the direction of my life often seemed beyond my control. My emotions were unpredictable during this period, wildly fluctuating between hope and despair. Soon after I met Jo Luck, Zuda came to my mother's village to fetch me, claiming that he had changed. He was contrite in front of my mother, and I gave in to him and to the societal pressures that encouraged my return to the marriage.

It was a terrible decision. I learned soon enough that Zuda

had not changed at all. But the difference this time was that *I* had changed. Despite the continued abuse, my conversation with Jo Luck and my buried dreams gave me continuous hope.

In the worst moments, I remembered my mother's inspiring words: "If you believe in your dreams and you achieve them, you will define who you are, as well as each life that comes out of your womb and those for generations to come." Believe, Tererai. Believe. I clung to the words. The word "believe" became intricately woven in me: its promise was to heal my past, and the deep wounds that I carried at the time, and to help me build a bright and beautiful future.

I began classes in my first correspondence school, paid for by my mother's hard-earned money. This school was not a physical building; instead, correspondence and reading materials were sent to me at home. As a former colony of Britain, to qualify for a Zimbabwean Certificate of Secondary Education Ordinary ("O") Level, which is comparable to a high school diploma in the United States, I had to pass at least five subjects, which were graded at Cambridge in Britain.

Due to lack of money and time to study, I could take only one class at a time and wait for my results. For me, correspondence learning required commitment, discipline, and an unstressed environment. While I had the former two, the latter proved to be difficult. Without my commitment to my faith in a better future, I have no doubt I would have abandoned my studies.

As a newly independent country, Zimbabwe attracted the donor world and the demand for empowering women saved many families. In 1994, I had a job interview with a nongovernmental organization (NGO) based in rural areas, facing seven men and one woman. My hope was in two people in the room, one woman and one man. Both looked interested as they nodded their heads, and they would not only look at me but also at each panel member as though trying to pull them into agreement.

I felt like I was sitting in a storytelling ritual where there are individuals who become so enthralled with the story that their buoyancy intoxicates all listeners, forcing the collective energy to center around the storyteller. The odds were stacked against me: I was a woman and I had no degree. I feared I would not get the job. On the other hand, I felt that the two panelists were rooting for me. Moreover, it was common knowledge that our newly independent Zimbabwe needed women in the labor force as part of fulfilling their donor requirement. It could go either way, I thought as I made my way home after the interview.

A week later I received a message that I had passed the interview. I was thrilled and knew Nyadenga, the Creator of the Universe, was in agreement with my buried dreams. My main function in the job was to mobilize women to join savings clubs that would allow them to securely save money and take out loans from development aid organizations. I knew from the start that here was a piece of my healing. A deep connection to my fifth dream was being forged well before achieving the other dreams, because I was already empowering women in communities like mine. And despite the small paycheck, I managed to save enough to pay for more classes.

At this time, Zimbabwe's currency was stronger than the American dollar, since we used British pounds before independence. Every payday, I put aside money for my dream to get an education in America. I hid my money in different places, changing the locations often, because I was afraid my husband would find it. Becoming paranoid, I started having dreams that he would find the cash, and often I could not sleep because the dreams were so real. I was known for walking and talking in my sleep, so I became afraid to sleep at all and developed terrible insomnia. I always looked tired and irritable.

Despite my belief in my dreams, fear became my worst enemy and I knew this way of living was not sustaining me. I decided to give my money to different people I trusted for safekeeping. I wrote their names down hoping to keep an accurate record of the amounts. Then I finally gave up counting because I was afraid someone would find the paper with the information.

Without any record, I continued to give money to my sister,

mother, and sister-in-law, and prayed they would not be tempted to spend it. They promised to safeguard my savings, which they jokingly referred to as "sacred America," indicating that my money was destined to be spent there. How ironic! I was helping other women securely save, but I struggled so hard to do it for myself.

It was at this time that my husband Zuda joined a church commonly known as *madzibaba* or *postori* (apostolic or relating to the spiritual authority of the apostles). While Christianity is one of the major religions practiced in Zimbabwe, recent years saw an increase in the number of new denominations branching away from more traditional churches like the Methodists and the Anglicans. These churches are collectively known as *vaPostori* in Shona—or Apostles. Members of the churches are well known for their appearance and the way they dress. Men shave their heads, grow beards, wear long white gowns, and carry a long walking stick known as *tsvimbo yemadzibaba*—"the father's stick." On the other hand, women and girls remain in their white gowns, shave their heads or keep the hair very short and covered in long white head scarves. While many of the VaPositori derive their teachings from the Bible, their greater emphasis is on prophecy, belief in oil or water miracle healing, polygamy (some), and fasting in the wilderness. Generally, women believe in their subordination to men.

These churches mushroomed throughout Zimbabwe, particularly in poor towns such as Epworth, Chitungwiza, and Mbare, as well as in rural areas. Men commonly referred to as "bishops" ruled such churches. Believed to be God's "chosen ones," they exerted a great deal of influence. Power struggles erupted as male members fought to get closer to the bishop.

All around me, night prayers took place in homes and in the mountains. Church members wearing white garments worshipped under trees and sometimes spoke in tongues. Some members convinced the congregation that they could see into the future. In my mind, prophecy is used to manipulate women to become more subservient to their husbands and to control their individual freedom.

These so-called prophets claimed to have psychic powers, and they often accused nonbelievers of using ancestral spirits to bewitch other community members.

An unemployed young man might be told that his jealous older relatives have used juju, or bad omens, to prevent him from getting a job. A young woman who struggles in her marriage might be warned that her female relatives (usually dead grandmothers) are to blame for the problems she has with her husband. The prophets also caused much dissension within families. Some spent days gathering private information about a particular person and then made dire "predictions" about this same person in front of the entire congregation. The poor victim of the trick had no idea that the prophet had been playing detective; instead, the victim believed the prophet had divined her most shameful secrets using special abilities and second sight.

While women are generally deferential in the church hierarchy, some also became scammers. Even though they cannot hold senior positions in the church, women are allowed to prophesize, and they are often used by men to demonize those who don't conform. During services, they sway in a trancelike state as though imparting messages from God's angels.

I became a target when I tried to tell the women of the church that their prophets weren't seeing the future, but instead were secretly gathering private information and using it to spin false stories. I saw how belief was being manipulated, and I tried to stop it. For many months, I refused to attend church, which brought the wrath of its members upon my head. Word got around that a male demon on my paternal grandmother's side had made me stubborn.

Life at home was miserable. My husband forced my children to attend church, and because I was afraid that they would be brainwashed or hurt, I resolved to go with them. One particular Sunday, I was asked to confess. Not knowing what to confess, I kept my mouth shut. A prophet took my husband aside and before I knew it, several big men and women were holding me down. Screaming and yelling, they attempted to exorcise a demon. I was encircled by people speaking in tongues, which to me sounded like gibberish. As they sang and clapped their hands, one woman shook and twisted my head while another poured water over me. I concentrated on not passing out as a terrible headache surfaced. I assumed a rigid position because I was afraid that they might break my neck.

A woman and a man repeatedly told the crowd that they sensed a male demon in me, and it was about to come out. This announcement escalated the singing and praying. All of a sudden the church was hushed down because there was another prophetic message. I was told that I not only had a male demon, but also several she-devil spirits. The hurtful words stung me deeply, although I did not let my tormentors know this. When this failed, they gave up on me and decided to find my husband a good wife.

This was a dark period of my life. Although the church discourages wife beating, the emotional abuse I experienced had the same effect. Zuda considered marrying again, but thankfully, a senior church member, a Mr. Moyana, did not think that finding a new wife was the right decision for my husband. When Mr. Moyana confronted the prophets and my husband, several other senior people agreed with him. My husband resigned from the church and became the bishop of his own congregation. Some prophets followed him and as his church grew, so did my misery at home.

My husband's church was like none I had seen before. Young followers would do anything to make him happy. Out of favor, I became a convenient target. I was continually identified as evil and called a witch, a prostitute, a male demon within a woman's body, and a being with avenging spirits. I had had enough of this harassment! So one day as the men were enjoying tea and bread, I told them that they were a bunch of losers who needed education and good jobs. I confronted the women and told them that they were victims of the church. In response, my livid husband burned my study materials, which I desperately needed in order to write my exams. In doing so, he destroyed one of the only material things he knew really mattered to me.

Our life together became a cold war. I attended church in white garments but stubbornly remained silent. To maintain peace, I stayed away from any discussion of my husband's promiscuous behavior, finances, health, or the family's well-being. To escape further trauma, I let my imagination wander during services. What would life be like with an education? Dreaming of a better life was exciting and therapeutic. With my money hidden safely among different relatives and friends, I applied for a passport. When it arrived, I hid my precious documents in a bag of cornmeal. No man would think of opening a bag of cornmeal because cooking is a woman's job.

My sister, Tariro, and some close cousins were at a loss as to how to help because they could not openly intervene, but they lightened the mood by nicknaming me "Mai Bishop"—Mrs. Bishop, or Mai Vemadhirezi Machena—"Mother of White Garments." They encouraged me never to give up and to continue to hide every penny and dime in my possession. They told me to keep believing in my dreams.

Sisters, I have intimately experienced how belief systems can uphold and create unjust hierarchies. Yet even as I contemplate the hurt and pain my husband's faith caused many women (and many men), I know that as much as this is a story about how belief can be manipulated to do harm to people, rather than to set them free, it is also a story about how I held on to my own belief in the face of that hurt. I trusted my dreams.

During these difficult years, I exhumed and reburied and exhumed again my written dreams, I spoke of them to anyone who would listen, and I leaned on my community. To ground my resolve to stay on course, I took my mother's words as my mantra. I would often pretend to be my mother talking to this young and vulnerable Tererai: "Tererai, if you believe in your dreams and you achieve them, you will define who you are, as well as each life that comes out of your womb and those for generations to come." I saw these words as a priceless inheritance I had received from her.

Together with my daily prayers, this mantra became my morning, afternoon, and bedtime ritual. The place I buried my dreams became my own little church, my own altar. I created belief rituals that sustained me when the path forward seemed most hopeless. This place became my wall of resistance, the place that grounded my faith and helped me defy my own silencing.

This was my small act in my own small world, but I also know of so many women who have experienced the oppressive potential of belief systems in bigger platforms, and yet they were not deterred. I think of Anat Hoffman, executive director of the Israel Religious Action Center (IRAC) and director and founding member of Women of the Wall, who was arrested and strip-searched as she and two hundred fifty other women prayed out loud with the full power of their voices at the Western Wall in Jerusalem—rather than the silent praying with muted voices as most of the women who pray at the wall are encouraged to do. After her release, she went right back to the Wall.[3]

I think of Islamic feminist scholar and activist Amina Wadud, who, despite international condemnations and threats of violence, was the first woman to lead a Muslim prayer for a mixed-gender audience in the United States in 2005.[4] We are not all internationally recognized activists like Anat or Amina, but we can all take the same stand in our lives. My sisters, it does not matter if the toxic beliefs are your own or those of a whole institution; the power these beliefs have to silence us and the need to overcome them is hugely significant.

Whether it is dangerous or one-dimensional media images, economic inequality, or religious justifications for women's inferiority, we are so often encouraged to distrust ourselves, to see ourselves as limited and small, rather than spiritually infinite and cosmically significant beings. We are indeed at a pivotal historical moment when it comes to women and faith.

Let us take it back. Let us be spiritually whole, let us be spiritual leaders, let us dare to have wild and radical faith in ourselves and our connectedness to the universe. Let us be grounded and make our very lives a great ritual for divine purpose.

Cleanse Me: Belief Rituals

Although Zuda's church exemplifies the worst in belief practices, thank goodness my culture also gave me very powerful belief rituals. When my beloved mother died, many years after I had achieved my dreams of going to America and getting an education, I was thrown into such a state of grief that I did not know if I could go on—for how could I live without my mother, the woman who had so inspired and blessed my life? During this desperately difficult time, I returned home from America for her funeral, and the power of spirituality became clearer to me than ever before.

I found myself back at my familial homestead, needing to depend so deeply on my belief to help me continue living now that my mother, who taught me to believe, was no longer of this world. I could not help but reflect on my village's indigenous rituals and practices: What would sustain me in my deepest grief? What belief practices do I want to keep with me?

In times of loss and distress our elders perform sacred rituals consulting and seeking guidance from the power of unseen guardians. These guardians, our ancestors, are our channels to Nyadenga, the Great Spirit. Soon my mother would be such a guide for me. This is what I thought of as I waited near her coffin for the ceremonial funeral rites to begin: the Great Spirit. You see, the loss of my mother was devastating and I still mourn her, yet at the same time, I celebrate her gifts.

Named Shamiso ("a miracle"), my mother was the last daughter of VaHarusekanwi, the first wife of VaMuzanenhamo. Despite lacking a formal education, VaHarusekanwi healed the sick and delivered babies with great skill. She weeded other people's fields to ensure that her family had food and opened her home to sick relatives and even strangers in need. VaHarusekanwi set a powerful example, and my mother, Shamiso, followed in her footsteps.

During her lifetime, my mother took care of her siblings and stepsiblings. Like her mother and grandmother before her, Shamiso was abused by a promiscuous husband and expected to raise the many children he sired with other women. Like VaHarusekanwi, Shamiso also worked the fields to feed a growing family—and anyone else she encountered who was hungry. But it was not only food and clothing that my mother passed along. Respected by many for her wisdom and kindness, my mother served as a role model for others and had a big impact on the entire village.

Admired for her tenacity, many in the village called her "Shava Mhofu," signifying her eland totem, the animal believed to have the greatest spiritual power. To our people, the eland (a species of antelope) represents well-being, healing, peace, and plenty. This majestic animal is thought to lead people on a journey to the world beyond that connects them to God. From an early age, we are taught that the dead are not gone forever but rather remain as angels in our midst.

On the day of her funeral, I remember the rain falling at a slow, steady pace and a woman in her late thirties arriving at our homestead in a sleek black hearse. In our village, we hardly saw motor vehicles other than the buses that transport people to cities. It was rare to see such a fancy car in this part of Zimbabwe—and especially rare to see a solitary woman at the wheel. The woman parked the hearse, turned off the engine, and all that remained was deafening silence of the night. Neighborhood dogs stopped barking, and the singing and dancing at a nearby hut faded.

A short distance away, nearly forty adult men—some perched on benches and others on low wooden stools—quietly gathered around a big, open fire within a makeshift tent. Aside from the crackling wood, the only sounds came from frogs, crickets, and other creatures that do not concern themselves with human affairs. Like a polished stone, the deep yellow moon shone down on the mud clinging to the car's steel rims. A streak of red earth spattered along the vehicle is proof of a journey ventured far from the paved road.

I looked around the mourners and realized that no one was going to sleep this night as my mother is welcomed and prepared to enter the Spirit World. The singing and dancing will consume each moment until my mother's spirit departs this world.

Lamentations from the room housing my mother's coffin stop abruptly when an ancient-looking man raises his hand. The room became so silent that one could hear a pin drop. All eyes were on the coffin, almost as if everyone expected the dead body to awaken. Crouching down, the old man's raspy voice rings out: "Those in the Spirit World, we bring Shamiso to her people." Then the Supreme Being and Creator takes her into the Spirit World, where it now belongs.

More silence prevails and still, all eyes face my mother's coffin. My mother's remaining stepbrother, Uncle Maka, announces that the journey to the Spirit World will begin before midday. Korekore tradition does not allow burial at midday because it is too hot. While spirits of the dead must be sent off in a cool environment, evenings are shunned for fear of witches. It is believed that naked witches, on the backs of ferocious hyenas or in baskets controlled by broomsticks, search for dead flesh to eat at night. I cringe as I imagine hyenas and witches feeding on my mother, and I wonder why all the evil things tend to be women. Ambuya Muzoda used to tell me that the Great Spirit had at one time been a woman until men made us believe that God is male.

In my mother's hut, some mourners begin the familiar movements of a traditional *chinyamusasure* dance. Three men slowly encircle the women, forming what reminds me of a cattle kraal, or enclosure. The women respond with a mix of fluid and shuffling movements, raising their hips to mark the earth's spirit as provider of fertility and life. Korekore dancers leave little to the imagination when enacting such scenarios as courtship, sexuality, friendship, and hunting.

I stare at the dancers with wonder, appreciating the beauty and strength of our indigenous rituals. The songs that reinforce and instill belief in the power of our ancestors and the traditional dance take me back to the war that shaped my childhood. The war that liberated my country from the Rhodesian regime was a violent one, with many unspeakable things happening to rural communities. Women and girls became the casualties of war and suffered at the hands of evil men. Believing in our freedom was what inspired us and enabled many of us to wake up every day and cheer the freedom fighters. While the Rhodesian soldiers' brutality succeeded in dividing us temporarily, they did not appreciate how our commitment to Mother Earth and our strong belief in the Spirit World would bring us together again and ensure our survival as a people.

Not only do the *chinyamusasure* dancers narrate their pain and sorrow from the war as they experienced it, they also encourage the next generation to believe in their freedom and demand their dignity whenever it is violated. More important, the dance is a reminder of what grounds our indigenous belief system as an expression of Mother Earth's ancient wisdom, which teaches healing and forgiveness above all. The colonial government was out of touch with this reality—this power of an inherently woven belief among the people that helped lead them to win an almost impossible war.

As the *chinyamusasure* dance ended, I marveled at the way in which music and dance enrich our lives and honor our deaths. My mother used to say that music feeds the soul and would always encourage us to sing when feeling happy or sad. She showed us how our people use music to lift us spiritually from the strain of dire poverty, colonial oppression, and the indignities of gender inequality.

In deep shock, I sat in my corner, and long after the dancers stopped, the sound of music and dancing feet still played in my head, bringing me peace. The sky was now a vast blue dome with spectacular patches of red and purple. I want to hold on to this special moment as the sun sets and the air is infused with the fragrance of the *zumbani* herb (from the lemon bush), a smell that reminds me of my childhood.

Once, as a small child, I suffered from whooping cough. When attacks of heavy coughing would leave me heaving and breathless, the *zumbani* herb would always help. In our hut, I'd watch my mother crush and burn the dense heads and leaves of the creamy white flower of this herb. I remember the strong and aromatic lemon smell as if it were yesterday. The fragrant smoke would fill my lungs while my mother would concoct another remedy, a drink made from the boiled leaves of *zumbani* mixed with *umhlonyane* (wild wormwood).

Today, the *zumbani* herb serves a different purpose. After the burial, village elders will conduct a cleansing ceremony for those who have come into close contact with my mother's body. I cannot think of my mother contaminating anyone. The elders say that the herb acts as an antibiotic and protects people from transporting the spirit of death into their homes. This belief is passed on from one generation to the next. My mother once told me this ritualized belief of body cleansing before burial is ancient, and was practiced even before the missionaries ever brought the Christian Bible to the Korekore people. While steeped in our traditions, my mother was also an enthusiastic member of the Methodist-Wesley Church. A holdover from the pre-independence colonial era of British rule, many villagers have integrated Christianity into our indigenous traditional culture.

Many of my people struggle with the contradictions between Christianity and Shona culture and beliefs. As new denominations arise in Zimbabwe, many believe in the Bible, yet the need to hold on to ethnic roots and ties to the ancestors has led to issues of divided loyalty. I grew up knowing families who attended church during the day and practiced ancestral ceremonies at night, ceremonies considered pagan by the church. In some circles, there is a hint of shame and judgment toward those who fully practice their rituals and follow the pathway of their ancestors.

While many believe in the power of indigenous practices, there is always fear of compromising the integrity and "purity" of their Christian beliefs. In trying to reconcile their African tradition and rituals, I have watched many of my friends and relatives struggling as they adapt to a religious heritage as a way to reconcile with their Christian faith.

My mother attended church but she never lost touch with her

cultural beliefs. She believed both the Christian faith and Shona beliefs were based in love. Just as she lived her life, she embraced what supported her soul when she attended church and left what violated her ancestors behind at the church door. For my mother, the church was a place to do good and to keep in touch with friends. If it spread love, it was part of her spirituality.

The Bible's Book of Psalms discusses purification rites associated with burial that support the cultural cleansing ritual: "Cleanse me with hyssop and I will be clean."[5] My mother loved this verse, which refers to David's need to be cleansed of sin after an adulterous affair with Bathsheba. My mother believed very strongly in the power of forgiveness, and felt that by forgiving, both the forgiver and the one asking for forgiveness are cleansed. I take this deep into my heart and let it inform my worldview. I feel my mother's wisdom speaking to the world: "We can only cleanse the world if we clean ourselves of hate and the hurtful things we do to each other."

These are the kind of spiritual faith rituals I claim for us, my sisters. I claim belief in the Great Spirit, our Mother Earth, for she is wiser and freer than any institution can fathom. She is certain in the face of our doubt and confident in the face of our fear. If we are willing to listen, she tells us of grandeur whenever we feel stuck in smallness.

I also claim for us a vibrant sensory healing: the body moving in dance, the sound of music and dancing feet, the vast blue and red and purple sky with its sun and moon cycles, the smell of crushed and burned herbs, the taste of freshly steeped tea. I claim the power of cleansing from mind and body whatever does not sustain and elevate and heal us. I claim forgiveness for ourselves and for the world. These are the things that ground our belief.

Zuda and his followers wanted to exorcise from me a demon because that was the only way they could understand my intelligence, my yearnings, and my power. They wanted me to be materially and physically vulnerable, afraid, and ashamed, so that I would comply. These are beliefs that demanded my smallness, a belief system based on ego: their need to make me small to make themselves feel bigger. Although I had very little at that time, I did have a source of inner power and strength that they could not take from me: my belief in myself and in the sacred connection of my soul to something greater than human limitations.

That is the difference between these faith stories: the indigenous traditions of my people gave me strength, a sacred, spiritual ground on which to stand. They awakened my senses so that I was fully present and fully alive, in touch with the powerful life force of the blessed Mother. They grew not my ego but my soul.

Forgiveness at the Heart of Your Belief

One important way to grow your soul rather than your ego is to practice forgiveness, to place forgiveness at the heart of your belief. I was only nine years old when I learned the power of forgiveness from my mother, when she showed me by her actions how freeing your heart from bitterness empowers you to transcend the gnawing of the Little Hunger in favor of seeking the sacred.

When I was nine, my father disappeared without a trace. My mother could not imagine him joining the freedom fighters, and in any event, he was too old to walk the long distance to Mozambique for training. She thinks he might have gone in search of a job at a nearby tobacco farm. We suspect this is not something he would be proud of, and worse, it would place the whole family at risk of being killed if his work status became known. The freedom fighters would consider him a traitor, the punishment for which is terrible to imagine, while the Rhodesian soldiers might torture my mother to death if they suspect her husband has joined the freedom fighters.

As the war for Rhodesian independence intensified, so also did poverty and anxiety. Few of the villagers had the means to sustain their families, and worse, we begin to hear of increasing random acts of atrocious violence. There are almost too many horrible stories to tell: of women being gang-raped and tortured by Rhodesian soldiers, and from distant communities, we hear that soldiers raped young girls and poured hot porridge into the vaginas of older women who refused to reveal the identity of the nonfamily members who last had supper with them.

Not long after my father's disappearance, it is our turn to buy hiking boots for the freedom fighters. It falls upon my mother to find the money to fulfill this obligation, and because she hopes to squash any rumors about my father's relocation, she also decides that we must find him.

Early one morning, my mother, sister, and I leave the village under the pretense that Tariro is sick with malaria and must go to the hospital in Karoi. Playing the part of a sick child is easy for my sister because she is not as talkative as I am. A half-empty bus arrives at our terminal. While we are excited about the ride, no one talks. Fear is written on the faces of the bus driver and conductor.

The driver's eyes dart back and forth as he orders the conductor to get people onto the bus as quickly as possible. The conductor warns us to refrain from eating guavas or drinking water, as it is risky to make pit stops. Unfortunately, this also means that we cannot eat *mutakura* (boiled maize mixed with bambara nuts), which our mother has prepared for the journey. Because eating *mutakura* makes one very thirsty, our mother hides the food.

Halfway to our destination, a dozen men with machine guns block the road. Pointing their AK-47s at the bus driver, they order everyone off the bus. Passengers are told to show identity and government travel cards. Frisked at gunpoint, we are shaken and terribly afraid.

We endure many hours of harassment. They ask my mother if she is carrying food for terrorists. Young mothers who cannot produce enough milk try to comfort distressed babies. The soldiers go berserk: one shoves and yells at a young woman who cannot calm her baby. The mother cowers in fear, placing both hands tightly around her head as if to protect it from bullets. Not knowing what to do, we freeze. The heavy silence turns the soldier's attention toward the rest of the crowd. One soldier's glittery eyes send chills down my back. My mother slowly and gently places her hands on our laps and nudges us. We understand that she wants us to avert our eyes from staring at the soldier.

The bus conductor makes the mistake of telling the soldiers that some people on the bus are sick and in need of a hospital. A soldier asks the sick people to raise their hands. My mother cannot bring herself to say or do anything nor does anyone else. We watch in horror as the conductor is taken into a thick forest nearby. He does not return. The remaining armed men order the bus driver to continue the journey. There is deathly silence as we drive away. It is heart-wrenching to watch my mother age before our eyes.

When we arrive in Karoi late that night, my mother decides that we will spend the night at the bus terminal. As women vegetable vendors regularly sleep there in order to guard their produce, it feels like a safe place. That night, we sit around a fire built by the women and talk about the war. These women vendors know more than we do because they gather war stories from different parts of the district from people passing through. Some even help freedom fighters penetrate the urban areas.

My mother spots someone from our village who has recently seen my father in a beer hall. This person tells us that he works on a tobacco farm about twenty miles from Karoi, so that is where we will go. The vendors warn us that all roads to commercial farming areas are safer during the day although no buses or public transportation follow these routes.

We begin our journey very early the next morning, walking for hours and only stopping for water and food. Even though our food is spoiling, we have no choice but to eat it. Fortunately, women at the terminal have sent us off with water in empty Orange Crush soda bottles.

When it begins to rain, we are surprised to see white farmers pass by in open trucks with black farm workers huddled in the back while Rhodesian ridgeback dogs sit up front. The workers' tattered clothes expose soaking wet, bare backs—what a miserable sight. I cannot understand why the dogs receive better treatment than the human beings. I later learn that some white farmers actually train this breed of dog to attack black people—the darker the skin color, the more vicious the dogs become.

We arrive at the farm after our endless hike, tired and barefoot, our old tennis shoes now rags. We eventually locate my father's hut, one of many in the large compound. As we approach, the setting sun saturates the sky with multiple shades of red. Nearby, barefoot boys play with a ball made of plastic bags tied together with an old bicycle tube. Later, we learn that these children attend a dilapidated one-room classroom where a teacher who only has a fifth-grade education teaches them. The school only goes up to fifth grade and the teacher is a former student of the school.

As we head to the compound, the heavy chemical odor that fills the air is the same nasty smell of cotton fields near our village. The earthy, red soil also reminds me of home except that the soil seems thin—like powdered skim milk or sifted cornmeal—which is a stark contrast to the dense green growth bordering a nearby soccer field. Perhaps water from irrigation pipes has found its way to the bushes and trees at the edge of the field.

In my father's one-room hut, a light-skinned woman is cooking food. My father does not introduce her but my mother politely greets them both as my sister and I go sit quietly in a corner. With his old tobacco pipe between his front teeth, my father seethes with anger and the woman scowls and indicates that she "owns" the old man. Ignoring this hostile reception, my mother, older and "unsophisticated" in comparison, nevertheless asks the young woman about her totem. Before we know it, she has discovered that the woman's mother and my mother share the same totem! Tensions are softened when my mother addresses my father's girlfriend as "my child."

Despite our hunger, my mother tells the woman not to bother cooking for us because we have just eaten (not true!). All we need is hot water and a teaspoon of sugar. Melting the sugar over the flame and mixing it with boiling water, my mother offers us "dinner," and warns us not to pee in bed because it will be a long cold night. My sister whispers that my father does not know how to deal with the situation and, in response, I let out a muffled laugh. One disapproving look from my mother reminds me that I'd better behave.

The woman then ejects us from the hut and sends us to a nearby tobacco barn to sleep. She gives us empty burlap sacks so that we don't have to sleep on the ground. Unfortunately, the bags are not thick enough to protect our malnourished bodies from the moist and rotting floors, nor do they shield us from the big rats that run amok in the barn.

After a blackout sleep born of complete exhaustion, my sister and I wake up to long-winding red lines on our palms and fingers. We'd had no water to clean off the remains of the last meal we ate, so the big rats found us and had a feast, nibbling on our hands as we slept.

Before my father leaves for work the next morning, my mother tells him why we have come. She says that we plan to return to the village on this day. When my father hears about the encounter with the soldiers, he softens and invites us to stay until he gets paid. The girlfriend and my father disappear at night so we have the hut to ourselves. But he returns each morning to a cup of tea and a warm bath that my mother has prepared for him.

During our stay, my mother washes and irons my father's clothes. She scrubs his living quarters until every bedbug is gone. After work, my father spends time with us and behaves decently before disappearing for the night. One day, our mother asks my sister and me to bring lunch to him in the tobacco fields. Knowing that the men share food, she has prepared enough sweet potatoes, cooked vegetables, and *sadza* to feed six men.

We arrive to see a white boy of no more than thirteen years shouting at our father. We cannot move as the boy insults my father and demands that he refer to him as "sir." My proud father refuses to call this child "boss." Later we learn that he has defied other rules. For example, my father wears trousers despite an assumption that black men, known to white men as "boys," are supposed to wear shorts.

We cannot believe that a boy is challenging our father. But there he is, pointing a gun at his chest, demanding respect. "You bloody bastard!" screams the white boy. My father stares directly into the boy's eyes as though daring him, which agitates the boy further. Enraged, he shouts, "You're nothing but a fucking kaffir, boy!" My father's response to being beaten is to point an index finger so close to the young man's face that it almost touches him. My father yells, "I am a man, the same age as your father, and I deserve respect!"

These words infuriate the young boy, who points his rifle straight at my father's forehead. There is silence except for the sound of the boy beating my father and incessantly demanding that he say "Yes, sir." Even when my father complies, the red-faced boy is not satisfied. Showing off in front of the many spectators, he hits my father across the face with the butt of his gun, breaking his nose. I am not sure what power uproots my sister and me, but we run to him and try to lift him as he searches for an old rag in his pocket to soak up the blood. Before driving away in a Land Rover, the boy spits in my father's face. "Don't you dare disrespect me again!"

As my father picks himself up, workmates rush to comfort him. With a quivering voice full of rage and tears streaming down his face, my father repeatedly pounds his chest and says, "I am a man, I am a man, I am a ma—a—an." With blood splattering and about to faint, my father is caught by fellow workmates before he hits the ground.

I cannot look my father in the eye. Peeing in my pants, I run back to my mother. An elderly man accompanies my sister to the hut with the food. We do not see my father again for two days. When he returns home, he is in a drunken stupor. My mother behaves as though nothing has happened and we stay as far from my father as possible. I know that my mother wants to comfort him but she realizes that to do so will humiliate him. Silence is the best way to deal with the situation.

Although my mother and we kids experienced much abuse and violence at the hands of our father, this shameful memory remains at the forefront of my mind. The unexpected brutality—the way that the boy demeans my father—seems like a betrayal of decency. Knowing what he's been through makes me wonder if my siblings and I have judged him too harshly.

I intuited something then, even at a young age, about how bitterness and hatred work. My mother could have hated this other woman, but she did not. Why not? Because my mother understood that this woman was also a victim of a world in which women have more value, more food, and more protection if they are associated with a man. She did not have these words, of course, but she knew it all the same—and so she saw this woman as a daughter and a sister, not as an enemy.

My mother could have hated my father, too, but she did not. Why not? Because my mother understood what I was starting to learn: that my father was also trapped in the toxic power dynamics of a world that so narrowly defines masculinity, that values profit over people, conquest over shared humanity, and white over black.

Perhaps it would be easiest of all to hate or blame the young white boy, but is he not also poisoned by this bitter worldview? This white boy—so young that "boy" was indeed an apt description of him, not an insult, while it was to my father—was already being taught to brutalize another human being.

This experience was an awakening for me. I learned that my enemy was not this other woman, nor my father, nor this white boy, but the darkness in their hearts, and in the heart of the society that dehumanizes and devalues others. I realized that I did not need to excuse the bad behavior of people who hurt me, but I also did not need to waste all my life feeling anger for them while ignoring the larger dynamics that created these painful divisions among us. In fact, if I held on to anger, it would keep me from love and connection; it would keep me so busy with hating that I would have no time or energy to pursue my sacred dreams. What I needed instead was to cultivate forgiveness, just as my mother had done.

Let forgiveness be at the center of your belief practices. Let it be the lifeblood that shapes your destiny. You have the power to envision a better world. Be brave enough to look into the face of great challenges and let the truth of the struggles you see inspire you to imagine your way out, knowing all the while that your individual imagining is also a social imagining.

Grow Your Soul Through Ritual

There are seven billion people on earth and we're all searching for something: redemption, meaning, strength, and connection. How we express our spiritual belief is less important than our finding our own personal and social ways of connecting to something bigger than ourselves.

To achieve your dreams you need an authentic self that is built on belief. What are the ceremonies and rituals that guide your dreams? What is their foundation? Is that foundation strong enough to guide you through turmoil and unpredictable challenges? What will grow your soul? What will cleanse you? What will awaken your senses?

Belief becomes socially and materially real through action; rituals are the actions we can take to walk the path to our dreams, such as the sacred rituals this book offers at the end of each chapter. If you don't have your own personal rituals—rituals that may have been passed down from your great-grandmothers or culture—developing new ones will strengthen your goals and dreams. Your rituals are the time for you to tune in to the powers of the creator of the universe beyond your daily life. They enable you to call forth your goals and dreams from beyond the small you, reminding yourself that you are connected to a higher power—whatever name you give it—and should function from that place.

You might want to start by questioning or rejecting any belief systems that make you feel small, or that value your silence. Good rituals will feed and nourish your goals and dreams, rather than limit you. Rituals also take your dreams out of your hands and put them in the hands of the universal spirit. Engaging in rituals will help you to remain connected to your dreams, even when the challenges of daily life make you feel they are impossible.

Rituals can include prayer, meditation, visualization, gratitude, or any other forms of connecting with the creator of the universe, God, or a higher power. Rituals need to be authentic to you and give you a feeling of connecting to something greater than yourself. They are less likely to work if you simply go through the motions. I have found that the most life-giving rituals connect me to the past, present, and future. My own rituals connect me to the past by keeping me linked to my people and my traditions, and preventing me from losing touch with who I am and where I came from. This relationship has always given me strength and reminded me of my true identity.

I have a friend whose altar includes a little ceramic bowl filled with dried sycamore fruit from a tree that nineteenth-century suffragist Elizabeth Cady Stanton planted. Why? Because Stanton was a housewife, mother, writer, and activist who helped women in the United States gain the right to vote. This combination of mothering and bettering the world through social action is a piece of the past that inspires my friend, and the symbolism of holding in her hand the fruit of what Stanton planted speaks so profoundly to her, that she created an ancestral connection that gives her courage and strength. Connecting to the past, whether our own personal traditions or those we create, gives our faith a solid foundation.

Of course, the purpose of our belief is to enable us to achieve our dreams, our sacred purpose, and so your rituals should give you strength in the present moment as well as help you see a better future for yourself and the generations to come. In my case, the rituals of burying my dreams and honoring their importance acted as a focal point that kept me attuned to my desires. The power of my thoughts became a sacred space for me to experience possibilities because my imagination was boundless. The act of digging up, rereading, and then burying my dreams was also a ritual that sustained me, as was holding or touching the stone that I kept as a memento of my buried dreams.

Another one of the most powerful rituals I practiced on my sacred dreams journey was visualizations. Visualizations can be done on their own or included with other forms of ritual: meditation, prayers, chanting, or anything that brings you closer to your spirituality. Through my visualization ritual, I was able to channel my imagination, belief, and energy into a beautiful vision of my future reality not only for myself, but also for my children and my community. The ritual served as my North Star, guiding my journey, and whenever I went astray or felt weary, I just had to focus my attention back to this beacon of light.

SACRED RITUALS TO CULTIVATE YOUR DREAMS INTO REALITY

The sacred visualization ritual I offer to you is designed to make your dreams bold. You will envision the future you desire. The mental images you create should be crisp, detailed, and multilayered, so that they remain in your mind, never to be erased. Sacred visualization helps you to be ready to transcend problems and limitations when the path gets difficult and your belief in yourself wavers.

If my visualization practice feels too difficult or inauthentic to you, I encourage you to start with prayer. Prayer tends to get dismissed in the West, especially by those who associate it with a religious practice. But you don't necessarily need to belong to a church or religion in order to pray.

You can pray to your own personal and spiritual source. That might mean a creator of the universe, a universal consciousness. You can talk to and commune with the higher powers without associating them with any organized religion. Or you can talk to your great-grandmother's spirit, or to historical figures who exemplify the Great Spirit to you, or to future generations you have not yet met. A regular prayer practice, perhaps at night before bed or first thing in the morning, will also give you strength during setbacks and challenges.

The following is a three-step visualization ritual that I have used to create strong images about the life I knew I was meant to have.

Step 1: Trance-like Sacred Journey

My grandmother used to say that trancelike rituals have the power to take you to a place where ancient wisdom resides. In those moments of silence and reflection, our mind is filled with ancient whispers that ground our belief, and soon the body and soul knows what belongs to us.

In your holy-ground (*masowe*), your quiet, comfortable prayer place, adjust curtains and lights so that the room is dim. Light a scented candle or use essential oils with your favorite fragrance. I like sitting barefoot on the floor where I can be in touch with the earth. If sitting on a hard surface is difficult for you, sit on a cushion.

Sit still and let your physical body be loose, muscles relaxed, while your mind is alert. You want to achieve a state something like that moment right before sleep—totally relaxed in body, your mind open to daydreaming and the creative flow of images and ideas, but still awake and attentive.

Detach yourself from your physical surroundings. Be in the flow of your mind. You might find the surrounding noise distracting, especially if this is your first time in a trancelike state. Take a deep breath in through the nose, and out through the mouth. Gently let the sound around you wash over you without feeling irritated. Accept it as a lullaby in the background.

Let all things flow through you and around you. Awake and aware, yet deep in contemplation, a wave of silence washes over you. Listen for the whispers around you, little ideas and voices softly speaking. Feel the stillness until you sense you are in control of everything in your surroundings: in control of the power of concentration and in control of the images in your mind.

Nothing can interrupt the clear, quiet stillness you have created. Hold on to this stillness, it leads the physical body to meet with the yearning of the soul until all become one. There is no separation between physical body and mind.

Ask yourself, *What would my achieved dream look like? Like in a movie, can I see, feel, and touch it?* Think deeply about these questions. Continue to sit still, allowing your creative mind to take over, like a daydream. Create a mental image of what your world will look like after achieving your dreams. Stay in that moment.

Take three deep breaths. Zoom in on the image of your life. What it would look like. Remove anything from the picture that you don't like to see. Focus. Focus. Focus. Perfect the snapshot of your dream. Journey deep into your dream world, allowing the scene to form clearly and as vividly as possible.

Slowly breathe in and out. Hold your thoughts and consider what you have visualized: Take as much time as you need to see, feel, and breathe into your dream before you come back to the present. Is it uplifting? Does it fill you with a sense of possibility? If not, keep practicing and encouraging yourself to really dream. You will get there!

Step 2: Writing Journey Visualization

Now, beloved sister, take that pen and write or draw the mental images you have experienced and seen. Write a statement in the present tense about what you believe you are accomplishing (as though you are already living your dream right now). Describe people, places, resources, activities, and outcomes.

If the information becomes fuzzy or unclear, you might want to practice your visualization ritual again until you can see clearer and clearer the details of your dream. You might want to take a break and do it another time or sleep on it and return back another day. Remember writing is another powerful ritual to realizing your vision, so take your time. Make a work of art out of it.

Step 3: Celebrating and Affirming the Blueprint of Your Visual Image

After you are satisfied with your mental images and you have written or drawn the images, put the paper where you can see it. Now, sit quietly and reflect on the results. Take another three deep breaths, and then read the following poem to seal the practice. You can also come up with your own affirmation that works for you.

> I am a dreamer, the mistress of my own destiny
> I refuse to let the past and its fears define who I am
> I defy the rules and norms that silence my dreams
> I have the power to make this blueprint of my life a reality
> I have the power to right the wrongs of generations that have torn me down

As you leave the place where you keep your image, whisper, "*Tinogona!* It is achievable!" Let out that ululation of joy and gratitude to the universe and Nyadenga, your Creator. Return to this image as often as you like. Make of it an altar to your sacred dreams, a place where you remember, a place to remind yourself to believe in this vision of the future.

My sister, our circumstances may change us, but in the end it is how strongly we believe and how clearly we visualize our destiny that transforms us into the people we want to be. The power to redefine and re-create a new narrative is in our hands. We are the instrument for the positive change we want to see in ourselves and in our children.

*See yourself as the creator of your own destiny—
knowing that you have the power to shape
your future and achieve your dreams.*

7

BE COURAGEOUS, NOT SILENT: INSPIRING ACTION AND OPPORTUNITY

I change myself, I change the world.

—GLORIA ANZALDÚA

I often say that whatever we do to ourselves we do to the world. When you educate and empower an individual, especially a woman, you have potentially awakened a champion who will change the world. This is not just empty rhetoric; there is well-documented proof. As Kofi Annan, the former UN secretary-general said, "Study after study has taught us that there is no tool for development more effective than the empowerment of women."[1]

Empowered women change the world for the better. You might not know it from what you see or hear in the media, but all around us, in ways big and small, when women refuse to stay silent, they change the world:

- Six thousand semiliterate women tea-pickers in southern India calling themselves "Pempilai Orumai," or "women's unity," win better wages for themselves from a multinational corporation.[2]

- A twenty-nine-year-old single mother of two puts herself through college.

- A global outpouring of female scientists share photos on social media of their on-the-job footwear in support of an eight-year-old girl who was told by a shoe salesperson that dinosaur shoes are only for boys, sparking an international conversation about women in science.

- A sixty-year-old woman begins a flourishing career as a writer.

Whether through making your mind up to change old habits, marching in the streets, writing a letter, making big or small life changes, or engaging in social media, women across the globe are rooting deeply and speaking bravely—to themselves, to their families, and to the world around them. And they are making waves.

As they do, these women pathfinders lay a footprint whose impact invokes and awakens untapped potential in both young and old regardless of their gender, race, and class. These trailblazers not only become the fertile ground for seeding our potential, but also become the architectural templates of inspiration, a source of faith, enabling others to rise against their own silencing. "It's hard to be what you can't see," said Marian Wright Edelman, founder and president of the Children's Defense Fund.[3] Our dreams have to originate from the deepest, rooted parts of ourselves; they need creative space to grow; they have to be nourished by community; and they must be supported by faith.

We also need role models if we are to put our dreams into action, if we are to overcome all the forces that silence us. We need them to keep the spark going. If we are to act in service of our goals, it helps to see the footprints laid out before us and to be familiar with the known and unknown hands reaching back to pull us forward. This truly speaks to our connectedness—our *ubuntu*, or the essence of our humanity, knowing that we exist because of others and that it's our collectiveness that strengthens us. We need to know that every little step we take toward our sacred dreams makes us a part of a global collective. And yet, there is always that invisible stretch of road full of challenges that holds us back.

The Invisible Stretch of Road

There is an invisible stretch of road that lies between the idea of our dreams and the finishing mark of achieving them. This pathway is entrenched with barriers and potholes that seem to increase in depth as we women get closer and closer to claiming the prize. These barriers are universal, and we feel them deeply, but they are not identical across space and time: each woman faces her own impassable stretch of road in her own way.

Who are the champions who faced their own pervasive stretch of road and succeeded? My sisters, what are the inspirational stories that will awaken us from our own silencing and make our challenges feel recognized and help us to map out how to cross the rocky terrain that leads to our dreams? Who are these giants whose stories remain a song in our souls reminding us that it is achievable—*tinogona*?

Can we find them, and let their energy invigorate our passion? And do they have to be celebrities, or extraordinary individuals, or could they also be an unknown grandmother whose ancient call becomes our source of inspiration? An elderly woman in your community who gained perspective from her own struggles and now inspires others to dream big, or a mother whose resilience has become a torch for others to shine light on their possibilities, or, perhaps, an unlikely ordinary individual doing some extraordinary things to uplift others?

At each moment in my life, I can point to a person or persons who encouraged my ability to act. Despite the fact that I maintained three jobs, for example, I found myself without enough money to pay tuition for the last semester of my undergraduate degree. The kids and I were running out of food, and, in the midst of this, my abusive husband would take any opportunity to disparage me. I could feel the end of the road coming, and yet, what lay between where I was and reaching the finish line of achieving my bachelor's degree almost beat me. During this time, a group of philanthropic women who called themselves the Women's Giving Circle of Stillwater, Oklahoma, came to my rescue. Rallied by Grace Provence, a local realtor, these women converged and paid the $1,500 in tuition I needed to graduate, ensuring that I made it to the finish line.

Soon I was heading to graduate school to pursue my master's degree in plant pathology at Oklahoma State University. I chose this field because a degree in anything to do with the earth and its plants gave me a connection to my roots. Agriculture was not only a profession to me, it was a spiritual practice as important as survival itself. My people survive on the land. The land and its soil and plants provided everything we eat. We heal everything with plants. Plants are a major part of our rituals. And hence, coming from an agrarian society, I wanted to better understand the science and practice of farming and how Mother Earth can continue to sustain us. I felt that this direction would allow me to make a living while contributing to my people.

But just as I was about to begin the program, I got a call from the university administration saying that it would be almost impossible to continue unless I got a scholarship. I cried my way back to my small apartment after hearing the news. I was overwhelmed with the news and felt lost and rejected. My only option was to pack my belongings and go back to my country.

As I fretted about how I would go about moving our lives back home, grieving and desperately trying to hold on to any small shred of hope that this setback wouldn't be the end of my dream journey, I got a letter in the mail from the American Association of University Women (AAUW). I had been awarded a scholarship! Just a few months before, with the help of the vice president for student affairs, Dr. Ron Beer, I had submitted my application for a scholarship but never gave it much thought. I had struggled in vain to get scholarships before as an international student.

Tears of joy now streaming down my cheeks, I walked to the office to pay my tuition, overwhelmed by the reality that an organization founded in 1881 to promote equity and education for women and girls had just saved me, as did Dr. Beer, a man who stood with me through many challenges. You see, at each and every step of the way, there were heroines and heroes who helped me cross that dark and treacherous invisible road in my life. As I continue to hear, read, and speak about women's invisible stretch of road and the sacred sisters who come to our aid, I find my own inspiration to extend my hand. I'm no Mother Teresa, all I know is I stand on the shoulders of many individuals.

Our ability to effectively navigate the invisible stretch of road is improved if we look to those who have gone before us, pioneering leaders and everyday heroines, for inspiration and guidance. My home is full of notes to these women. Sometimes they become emails or letters that I send out, and many times, if I don't get their contact information, the note remains in my own space as a silent prayer and a testimony to how they inspire me. It is one of my monthly rituals to honor my heroines.

I was twenty-two, already an adult woman, and a mother of five, when I buried my dreams. It was not easy to remain steadfast. It was not easy to keep walking the path. I had plenty of social barriers to overcome. I was overwhelmed with poverty and an abusive relationship. I was desperately worried about the resources needed for child care if I was to pursue my dream of an education, and equally worried about where to get tuition for my children's education as I was to find money for my own. Like many women, my own inner voice became my worst enemy: What if I was not meant to achieve my dreams? Why spend the little money I had on myself instead of investing in my children's future? What if I fail after many years of trying to achieve my dreams?

Yet the most difficult time during the pursuit of my dreams was when I was just about to achieve them. I almost gave up until I listened and learned from some mighty women who helped me to navigate my own invisible stretch of road.

Many times since the blessed day on which I achieved my five dreams, and even still in my humanitarian work around the globe, I ask myself: *Was it luck or smarts that made all my dreams come true? Was it a coincidence that I met Jo Luck, who encouraged me to dream, or that my community gathered pennies, sold chickens, guavas, and mangoes to raise my airfare to go to America?*

Accepting how, why, and what had happened for me to achieve my dreams was not easy, because my ego kept clinging to the belief that the achievement of my dreams was due to my sheer hard work. It took many years for me to understand the true key to my success. My sisters, I began to hear the ancient wisdom in my mother's words. When she encouraged me to make my dreams sacred by adding the fifth dream of giving back to my community, she was trying to help me see that there is something hallowed—communal, spiritual, and holy—about achieving our dreams. I could no longer view what had happened to me through my ego filters.

I recognized my life's achievements as something inconceivably simple and yet deeply profound: *at the most difficult points in my life, I had superhuman strength because of other people who gave me opportunity.*

Without a shadow of doubt, I have come to realize that the chances of achieving our dreams are greater when our hunger for them collides with *opportunity*; once we have laid the foundation by establishing strong roots, cultivating imagination, and finding our voices, developing strong sisterhood support and putting our trust in something bigger than ourselves, we are ready to meet opportunity when it arises. It came to me in the form of a stranger sitting down on bare ground, simply telling me that my dreams are achievable. My sacred sisters, each of us can be a source of opportunity, a fertile ground that nurtures, inspires, and enables others' growth.

Let me share with you a story that illustrates the many unexpected ways we can receive and be sources of opportunity. I arrived in America late in 1998, prepared to commence my studies for a bachelor's degree at Oklahoma State University in January 1999. The school is situated in Stillwater, a small city in the north central part of the state. My possessions consisted of five new dresses, one pair of sandals, a knitted jersey, and a modest sum of cash wrapped in a pair of stockings tied to my waist. My children were to join me after I was settled, and so for a few months I was alone in a new country, poor and foreign, brimming with optimism and determination but also with sadness and uncertainty.

But it wasn't easy to bring my children.

In preparing to leave for America, I counted all my savings from my job at the NGO, including the money I had given my relatives for safekeeping. With the help of a friend who looked into the costs of plane tickets to America, I realized I had most of the money I needed, but was short six hundred and forty dollars. As I figured out a way to make up the difference, I continued with my plans, making my way to the visa office to get my passport.

The clerk at the visa office asked if anyone would accompany me to the United States. When I mentioned my children, an embassy staff member asked me to bring their passports. I never saw this coming. Passports for minors in Zimbabwe require the father's permission. Even if the Great Spirit is indeed female, in my village, there is no doubt that it is man who reigns. Although this presented a great challenge, I was determined to get my estranged husband, Zuda, to sign the applications.

I began by begging, repeatedly, at his workplace until he instructed the security guards to block my entry into the complex. Feeling desperate, I prayed as I never had before and begged God to help me. I made all kinds of promises to God: I will be a good person; I will help my community. If God melts this man's heart enough to sign the forms, I will educate my children and, in turn, bring education back to my community.

After everything else failed to move Zuda, I went back to my mother. We brainstormed together. She said, "Every family has someone who stands with the Nyadenga, the Great One-God and who knows right from wrong. Have you searched within your husband's family?" I had not. Zuda's cousin, Mai Machacha, agreed to talk to my husband, but even after we approached Zuda together, he continued to refuse me. When we left, she suggested that we needed the support of all the angels in heaven to resolve this difficult situation.

Mai Machacha belonged to the Pentecostal church. She rallied church members to pray for me and asked me to join her in a ten-day fast. I agreed—and found the experience to be one of the most difficult of my life. By the end of that time, I was still determined but quite physically weak. After the fast, I paid a visit to one of Zuda's uncles. The old man lived in a rural village with his three wives. Opposed to the idea of educating women, he initially tried to talk me out of my plan. The more I looked at his wives and children, particularly his meek first wife, the more I resolved to never give up on my dreams.

As I was about to leave his home, the old man said something that changed everything: "I do not know anyone from this village, let alone this country, who does not want to go to America. If you go there and your husband continues his abuse, I hear that the American system is not like ours. Here, a woman may report abuse to a policeman who himself abuses his wives. In America, abuse can get a man deported." I made my way home, shocked but reenergized. To this very day I have no idea why this old man shared this insight with me. Maybe he felt pity for me or perhaps he knew that I was not going to rest until I got what I wanted.

I approached Zuda again, this time buoyed by his uncle's insight and indirect support. It did not take long for my husband to sign the children's passport applications with the condition that I also bring him to America.

My estranged husband told me he wanted to tie up some loose ends before leaving Zimbabwe and suggested that he bring the children to America a few months after I was scheduled to arrive. I reluctantly agreed because I had no choice, and I told myself that Zuda's absence would allow me time to form my own social network. Even so, I was not totally willing to trust, so I decided to buy tickets for Zuda and the children in advance, well before I purchased my own. I did so for my own peace of mind.

During the negotiation with Zuda, I also made it clear that his decision to join me in the States did not mean we were going to be intimate. Zuda said he did not care; he believed he would come to America to find employment and be on his own.

I readied myself to leave for America with not only Zuda's permission but also with support from my entire birth village, for they had all contributed whatever they could to make my journey to America possible. Women and men had sold chickens, mangoes, and groundnuts for me. The headman told my mother and me that everyone in the village contributed, including the poorest, who gave pennies as a symbol of their love and good wishes. My community had ensured that I would move forward with my plans.

A Dream Come True

On my first morning in America, I woke up on the fourth floor of Bennett Hall, the Oklahoma State University dorm to which I had been temporarily assigned. I had no idea what time it was, but I felt tired and sick, which I later learned was jet leg from the long flight from Zimbabwe. While the cold was unexpected, and I felt it deep in my bones, the joy I felt was indescribable.

I heard young people talking outside my door, and I assumed they were students like me. They spoke so quickly that I could hardly understand what they were saying. I was overwhelmed and confused, but also excited about the new journey that I was about to take.

I then heard the sounds of a church bell, and I edged to the nearest window to determine where it was coming from. I wanted to follow the sound, as I was already yearning for some human contact. The young people on my floor were intimidating to me at the moment—at first glance, they struck me as too fast, too busy, or too into themselves. I was beginning to feel a bit lonely as I looked out my window and then noticed a tall building with a sign in front bearing a big red wineglass with a cross in an X-shape through the middle of it. It looked inviting and my room suddenly felt stuffed and small.

I wondered if I should dare venture out. The problem was that I didn't quite remember how I had gotten myself into the dorm in the first place. Plus, my money remained tightly tied to my waist. The mere thought of losing it scared me. On the plane I even dreamed of someone frisking me and grabbing my cash, so I remained wide-awake for the remainder of the flight.

I decided there was no point in being here if I wasn't willing to take some chances. After freshening myself and taking note of the room number, I stepped outside into the hall. I saw a young man going down the stairs and followed him. Once on the first floor, I saw a door leading outside, and I marched through it. The unexpected cold hit my face and I felt my ears and fingers sting. I did it! But I could no longer see the tall building with the cross.

I decided to follow a paved path and told myself to take note of key points that I may need in order to find my way back. There was no one around, except for a few cars on the road. Where were the people? Feeling terribly isolated, I exhaled into the cold air and was shocked when a thick smokelike fog came out of my mouth. I had never experienced this before, and it fascinated me.

Soon, I found myself within sight of the tall building again. It had a sign that read "First Christian (Disciples of Christ)," and I heard beautiful music coming from inside. I stood by the church door, freezing and unsure if I should knock. If someone opened the door, what would I tell them?

I was about to retrace my steps to the dormitory when suddenly the church door swung open. A man said, "Come in, come in, it's cold out there!" as he welcomed me into a room full of people drinking coffee and eating cookies. The group was getting ready for the morning church service. Too worried about what these strangers thought of me to feel interested in food, I politely refused the offer to try some of the biscuits. I remained transfixed as I took in my surroundings. The food, the people, and the elegant attire were a far cry from the village life I was used to.

I was brought back to reality when the man who first invited me inside introduced himself and his wife. His name was Ron Beer, the man who would later help me find the American Association of University Women (AAUW) to fund my graduate education, and his wife was called Cara. They were delighted to hear that I was from Zimbabwe—they had traveled to my country, and they did work in Mozambique from time to time.

Ron and Cara quickly became surrogate parents to me. Cara, especially, was a welcome addition to my American life. She is so loving; in fact, her demeanor and wisdom remind me very much of my own mother. My first impression of the Beers was indelible and in the years I've known them, they've continued to prove themselves to be as nurturing, encouraging, and compassionate as they were on the day we met.

In those first weeks at OSU, the only thing that seemed certain was that my life would never be the same. I had trouble understanding American English, which added to the stress of getting acclimated to a new country, a colder climate, and the demands of studying in a very different kind of school system. To make matters worse, I thought of my children constantly. My mind swung to them when I should have been concentrating on school. I tried to feel encouraged that four of them would soon join me in Oklahoma. Unfortunately, my other two children remained behind in Zimbabwe to finish high school.

———

As the day neared for my four youngest children and Zuda to arrive in America, I prepared for them. The university had allocated a small two-bedroom apartment to me, and I expended a great deal of effort trying to make it as cozy as possible so that the children would feel at home. I was lucky to find some useful furniture, including three beds and two old sofas, by the dumpster outside my building. A new church friend contributed an old microwave and plenty of bedsheets. I scrubbed the apartment until it sparkled and squeezed a bunk bed and a single bed into one of the tiny bedrooms. Everything looked crammed in with a shoehorn, but I was so happy that the children would soon be there that I barely noticed.

New acquaintances introduced me to secondhand shops such as the Salvation Army, where I purchased pots, dishes, and blankets. Since we came from a much warmer climate, I worried that the children would freeze when they arrived in Oklahoma in the middle of winter. We needed extra-warm jackets, which were hard to find for an affordable price. A Nigerian friend told me about St. Andrew's Thrift Shop. Here, in a small thrift shop in Stillwater, Oklahoma, I met yet another unlikely source of opportunity: a stranger and a Winnie the Pooh toy.

The first time I walked into this downtown store, I saw a huge teddy bear with a shiny nose. The bear looked so appealing and real! His red shirt covered bright yellow fur, leaving a big, soft belly exposed. Looking vulnerable and mischievous at the same time, this was the biggest stuffed animal I had ever seen. I picked it up, hugged it, and returned it to the shelf before anyone saw me. As I searched for clothes, my eyes repeatedly returned to the bear. Something about it reminded me of my childhood and my children. I resolved to buy the teddy bear for my two youngest children, Sibusisiwe, "Cici," and Thembinkosi, "Thembi."

At the counter, I realized that I did not have enough money for the jackets, let alone a ten-dollar teddy bear. I held several jobs within walking distance of campus, primarily as a dishwasher, and my next paycheck would not arrive for two weeks, so I bought what I could afford and headed home. That night, I prayed that the teddy bear waited for me until my next paycheck.

Two weeks later, I returned to St. Andrew's and headed toward the shelf where I'd left the bear. It was gone! I had no idea where to find a replacement that would bring me as much joy. My eyes filled with tears and all of a sudden, I felt the intensity of the past year—the transitions, the cold weather, the homesickness, and the impending reunion with my children. I saw my own childhood, the challenges of being a mother when I was still a child myself. I could feel the lost little girl in me, filled with doubt and longing for love and connection in this foreign place. It was an emotional moment.

As I was about to leave, an elderly salesperson asked me if I was looking for Winnie the Pooh. I had no idea what she was talking about so I shook my head, indicating that she had made a mistake. She told me that she remembered my visit of two weeks ago. At the time, she'd guessed that I was a foreign student new to town.

The woman asked if I could wait while she answered a call. Closing a door behind her, she soon reappeared with the teddy bear. Placing it in my hands, she told me that she had kept Winnie in the back, knowing that I would return. Hallelujah! What were the odds of a stranger reading my heart and saving the teddy bear for me? She must have noticed me returning to it several times, and she probably watched me count my money before setting it back on the shelf.

This good soul would not let me pay for the bear. I did not know what to say. Do I thank her or hug her? Doing both, I began to cry as I left the shop.

Is this a silly story about an adult woman crying over a giant stuffed animal? Or a story of a stupid woman who welcomed her estranged and untrustworthy husband back into her home? That is not my experience of it. This is a story about how unlikely ideas and actions reverberated in the universe so that I could pursue my dreams, and so that I would have comfort on the long road ahead. Zuda's uncle gave me a way out of no way; this salesperson saw my heart's longing, my grief mixed with embarrassment and my need to be held, and she held the space for me.

How can I say that these acts were not essential to helping me walk the path toward my dreams? I needed to find a doorway at a dead end, and Zuda's uncle showed me how. I needed to be held and the stranger held me: she gave me the opportunity to grieve, to be warmed by memories of my childhood, to feel seen and heard in a foreign place, and to bring joy to my children as they made the difficult move away from their home.

My sisters, there are so many ways—big and small—that we can be a source of opportunity for others, and it is just as important that we are prepared to receive opportunities when they come to us. In my own life that meant I needed the courage to speak to the stranger Jo Luck when she asked me my dreams, the open heart to accept the teddy bear—and a thousand other moments along the way. Perhaps my story can be an opportunity for you, or perhaps the other women in this chapter will hold you like a giant yellow stuffed bear offered by the generosity of strangers.

Other women's successful actions are not your competition; they are your inspiration and your opportunities. Sometimes the best way to overcome our own silencing is to see how others are rising above theirs. When we truly understand other women's journeys, the contours their paths take, the steep climb and the silent terrain that become more visible when we share them, we can know for sure that we will also make it. We need the wisdom of those who have traveled the same paths, these women pathfinders, the torchbearers, the ones who have been silenced but have found their redemption against all odds, claimed their own voices, and then remembered those left behind.

Native American poet, novelist, and activist Paula Gunn Allen writes that one of the weaknesses of women's empowerment as imagined by white women in the West is that there is little sense of history or memory of past successes. The Native American emphasis on continuity, heritage, and lineage offers an important contrast to the Western emphasis on the new, the modern, the future, and the young.

When we emphasize forgetting rather than remembering the past, Gunn Allen writes in "Who Is Your Mother?," we forget that we have successful egalitarian and female-centered social models to build from. This knowledge is crucial to making the invisible stretch of road feel passable. She writes, "Feminists too often believe that no one has ever experienced the kind of society that empowered women and made that empowerment the basis of its rules of civilization. The price the feminist community must pay because it is not aware of the recent presence of gynarchical societies on this continent is unnecessary confusion, division, and much lost time."[4]

For Allen, this means bringing the recent past of indigenous cultures back into the conversation, from the history of the women-affirming Iroquois and their Council of Matrons who influenced policy, worship, lawmaking, and matters of lineage, to my grandmother's secret women's society and their celebration of women's bodies, to modern sayings illustrating the prominent place women hold in society, like this from the Cheyenne: "A people is not conquered until the hearts of the women are on the ground."[5]

I also imagine it to mean that we stop ignoring or cutting down the many examples of strong, successful women we have all around us, not just from the past but also in the present. Let's stop losing that time; let's embrace and celebrate models of female equality and empowerment without fear of competition.

Let's learn and remember—and be prepared to give and receive encouragement wherever we can. We must always be getting more and more familiar with creativity, with finding pathways when none are clear, with resilience and perseverance in the face of adversity. Submerging ourselves in inspirational stories by fellow women can help us act.

Torchbearers

Today Jo Luck remains one of my torchbearers. Soon after I obtained my master's degree, and before I began applying to doctoral programs, I landed a job with Heifer International at their headquarters in Little Rock, Arkansas. I was elated to be named deputy director of planning and evaluation, responsible for the organization's impact assessments. Who would have thought that one day I would work for a global organization known for its focus on ending poverty in the world?

I had no idea that Jo Luck also worked for Heifer International. When I met her all those years ago, I thought she was one of the organization's donors. Little did I know she was now the president and CEO of the organization that had just hired me. It was then that we reunited and began a long friendship, both amazed and overwhelmed by the miracle of our connecting once again.

My job with Heifer International involved traveling to all the places the organization did outreach and evaluating the outcomes. In the summer of 2003, my first trip with Heifer International took me to Africa, which enabled me to visit home for the first time since 1998. One of the first things I did was to visit my rock to dig up my list of dreams. I checked off the first three dreams and reburied the container. I sat for so long by the rock that protected the now dirty handwritten list that I'd written fifteen years ago that my mother came to fetch me.

Yet to this day, even with all these synchronicities, I never asked Jo Luck about that day in 1989 when she sat with me on bare ground and asked me my dreams and told me that they are achievable. I thought perhaps she could tell me something about the magic of that day so that I could give it to you in this book, dear ones. Was there something that pulled her to our group? What beckoned her to nudge and ask me about my dreams? Was there something in the weather? Her responses were more than I expected.

"I am certain that our bond is more than coincidence," Jo Luck said in her beautiful Southern drawl. "However, it is stunning when one thinks of the odds that we met in an African country, shared life-changing words in a brief time together, unknowingly documented the encounter with a happenstance photo on my small camera, and have remained connected over the past two decades as our paths continued to cross."[6] Jo Luck continues:

> On that day in Zimbabwe I was scheduled to meet with the men of the village, as was the usual custom. Afterwards, I asked to meet with the women, which was unexpected but was agreeable. We gathered under a tree near a small mud hut in a circle, and Tererai and I sat next to each other. As we talked I asked someone to take a photo. I wanted to share the picture at headquarters to stress the importance of talking and listening with both the women and the men of the community. We were launching a participatory approach as a governance model for local leadership as an important component for sustainable development.
>
> Several years later amazingly Tererai was hired and working at Heifer's headquarter offices. She told her story about the dream circle and the resulting wishes she made and had at that time nearly achieved. That was the first time I made the connection that she and I sat together in that circle. I found the photograph to show her, and we marveled that our acquaintance had come full circle.

Do you hear what I hear in this story, sisters? I had hoped for magic from Jo Luck's telling: some formula for giving and receiving opportunity that would help you traverse your own invisible stretch of road. Yet once again, Jo Luck offers me wisdom I could not have seen coming. The magic is that there was nothing special in this encounter and yet everything was special. Jo Luck was doing her job.

She had no idea that I was in the middle of a storm, or that my life was falling apart.

She had no idea the effect she had on me until years later. She asked to talk to the women, and the simple, profound act of two women's conversation—our call and response—was a transformational moment. Her act was simply her presence and her asking without realizing the seed she was planting. My act was simply my responding and my receptivity to her answer: it is achievable. With that, my world changed forever; with that, thousands of girls' and women's (and boys' and men's!) lives changed forever through my educational outreach.

This, sacred sisters, is the profound power of your actions. Only you can decide: Will you be present enough to ask another woman about her journey, her dreams? Will you be able and strong enough to discern the depth of what is being said and the meaning of the silences in between the words? Will you be prepared to answer when she asks you?

The stories I share here profile some of the world's unheard sacred sisters whose great hunger, self-determination, and belief in their purpose and its sacred responsibilities are making the entrenched road possible for their sisters. When asked, they were brave enough to answer, and then they promised to be present to all those who have yet to be asked. Using their dogged determination, and without much moral support or financial aid, these heroines of their own stories are addressing the root causes that first brought us here, and rejecting the external and internal barriers that continue to perpetuate the silencing of adult women.

I am sure you will love these women as I do. Some of these unsung heroines come from less than desirable circumstances in life but went on to overcome their own silencing, becoming pathfinders, giving us hope and a compass reference that *indeed, it is achievable*. I offer these stories to you so that you may reflect on how nothing and yet everything about them is special: flow with the presence found here, the purpose, the dreams, the acts of finding voice, the answers given when a call is made, and the power of calling out to others, that are all so beautifully and diversely portrayed by these women.

Taking a Chance on Your Dreams

In 2009, Diane Ramsey had a well-paying, impressive corporate job. She also volunteered her time as conference chair for an organization that would subsequently become Iowa Women Lead Change (IWLC), a nonprofit whose sole focus is to advance women's leadership. For months leading up to the conference, Diane spent nights and weekends and every free moment of her seventy- or eighty-hour workweek helping to make their annual conference a success.

One day Diane and her supervisor, the highest-ranking woman in the organization, had a meeting in Diane's office. Her boss flippantly picked up the conference program and then flicked it back down on the desk. "I haven't even looked at this," she said. "I don't believe in women's conferences, or women's leadership for that matter."

These words were profoundly destructive and hurtful to Diane. "With those few words," Diane recalls with impressive clarity, "she had entirely devalued that experience and my contributions." Diane remembers that this woman did everything she could to undermine the strong women who worked for her. In that moment, she says, she knew that in too many instances she had allowed her boss to take her power.

Not long after this exchange, Diane left her job. She had no plan, no idea of what she would do. All she knew was that she had a dream: the desire to do something that was mission driven. Then she was approached to lead the grassroots organization that would become IWLC.

"After working in corporate positions my entire career," Diane reflects, "my husband wondered if I'd ever be hired for a 'real' job again. People did not understand why I would give up the security and compensation of my position and want to work that hard for something that many people didn't understand, or value." Deep down, though, Diane knew this was something she had to do. "I had not been born with wealth or privilege, yet have had opportunities and experiences that I could never have imagined having." She had to share that with other women.

As Diane began devoting more of her time to the next Iowa Women's Leadership Conference, she also began transitioning the grassroots group from an event to an organization focused on advancing women throughout the region—and she was offered a brand-new role: chief executive officer.

In the fall of 2012, I spoke at a luncheon in Des Moines, Iowa. Diane was in attendance. I provided each attendant with their own "dream can" and asked them to write a sacred dream down and bury it somewhere safe. On Diane's slip of paper, she says, she wrote "make IWLC self-sufficient."

Her planted dream quickly bore fruit: "After I wrote down my dream for IWLC to become self-sufficient, we had our biggest conference to date with Martha Stewart and Gloria Steinem (among others). Conference registrations for nearly a thousand seats sold out in two weeks. That gave us a cash reserve so that our fledgling organization could move out on its own."[7]

On November 1, 2013, Diane moved into IWLC's first office. The organization continues to grow. They have had more than nineteen thousand women attend their events. Diane reflects, "Every day I get up knowing that I am helping other women. I have so many ideas about new programs and projects flowing that it can be difficult to prioritize. I have surrounded myself with women I respect, who share the passion around our mission, and with whom I enjoy working."[8]

Diane often hears from women for whom IWLC has given them back their voices. One young woman who was completing her PhD in psychology decided not to go into private practice after attending the conference on an IWLC scholarship. Instead, this young Latina chose to move to a community in Iowa with a large Hispanic population, because she believed it was the best way for her to impact the greater good. Diane's mission continues to expand.

"We have fueled a passion for women to invest in themselves and not settle for the status quo," Diane says proudly.[9]

Women Educating Women

Hope Sadza is the founder of the Women's University in Africa, the only university in the region that focuses on promoting gender equity and women's access to college education. Hope was born and grew up in the African suburb of Salisbury, now called Harare, the capital city of Zimbabwe. Her mother was a trained teacher and her father was one of the first African men to buy a fleet of taxis to ferry Africans from their poverty-stricken townships to the city where most of them worked at low-level jobs.

Hope always knew that education was her calling and she wanted to be a teacher. After she obtained her degree from the University of Missouri in 1980, soon after her country's independence, Hope's passion for adult women's education became her hunger, a sacred calling. She went through several jobs, and in 1989 was appointed public service commissioner of the Republic of Zimbabwe. Here she realized that there were very few places for promotion of women. Many women lacked degrees, confidence in the interview room, and the ability to express themselves even when they knew the answers or had ideas for the jobs. A nagging desire empowered Hope to ask, "Would there ever be a time when the government of Zimbabwe would have great numbers of women to steer the ship of economic and social development?"[10]

Hope realized that many women were very smart, but they felt inadequately prepared because they lacked the education or even professional training needed for higher positions within the government.

An academic certificate, a degree, more professional preparation—something to boost their confidence was needed. It was their last mile to promotion, and that entrenched mile represented a good salary, independence, and importantly, equal participation in society.

There were many barriers that kept women from attaining these goals: the policies in place, of course, but also the blindness of the policy makers to the root causes that created this situation in the first place, and their failure to address the structural needs that would make education accessible to women and girls (access to education, child care, economic empowerment, changing social norms and practices). Hope also realized that some of the inequalities in sub-Saharan African countries are remnants of British, Portuguese, Dutch, and Italian colonization, which to this day perpetuates current inequities in education and the silencing of women's voices.

How in the world do you close this invisible stretch of miles when there are no universities to take care of mature women? Even those who can afford to go back and finish their secondary (high school) education had no time to go to school as they had to balance work, taking care of children, and, if married, taking care of the husband and his extended family. All of this falls on the shoulders of the woman! "Every day, I went to bed asking myself, how could the women I saw around me, from age twenty-five and beyond, even up to sixty plus years, access higher education?" Hope's desire to change things—to make this seemingly impossible passage from women who are devalued and undereducated to women who are educated policy makers in all areas of the national fabric—became her only thought. "I had many sleepless nights," she says.[11]

Hope strongly felt Africa could not develop economically and socially if half of its population (women and girls) could not take part in discussions, policy-making, and decisions for development. "Women should learn about why they are on the bottom of the development pile. So many women are lost at the bottom of this pile, kept from using their voices, and the lack they represent disempowers the next generation of women as well," declares Hope. "I resolved:

I was going to create a university for silenced African women and for any woman who is struggling."[12]

This was not easy. "I was in for a shock," reflects Hope. "I felt silenced, dejected, and rejected when I shared my dream to open a university for women. Many friends, and most men, thought it was just sheer madness and impossible. I heard negative statements like 'Why don't you start by having a high school first before you jump to open a university?' Some men said, 'Has a woman in Africa or in the world ever opened a university?'" Devastated, but still firmly committed to her dream to establish a university for women, Hope's simple response was "Yes, this woman is called Hope and she dreams of success. I will empower women to have a public voice."[13]

Teamed with her friend and colleague Fay Chung, Hope opened the first university in the region that caters mostly to adult women. Women's University in Africa (WUA) opened its door in September of 2002 with a staff of ten and a student population of 147.

Today, WUA has graduated more than three thousand women from all over the region. Hope's university has seen many women graduates rise to do great things. Some women went on to run big companies in different parts of the world as well as make impressive strides in politics—for example, Joyce Mujuru, who earned two degrees from WUA, became the first female vice president of Zimbabwe, one of the few women *in the world* to hold such a post. Joyce went on to get her MBA, and then embarked on her PhD studies with the University of Zimbabwe, and now carries the title Dr. Joyce Mujuru! Hilda Suka, the ambassador to Sudan, got her position after graduating from WUA.

WUA continues to grow and impact many countries. For example, Hope has opened classes in Malawi and Zambia, where the university is attracting women who would otherwise not have such an opportunity.

Hope Sadza's crowning achievement came in 2014 when she was one of twenty women inducted into the Women's Heritage Society World Organization Hall of Fame. The list included prominent women like Hillary Clinton, Angela Merkel, Oprah

Winfrey, Beyoncé Knowles, Joyce Meyer, and Elizabeth Glaser. The WHSWO Hall of Fame is the hallmark of the highest symbolic preservation and historical recognition and honor bestowed upon any woman in the world who has lived a life that inspires another life, a life worth celebrating, a life worth emulating, an inspiration to humanity, and a legacy worth preserving for generations present and future. Professor Sadza continues receiving honors for her work—in August 2016, for example, she won a lifetime achievement award from the Southern African Development Community (SADC) for Women in the African Education Sector. "I want to see women refusing to be silenced in their quest for equality," says Dr. Sadza, and she has helped so many women do just that.[14]

Resolving Personal Silences, Creating Sustainable Futures

For more than two decades, Michelle Stronz has set a high bar for leading organizations across business, government, and other sectors. And yet, in her personal life, she suffered silently in an unhappy marriage for twenty-five years. Making a major personal change after attending one of my talks, Michelle also made powerful professional changes, moving from a more traditional CEO track to a position that empowers and creates sustainable development across the globe.

Michelle reflects:

> The several-year process in which I was closing my twenty-five-year marriage was transformative for me. It is difficult, even now, to understand how my voice was silenced by my husband for so long. I was a bit paralyzed by my "commitment to commitment" and, looking back, I think it was also my own deep questioning about self-worth. One thing is clear, the further I got from speak-

ing my truth, the further I was from my true calling. Without this difficult process of closing my marriage, I would not have come home to me.

I was in the early stages of "waking up" from my emotional prison when I met you at the United Way Women's Leadership Council annual event in Hartford, Connecticut.

After hearing your compelling story, I found the courage to envision a future where my voice would have value and where I could embrace my freedom with a renewed purpose.

You held up a mirror to my experience as you spoke of your poverty in Africa—not just financial but a sort of *poverty of the soul*. Your words resonated for me and I responded. After your presentation, I drove home with tears streaming down my face, found a scrap of fabric and an old tin. I wrote down my dreams and buried them underneath my favorite yellow magnolia tree.

They read: "To be free to tell the important stories, to mentor others whose leadership stories have a healing quality, and to be loved for who I am."

Today, I do not see any limits on what I can do to contribute to a better future. With the help of mentors and "mirrors," I rediscovered my authentic voice. Now, I am pursuing what I love the most—working with purpose-driven leaders to help them reimagine their lives and their organizations as both centers of economic value and engines of impact around the world.[15]

Turning Rejection into Opportunity

Shirin Ebadi grew up in a loving home in Iran, with parents who respected gender equality and treated her the same as her brother. Shirin is Muslim, and she went to a Zoroastrian school, which taught her respect for other religions. "This was a very important factor in forming my mind-set later when I grow up," says Shirin.[16] But her life was far from easy; the sixty-nine-year-old Iranian lawyer has had her share of being silenced. Shirin was very successful in school and eventually made her way through law school.

Prior to the 1979 Islamic revolution, Dr. Shirin Ebadi became a hero to many when she was selected to be the country's first female judge. But soon after, her dream was shattered when the government stripped her of the post because the new ruling clerics decided that women are unsuitable for such a responsibility.

Shirin remembers she had a trial on the day that an employee from the recruitment office gave her a closed envelope. "I opened the envelope after the trial and then I realized that they had removed me from my position. It was even written in the letter that according to the decision of the committee for clearing employees I am dismissed from my job. Other female judges received the same letter. I gathered all my belongings, and before leaving the court I informed the head of the department about the letter I had received. He was not aware of the decision and was very sorry but he could not do anything."[17] Despite her loving and encouraging parents, the excellent education and qualifications that got her to be selected as Iran's first female judge, Shirin was still a victim of a cultural worldview that does not respect women in leadership positions.

Shirin did not let her dismissal stop her from working—instead it fueled her. She doubled her workload after they dismissed her. She's written fourteen legal books and many articles. This lawyer and former judge is now a human rights activist who founded the Defenders of Human Rights Center in Iran. In 2003, Shirin became the first Muslim woman to win the Nobel Peace Prize. This was in honor of her significant and pioneering efforts for democracy and human rights, especially women's, children's, and refugee rights.

Listening to the Voice Within

In her mid-twenties, after majoring in finance as an undergraduate and then continuing on to pursue a law degree, Leah Campbell became deeply depressed. She had a recurring sense that there was a light within her that was dying out. She kept trying to push herself to study, and to apply for internships and jobs, but it was getting harder and harder to get through days that she dreaded, especially when she felt like she had to keep up the appearance of "having it all together."[18]

Leah had always been very spiritual, which was another thing that made law school a challenge, as the culture there seemed to make intelligence and spirituality mutually exclusive. She was also aware, though, that she kept God at arm's distance when it came to the "Thy will be done" beliefs. Ever since she was a child, she had a strong sense that God *did* have a special intention for her life, and then, somewhere between the ages of seven and twelve, she says, she had "enough Catholic religious education to be scared to death about what God might have in mind for a girl with great faith." So she made up her mind that she would take matters into her own hands.

She'd had a childhood that was idyllic in many ways, growing up on a farm surrounded by a loving family and wide-open spaces that encouraged her imagination to roam free and grow wild. As a child, she was drawn to anything to do with beauty, imagination, storytelling, spirituality, reading, writing, drawing, exploring, and helping others. But other than her beloved grandmother, who became an art teacher later in life, she didn't know of anyone who made a living doing just these things. She was quite familiar with the phrase "starving artist" and at an early age acquired the belief that artists, writers, poets, healers, and explorers were a special, almost mythical class of people to which people like her—a white girl from a very small, rural, agricultural community in the Midwest—didn't belong.

By age twelve, she came to the conclusion that the only way she could afford to have all of those loves in her life would be if she were successful enough using her brain at something "practical." It seemed like a smart, responsible plan. Becoming a lawyer got her positive reinforcement from family, teachers, and friends, and it was a career supported by society in general.

Once, during law school, Leah visited her grandmother for a few days. "Grandma Donna" had been a farmer's wife but became an art teacher at forty after Leah's grandfather died of cancer. Grandma Donna, always one of Leah's greatest fans, encouraging her creative inclinations, could see how unhappy her granddaughter was. She encouraged Leah to drop out of law school and come live with her. She'd teach her everything she knew about art and that would get her started. Donna was sure Leah could be a great artist.

Leah appreciated the love and vote of confidence, though secretly worried that her grandmother was incredibly overestimating her abilities, especially since she'd hardly done more than some sketching her entire life. She'd always wanted to paint, but was too much of a perfectionist and too scared to begin. Leah thought about her grandmother's offer, but it seemed like such a big risk and, besides, what would everyone think? Her husband? Her parents? Her classmates and friends? At best, they would think she had gone off her rocker. At worst, they'd think she was a failure, a quitter, and couldn't hack law school. *She* would think she was a failure. So she went back.

Several months later, Leah's grandmother suddenly became ill. Leah drove hours through a snowstorm to see her in the hospital. The doctor said Donna was in a coma and couldn't hear her, but Leah sat by her side and talked long into the winter's night anyway.

She said she was so sorry she hadn't made the time to come visit more, but she would, and they could start on those painting lessons her grandma had offered. "We'll start by learning to paint poppies just like we said we would," Leah told her grandma. "I've been using the pastels you gave me for Christmas last year," Leah said. "I even tore a picture of a sunflower out of a magazine. It had a caption that read 'Sunflower your elders.' One day I'll give you my drawing of the sunflower, Grandma."

As Leah told this to Donna, tears started to flow down the corners of her grandmother's eyes. Leah held her hand tighter and said "I love you, Grandma. I love you so much, I love you, I love you, I love you" over and over again.

A few days later, Leah's grandmother passed away. Leah soon found she inherited her grandmother's large collection of art supplies. In the boxes Leah also found some of her grandmother's journals. As Leah read them, her heart was torn in two. Many of the journals would start with lists of ideas, the beginnings of things—ideas for art or for stories or articles—and then the writing would turn into reflections of self-doubt and harsh self-criticism. Then even this would trail off into nothing but blank pages. Blank pages. So many blank pages. Almost every single journal was at least half-empty.

Leah was devastated to know that her grandmother, the woman whom Leah had once seen in a black-and-white picture at age sixteen standing on the bare back of a running horse—Donna told Leah that when this picture was taken she was secretly plotting to run away and join the circus—had experienced so much agony around her creativity. So much of her beautiful, feisty, spirited, pioneer of a grandmother's spirit had been trapped inside her, unexpressed.

As she considered her grandmother's life and so many family stories she'd grown up with, stories of almost-but-not-quite success and thwarted creativity and greatness, she felt as if a giant wave was crashing over her. The weight of that kind of lineage, that kind of tradition of living good, respectable lives but with so much inner disappointment seemed like it would bury her.

But she refused to let it. She promised this to herself and her grandmother and anyone to come after her. She would set about figuring how to live a fully expressed, flourishing, vibrant creative life. Her sacred dream was to eventually be able to help others set their own creative spirits free as well.

She started to think about law school and the practice of law in this light. Much attention is given to citation. Whether you're citing precedent when constructing an argument or citing primary or secondary sources when writing a research paper, you are required to back up your argument and thoughts by referencing an already established, external authority.

Leah began to realize that she had been living and planning her life this way. She had many references to support the argument for being an attorney as a guaranteed way to help others and make a good living, thereby becoming "successful." But there was a source within her that clearly persisted in saying, "No, this is wrong! This is so wrong for you!"

In all the years Leah had been trying to ignore it and stuff it down because it was such an inconvenient, uncooperative wrench in the plans she had been making, that same internal source also insisted on continually handing her an unexplainable desire to paint, an urge that seemed to spring from so deep within her that she didn't know the source, but it radiated energy out through her limbs and fingertips, like she held paintings inside of her that were just waiting to be danced out!

Today, Leah's life is in tune with that inner source. She is a thriving artist who paints and coaches others in their creative lives. She also collaborates with poets and artists. In her own experience and from being a witness and midwife to the experiences of others, Leah has seen proof of something that was a faint whisper inside her so long ago: that the energy of creativity carries with it the divine essence of who we really are. She's become convinced that this kind of creativity has the power to heal, enliven, and enlighten. Her new goal: one million plus revived and restored souls.

The one thing all of these leaders and stories have in common is that when they empowered themselves, they improved the world. By developing healthy businesses, pursuing our passions even after a major setback, getting in tune with an inner spirituality that serves your deepest hungers, these women recognized the treacherous stretch of road they had to traverse, and they turned around and worked to lighten the journey for others.

We all have so many reasons not to pursue our dreams, so many things that keep us from walking those last few miles. Maybe it's a corrupt government that oppresses and divides—or even attacks—its own people; maybe it is poverty, or racist or sexist cultural norms. Maybe it is a "commitment to commitment" that keeps you stuck in a dead-end marriage; maybe it's a career that doesn't satisfy your sacred purpose. Maybe it is age, or isolation. Maybe no one has ever asked you, or maybe you have never been ready to answer.

I do not know what barriers line your pathway, but I know that you will only traverse them when you open yourself to the wisdom of those who have gone before. Find your giant teddy bear. Find the cracks and fill them. Find the seeds that you can plant. Find your Hope Sadza. There is a space being held open for you by millions of people and their actions across the world; will you let them help walk you to your sacred purpose?

SACRED RITUAL TO INSPIRE ACTION AND OPPORTUNITY

Taking guidance from elders' wisdom and from those who've taken the journey before us is vital. Inspiration from those who have already walked your path can save time as you learn from their triumphs and errors. But there is also something greater that happens when you tune in to the energy of the successful, authentic women who inspire you. On a vibrational level, you will be able to attune to the energy of what they have already created, while also adding your own energy and enthusiasm. The harmonious outcome is a mixture of your energy and theirs. In other words, once you tune in to their collective creation, you expand the potential of that creation—to everyone's benefit.

In order to tune in to this vibration we need to be able to recognize opportunity when it calls us, and offer opportunity to others whenever possible. So often we say no, implicitly or explicitly, when opportunity arises. We are trained to say "fine" or "busy" when someone asks "how are you?" or to stifle the deepest parts of ourselves for the sake of making nice, keeping harmony with friends and family. Too often we get in the habit of ignoring the fact that interactions with others are *opportunities*—not for material gain or selfish ends, but opportunities for creative thinking, for acting on our dreams, for lifting up the dreams of others. Opportunities for inspiration.

You need to give *rukudzo*, honor, to those heroines who have walked the path before you if you are to get into the habit of saying yes to inspiration. These heroines have made the invisible stretch of road more visible to you, more passable. They reach back for you, whether literally or with the force of their example, waiting for you to thrust out your hands toward them. You inspire action in yourself by paying homage to these trailblazers in your thoughts and actions. Knowing their actions make yours more possible.

Honoring the Torchbearers

A dear friend told me how tears poured from her eyes upon hearing American civil rights activist Diane Nash speak. Nash told the audience that whatever she and her compatriots in SNCC (Student Nonviolent Coordinating Committee), the Freedom Riders, and more did for social justice—being arrested, marching, organizing—they did for the next generation; "we loved you before we even knew you," Ms. Nash said.[19]

Many women before you have done the hard work of awakening. Whether they knew it or not, whatever they did not only improved their lives, but was an act of love for your life, too. They loved you, the next generation, before they knew you. They worked hard not to pass down their soul wounds; they worked instead to give you a gift of passion and purpose, a better world.

Feel that love coming to you from the past. Breathe it in, dance in it, hear it without reservation. As a tribute to that legacy, begin a monthly practice of honoring the gift of that love. Each month, make a short list of women who inspire you. Include women you know and women you've never met. Use the following questions to help you make your list:

- Think of a successful moment you've had in your life and all the little moments that got you there. Who had a hand in making that moment possible for you? Even down to the smallest encouragement?

- Who are the inspirational women in your life? In your family? In your community? Who has achieved something that makes you long for the same success? Whose work tugs at your heart?

- Think about a woman who inspires you who you have not met. Include the heroines and superheroines that inspire and fire you, and that speak to your spirit and your soul, beyond the conditionings of what you have learned in this lifetime. What do you admire in them? What one quality of theirs can you begin practicing today?

Once you have your list, clean off your writing space, put on music and a nice, comfortable outfit. Make sure you are not hungry or tired.

Get your best pen and paper and write a note of gratitude to this person. Be specific, thanking them in detail for what you appreciate in them, their work, and their attitude.

Put it in the mail. If you cannot get their address, place the note on a little altar of your own making, or stick it to the wall of your room or office. With this practice you will not only be cultivating humility and gratitude, which in itself is a significant action to take in pursuit of your sacred purpose, but you will also be creating a robust and ongoing catalog of actions and ideas that you, too, can use.

Draw upon the wisdom of your elders, as well as those who have walked a similar path before you. Be in touch with these torchbearers daily, whether in prayer or in reflection. Listen to or read their words frequently. Feel them in your heart and let them be the messengers that guide you, even when you feel you cannot guide yourself.

After you've gotten comfortable with this monthly practice, I invite you to add a final exercise for recognizing opportunity. Make a deliberate plan to inspire action for another woman, or to find another opportunity to be shared. This may mean taking a moment from your busy day to ask someone "What are your dreams?" It may mean volunteering your skills to women at a domestic abuse shelter, perhaps helping them on the path of education or employment. Maybe you watch a friend's children so that she can take a class or build the website for her sacred dreams venture.

There are so many ways we can show up for each other. The actions of others will not drain you; they will encourage you to act on behalf of your dreams as well. When we are willing to show humility and gratitude for our heroines, when we support action in other women, my sacred sisters, our own actions will be infused with a mighty energy that cannot be stopped.

As you become lighter on your feet you will notice that you are able to dance more freely with the world around you. You will find yourself responding to the circumstances of your external world, and being more resourceful with what is available to you.

New opportunities will appear when your heart is open to receiving the resources available to you. You will find that people who cross your path can help you with your dreams. At first it may seem like coincidence, but as it happens more and more, you will come to realize that the universe is supporting you to achieve your dream and you are lining up to receive all it has to offer.

As more and more opportunities come your way, a two-way process occurs. You open your heart to receive the gifts of the universe and at the same time you cultivate your own generosity of spirit, so that giving and receiving become a constant exchange.

As your dream project contributes to improving the lives of others, you will begin to connect with them, too, engaging them and listening to their needs, grounding your dreams in their reality. You will naturally adapt your vision to the real world, allowing it to be received in the best way possible for all involved.

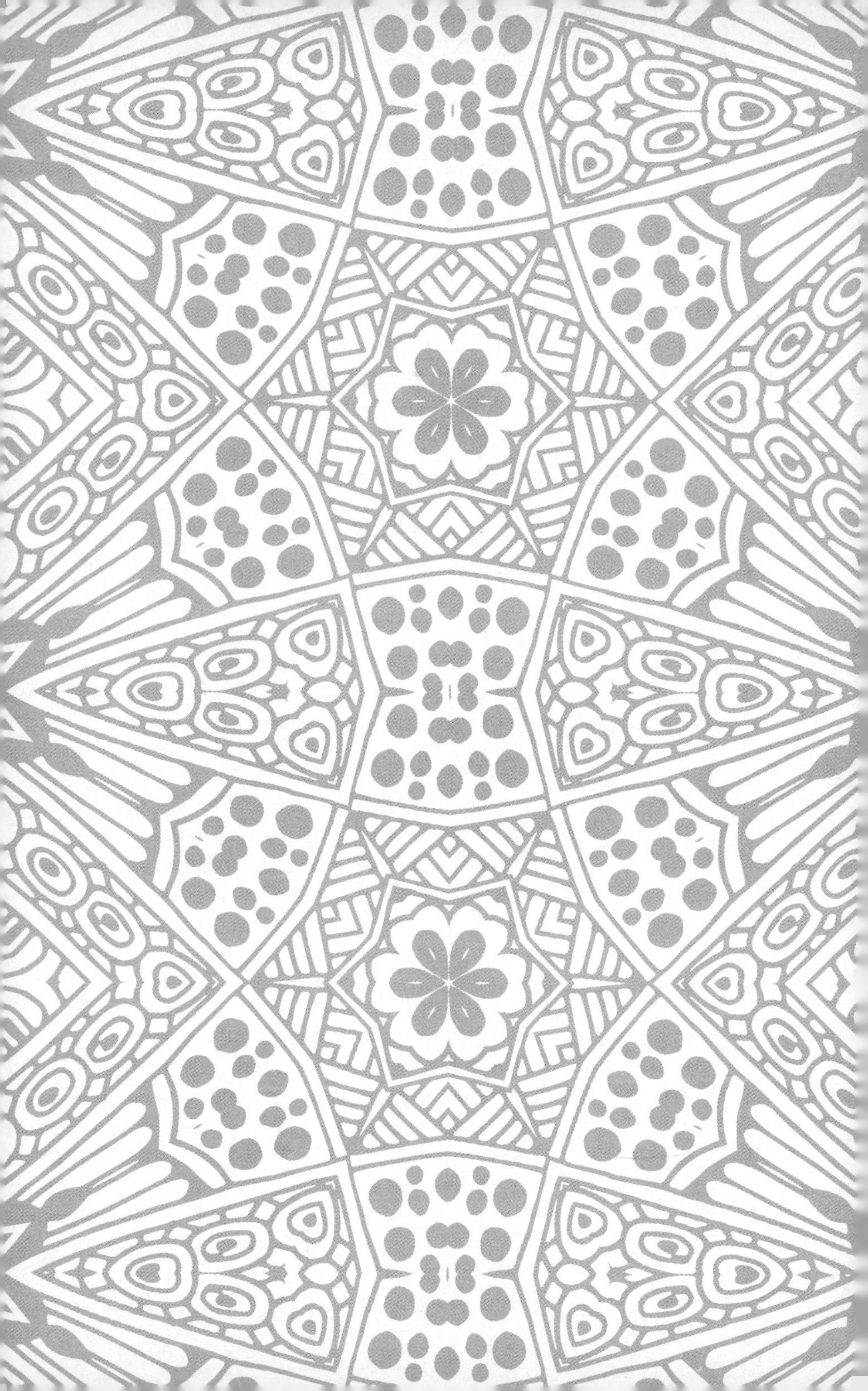

8

THE SACRED SISTERHOOD: CULTIVATING YOUR *SAHWIRA*

> *If you want to go fast, go alone. If you want to go far, go together.*
>
> —AFRICAN PROVERB

The driver of the hearse carrying my mother's body smiles nervously as she gets out of her car. Wiping raindrops from her forehead, she shakes thick strands of dreadlocked hair. Striding deliberately toward the back of the hearse, she unlatches the tailgate, which opens with a soft, hydraulic sigh. Inside, a dark brown mahogany coffin decorated with a patch of black leather blends into the darkness.

Moonlight reflects off the coffin's steel handles as the woman carefully opens the car's side window curtains. With perfect synchronicity, six middle-aged men emerge from the circle of silence to lift my mother's coffin. As the coffin is slowly raised, the sound of an eerie, shrill ululation fills the dark rainy sky.

The driver of the hearse closes the door, my mother's dearest friend, Mai Chigowo, asks, "What took you so long?" but she continues speaking before there is an answer. "Has anyone brought lamps or candles?" By now it is completely dark but for the light of the moon and a nearby fire.

My mother has just died and the hearse has brought her body from the hospital to her final resting place—our rural home. In my culture, no dead person is buried without her *sahwira* (pronounced sah-wee-ra), a Shona word that translates to "friend for life," to make sure burial protocols and rituals are observed before the dead's final departure on earth. The *sahwira* also presides over burial activities, overseeing food preparation and entertainment. But the *sahwira*'s role transcends beyond burial and is cultivated early in life.

As mourners gather around my mother's coffin, a voice imitating my mother's brings my daydreams to an end. The *sahwira* imitates her friend in order to represent her values. It is common practice in our community to use role-playing and "stand-ins" in a variety of different circumstances. Likewise, the *sahwira* becomes my mother to elevate our mourning. Our identities are fluid and transferable.

Mai Chigowo makes people laugh and cry at the same time. She emerges from my mother's bedroom, wearing her favorite dress, eyeglasses, headdress, and hat. Walking with a limp, she holds my mother's walking stick just as my mother did. Because Mai Chigowo and my mother were approximately the same height and weight, the *sahwira*—with her face partially covered by the hat—seems to bring my mother back to life.

Mai Chigowo approaches the mourners and pretends to talk to a young man with a cell phone. She dictates this message for the invisible young man: "*Wanyora here zvandataura, umuudze Tererai kuti kana ouya, atiigire mabrofeni*"—"I want you to send a text to Tererai! Tell her that on her next visit from America, she must remember to bring back ibuprofen pills for our headaches!"

In response, some in the room begin to laugh while others wipe away tears. Even I laugh—for the first time since my mother died. Mai Chigowo smiles at me. I smile in return for she has fulfilled one of her fundamental roles—to lighten our grief and to remind us of my mother's special qualities and extraordinary capacity to care for others.

Unlike in the West where such a role is either left to family mediators—social workers, psychologists, or the "Dr. Phils" of the world—in my village it is common to have someone in the family or close circle who gives advice. The *sahwira* is such an adviser, a resource of information on all matters that one might not fully understand, a friend who grounds you and brings a better understanding to some things in life.

A *sahwira* can be closer than your blood siblings. She is the one who becomes your sacred sister because she believes in what drives your soul without judging. Sometimes it is not easy for families to listen to pain, to empathize with what hurts us, or to acknowledge and understand the source of the hurt. The code of silence in our families is often much preferred, as it makes it easier for family members to stick together rather than pointing fingers of blame and shame. A *sahwira* has none of that; rather, she gives honest and direct feedback, helps us to face the good and bad, including the source of our pain, and the part anyone played in our suffering, including ourselves.

The choosing of a *sahwira* is an organic practice established among many generations. For example, if my family was *sahwira* to your family, then my grandchildren are more likely to play the role of *sahwira* to your grandchildren. Like a beneficiary inheritance, however, only good *sahwiras* take over the relationship as they replace a late *sahwira*. In informal discussions, members of the community play a role in pointing out good characteristics they see in a potential *sahwira* that resemble those of the previous (late) *sahwira*.

People establish their potential as a *sahwira* through their behaviors in daily life: we recognize the importance of a person's role in helping families raise their children, the care and frankness a person uses as they facilitate difficult discussions, and how well someone lightens bereavement and brings joy to celebrations. *Sahwiras* are also notoriously known for playing the devil's advocate in difficult discussions that might need out-of-the-box thinking, as well as for exposing destructive secrets that otherwise might have remained hidden because others are afraid to share. Our Korekore families depend upon this close friend to initiate difficult discussions about such sensitive topics as sex, incest, rape, and domestic violence—in other words, it is a socially acknowledged and valued relationship that offers women solidarity with other women.

You can see then why Mai Chigowo was a woman on a mission: she was my mother's *sahwira*, and while she is not a blood relative, she has a special place in the family. My mother's *sahwira* helped us see the bigger picture. She kept us attuned to our higher purposes when some of the issues that could trigger us into pain or sorrow were ignited. As a result of her guidance, my mother's funeral was a meaningful celebration for such an exceptionally beautiful soul.

My mother and Mai Chigowo were inseparable friends. As widows in their later years, my mother convinced her friend to attend church to alleviate the burden of parenting grandchildren alone. But what cemented their lifelong relationship occurred many years earlier.

During an era of economic collapse, Mai Chigowo had a land dispute with one of the most powerful men in the village, who also happened to be the son of the village chief. Not surprisingly, when she took the case to the chief, she lost. Without an education or money to hire a lawyer, she and my mother decided to take the case to Chief Dandahwa, the senior chief presiding over all other chiefs in the Hurungwe District. This took real nerve: among the Korekore, women don't do such things. But the two women were determined. Undaunted by the lack of bus service to Chief Dandahwa's homestead thirty miles away, my mother and her *sahwira* walked for days to speak with him.

The matter was decided in Mai Chigowo's favor.

This was a hugely important achievement, one that is rare among the patriarchal Korekore people. In our community, it is rare for a woman to prevail in a formal dispute with a man, as Mai Chigowo did, even if it appears that the woman is in the right. As children, we are taught to believe in a natural disparity between male and female worth, and many of our daily customs help to reinforce the notion that boys have more inherent value than girls. Growing up, my brother Tinashe is addressed with respect as "Moyo Sinyoro" (our heart totem) while I am simply "Tererai." The message underlying these different greetings is not lost on me.

Therefore, this experience was a major awakening of these two women's feminine energy, and they could only have done it together; they knew that an insult to one was an insult to the other, as well as to all women. You could hear Mai Chigowo and my mother's celebratory ululations a mile away as they danced and let everybody know of their victory. A few days after their return to our village, the two women role-played the whole thing for us.

My mother took the multiple roles of Chief Dandahwa, the presiding judge, and Mai Chigowo, the plaintiff. Mai Chigowo played the local chief's son, the defendant. My mother's voice changed as she switched roles from Chief Dandahwa to Mai Chigowo. She put on the chief's hat as she addressed the audience in mimicry, and in another minute she wrapped a Zambia cloth around her waist as she impersonated Mai Chigowo. The audience was in stitches with laughter as both women entertained the village, and yet, we could all feel their pain and their victory.

In that moment, not only did we experience their journey and gain insight into the court's proceedings, but we also shared in the deep friendship that binds these women together and enables them to fight for what is rightfully theirs. In this way one's pain becomes shared, their fight becomes a symbol of their commitment to social justice, and makes others realize that women's narratives and dreams will remain disjointed unless they are willing to not only voice their own pain and longing, but also witness each other's pain and longing. This empathic *sahwira* relationship is how we band together.

Friendship. Mentors. Community. *Sahwira*. There are many ways to name relationships of support and guidance. In my village and most of Africa we have these formal social support systems, such as a *sahwira*, that counsel us with vital wisdom, but regardless of your culture, everyone needs these relationships for survival. Sacred sisters, embedded in the *sahwira* dynamic is the ability of women to rely on each other, and to take risks by being open to love, hurt, and disappointment. This is because to rely on someone means you are willing to share ambitions, joys, and sorrows, and to reveal your own vulnerability.

Researcher Brené Brown defines vulnerability as an emotional risk that exposes us to uncertainty, and she puts forward the notion that vulnerability is a healthy part of daily life. Brown shares a conclusion that relates directly to the *sahwira* concept: that vulnerability is "the birthplace of joy, of creativity, of belonging, of love."[1] We do not simply depend on each other, we also build each other up, and when this happens, we create something greater. In the case of my mother and her *sahwira*, they banded together and conquered a corrupt local chief, a success that was practically unheard of at the time.

If there are no formal support structures in place, we must build a *sahwira* network for ourselves. This is not easily done; just the idea of building such a support network can conflict with the cultural norms with which we were raised, as we so often hear when someone says, "I lifted myself up by my own bootstraps." We are taught that everyone must exist for themselves, and that we must somehow do it all alone if we want to be successful.

How many mothers feel isolated and overburdened because we emphasize individual responsibility for child rearing over the social aspects? How many women are unaware that it is sexism that pays them less than their male counterparts at work? Or, sexism keeps them from getting a promotion, because they are socialized to believe that they are individually responsible for getting ahead, rather than to see that their personal concerns are indeed shared by women across the world?

I am a firm believer in the power of hard work to lift us up and achieve our hearts' desires, but even the hardest worker cannot do it on their own. Maybe this is possible if we are so powerful that we can impose our individual will on the world, but even then, we would need others to carry out our will. It is not a realistic vision of achievement. There are always other people and other forces that play a major role in our success. Even more important, there is another kind of power accessible to us: not the kind of power that comes from imposing our will on others, or stepping on others to achieve our dreams, or buying into the false belief that we both achieve and fail on our own, but *the power to lift ourselves up by lifting each other up*. This is the heart of the *sahwira*.

When we operate as an island, a number of things occur. We cut off our ability to receive. It is as if we are saying "no" to the creator of the universe on some level. We are also much less likely to help others if we close ourselves off from receiving help. Having a tremendous capacity to receive can also come from our willingness to be generous. I am not necessarily talking about giving away material possessions, but giving love, support, time, and energy to others. If we give without the capacity to receive, we become self-sacrificing. And if we only receive without the capacity to give, then we lose touch with the needs of those around us.

The *sahwira* tradition helps us remember that our identities are fluid and transferable; it offers us the powerful insight that we are social by nature. The *sahwira* tradition helps us hold in harmonious balance the seeming tension between personal and communal, for the *sahwira* shows us that each person has an individual responsibility for the well-being of the entire community, and that the community has a responsibility to the well-being of the individual.

The Power of Female Friendships

The first item on writer and professor Roxane Gay's insightful list of tips for having successful female friendships is: "Abandon the cultural myth that all female friendships must be bitchy, toxic, or competitive.

This myth is like heels and purses—pretty but designed to SLOW women down."[2] Why is this so important as to be front and center in advice on friendships among women?

We all know this myth. It is pervasive in the media, in everything from reality television to the lyrics of pop songs. It's Alicia Florrick getting slapped in the face by Diane Lockhart in the final moments of *The Good Wife*, ending a season that had Diane and Alicia flirting with the idea of starting an all-female law firm with a bitter strike at women's friendship. And although Gay writes about it with such smart humor, it is also quite serious: the cultural myth of toxic female friendships keeps up from the power of each other. We need to celebrate instead the power of female friendships by showing healthy and supportive intentional relationships among women; we need to introduce the *sahwira* concept anywhere this toxic myth pervades.

Sometimes it is not competition that threatens female friendships: sometimes it is fear of the depth of our own feeling; or the fear of being vulnerable, the apprehension of not knowing how to love and be accepted despite our flaws; or the fear of not trusting others to have the wisdom to get it right; perhaps it's the fear shaped by our need for control that keeps us from trusting others; or the fear of failure shaped by years of wanting to prove we are the best at what we do. And then there is the fear shaped by our culture that discourages us from venturing into the unknown, fear steeped in our culture that says exposing our vulnerability is not woman enough, or Western enough, or African enough, for it is a sign of weakness.

I was going through some personal family issues at one point in America and I needed someone to hear me, to provide some emotional support, so I called a friend in Oklahoma. Beth listened and for a long time remained silent. I talked more and still there was silence ... the silence soon became unendurable. "Beth, are you still there? Has the phone gone dead?" I panicked as I assumed I had been talking to a dead phone all this time. She said, "No, dear, I am still here ..." I waited for a response to what I had shared and none came. I was at a loss.

As I was deciding whether to continue or to hang up the phone silently, I heard Beth's voice sounding strained and strangely contrite as if she was feeling sorry for my lack of understanding. She said, "In this culture, we find it difficult to discuss such personal issues." Taken aback, all I could say was "Oh, I'm sorry, I didn't realize . . ." I didn't know how to finish that sentence.

"In this culture, it's not appropriate to involve others in one's personal problems, particularly when related to family issues," she went on. As though she wanted to get it all out, Beth hurriedly continued, "I know this might be different from Africa, which by the way I admire the culture very much, however, we just don't divulge such personal things in this culture." All I could do while she spoke those words, and she said them slowly, as though trying to convince a toddler in that beautiful Southern drawl of hers, was to scribble down each word.

Afterward, I looked at that small piece of paper and felt the deep echoes of our silences, my own silencing and hers, and the gaps that our love, healing, mentorship—perhaps even the tears of exposing our vulnerability and tears of comradeship—could have filled. The silence of this beautiful woman and how her silences shaped and confined her saddened me. How can we thrive if we allow ourselves to be so cut off from one another?

In response to the myth of toxic female friendships and to the reverberating silence of those who struggle to enter into the deep, vulnerable power of relationship, we need to raise up the *sahwira* tradition. The *sahwira* tradition helps us recover and value female friendships, empowers us to work on cultivating healthy female friendships, as well as to normalize and name support networks in cultures where there are few.

I was reminded of the *sahwira* recently when reading Rebecca Traister's *All the Single Ladies*. Historically and in contemporary society, Traister reminds us, female friendships have great significance in women's lives. We may know this, but often we do not hear about them, and certainly, there are few rituals to honor these relationships. Historically speaking, when marriage was still mostly a social contract entered into for economic purposes rather than for love or friendship or sexual fulfillment, Traister reveals, "friendships often provided women with attention, affection, and an outlet for intellectual or political exchange."[3]

Although today many do marry for love, affection, and intellectual exchange, Traister helps us to see that female friendship remains central to women's lives: "Among the largely unacknowledged truths of female life is that women's primary, foundational, formative relationships are as likely to be with each other as they are with the men we've been told since childhood are supposed to be the people who complete us."[4] Let us recover this history and let us proclaim the truth of our own time: women's relationships with each other are significant, foundational, and lifelong. We have so much power to lift one another up; we have been doing it over the course of human history and we shall and must continue to do it.

How are these friendships honored? Traister points out that as powerful and significant as female friendships are to women's lives, these relationships are largely unacknowledged in any socially meaningful way. "There has not yet been any satisfying way to recognize the role that we play for each other," she observes.[5] "There aren't any ceremonies to make this official. "There aren't weddings; there aren't health benefits or domestic partnerships or familial recognition."[6]

We have all sorts of holidays and rituals for celebrating and acknowledging spousal relationships, but so very few when it comes to female friendship. On the contrary, we have media messages showing women fighting over men, competing with other women for everything from love to clothing to beauty, and with so few women in top leadership positions, it seems there's only room for a few of us.

This notion that female friendship is toxic, competitive, a sign of weakness, and not socially valuable is a dangerous myth, one that highlights how much we need to proclaim and celebrate the heart of the *sahwira*. The *sahwira* will help us recover and uncover the illuminating potential of female friendships.

Research suggests that in addition to being spiritually and emotionally good for women's lives, there are quite a few physical benefits to female friendships. Melissa Pandika writes about a number of recent studies in her funny and informative article "Why Girl Gangs Make for Good Health."[7] As Pandika reports, research shows that "a tightly knit group of girlfriends might lower the risk for diabetes, cancer and other chronic diseases, possibly resulting in healthier, longer lives." In addition, "studies hint that friendships help women weather stress, lowering their risk for disease." But it's not just about having friends; it's about having quality, meaningful friendships. Pandika explains,

> A recent breast cancer study found that, compared with socially integrated women, socially isolated women had a whopping 34 percent higher risk of death. But the quality of their relationships mattered, too—women with small social networks and low levels of support had a 61 percent higher likelihood of dying than those with small networks and high support. That means ditch the crappy friends and focus on the real thing.[8]

I adore Pandika's humor and at the same time, my dear sisters, I shudder at the thought of all that we are deprived of when we are deprived of one another. I also ululate at the healing and uplifting possibilities available to us and to generations to come if we embrace the heart of the *sahwira*.

During my time at Oklahoma State University, I established many *sahwira* mentors, but one in particular stands out: Regina Henry, coordinator of international students and scholars. The first time I met her she was addressing the new international students. Strong and beautiful in her brownish suit, she stood by the podium leaning out toward us as she warned against letters that we would soon receive. "Welcome to America, dear students," she said, clearing her throat. All eyes were on her. "Very soon some of you will be receiving bogus letters claiming you have won lotteries worth millions. Soon you will think you are so lucky and have become millionaires.

Be very careful, it's all a scam. There is nothing for free in those letters; rather, you will end up losing your money trying to claim the so-called winnings." Friendly, and yet firm, Regina never minced her words. She instantly reminded me of my mother's *sahwira*.

I wanted to know her more and so I soon made my way to her office. We quickly became friends as she connected me to the wider community of Stillwater. Regina invited me to participate in a campus event where I shared cultural dishes from my village. Over the years, Regina mentored me through visa changes that allowed me to continue working in the United States.

She also warmed my children's hearts in many ways. One day she noticed my son crying as he watched other children riding bicycles. Not long after that, she surprised him with his own bicycle that another family had donated. This act of generosity had a huge impact on him. When at seventeen he was ready for college, he easily chose OSU, saying, "After all, it's the place where I first rode a bicycle." It surprised me to know that after years away from Stillwater, he so clearly remembered the *sahwira* mentor and the community that helped us to thrive as a family. To this day, when people ask my son where he is from, he smiles and says, "Stillwater, Oklahoma." And Regina remains in my circle of *sahwiras*.

You see, when I held my dreams alone, they were unstable, but when I added the energy of another who believed in me, my dreams could take root. My dearest friends, we cannot deny love that comes from our fellow women. As humans we are social animals. Our collective empathy, friendship, and responsibility toward one another are what awaken our humanity, and therefore, each of us is fertile ground that nurtures, inspires, and enables growth in each other.

This fertile ground has unlimited power, if we would only plant in it. Female friendship is good for our physical, emotional, and spiritual health. It crosses so many barriers meant to keep us apart. It has always been there for us, for our mothers, and our grandmothers, and many more before them. We have to claim it, with intention and an open heart.

I See You/I'm Here

Many native South Africans have a particular way of greeting strangers and familiar people that recognizes the essence of the moment, which we believe is not a "hello" but a deeper interaction of our *ubuntu*. Our greetings express the power of our collectiveness, acknowledging and giving space to each other's joy, pain, and dignity.

For example, the Zulu greeting starts with "*Sawubona*," which means "I see you." The response is "*Ngikhona*," "I am here." The person being greeted is saying to the greeter "by recognizing me, you brought me into existence." The "I see you" invocation is a spiritual ethic that magnifies our shared humanity. This greeting is a mutual, reciprocal way of recognizing not only each other's existence but also each person's significance and value to our existence here on earth. By saying, "I see you/I'm here" we affirm that we are inextricably connected in ways beyond human understanding, and our survival is dependent on one another.

"I see you/I'm here" proclaims that we are both equal, and a gift to each other. We see each other's greatness as Nyadenga, the Great Spirit, the creator meant us to be. This is a declaration of intent to fully inhabit the other person's spirit and presence.

The most powerful part of the "I see you/I'm here" invocation is the eye contact between the two speakers. Facing each other, eyes looking deeply into the other's eyes, there is a moment of silence before the greeting. A deep connection and a sense of oneness are established without any words. Eye contact provides a great mirror into the other. Looking into each other's eyes, they see the reflection of themselves, their joy, pain, and their dreams, and recognize their oneness.

"I see you/I'm here" encourages us to appreciate the gift of the moment. It calls us to be grateful to what is in front of us, to see joy and vulnerability and to reach out to others. There is no stronger foundation upon which to build dreams than gratitude, forgiveness, and empathy! "I see you/I'm here" nurtures our dreams, because when we recognize the presence of others and their gift to us, we nurture their dreams and help sustain our own.

An understanding of building relationships that are authentic and based on the power of our collectiveness and the gift found in our oneness is critical for our survival. Is the foundation of your "I see you" strong enough to bring joy and healing to others? Is your "I see you" authentic enough to pass on this ritual to the next generation? The "yes" to these questions should be matched with how we show up in the world. I know there will be setbacks, and sometimes enormous challenges, but the invocation of "I see you/I'm here"—when practiced in an intentional, *sahwira* relationship—is about showing up despite whatever changes are occurring in our lives.

The Heart of a *Sahwira*

We find powerful friendships by embodying the heart of a *sahwira*. Each of us can be a *sahwira*, just as we look to others to fill that role for us. What defines the heart of the *sahwira*? For me there are three central and interwoven characteristics:

- Sacred sisterhood is embedded in the *sahwira* structure. It is a pact you make. It enables women to rely on one another, and to take risks by being open to love, hurt, and disappointment.

- For the *sahwira*, giving and receiving takes all forms and should not be restricted to material things. It is important that you also remain a giver of your knowledge, wisdom, love, and empathy, and that you receive gifts from others with grace and gratitude.

+ The *sahwira* is authentic in both receiving and giving. Give what is needed without being overbearing, and receive what you need without making it a duty to impress the giver.

My fellow women, we need each other. We need to stand on each other's shoulders and believe in the power of our collectiveness and how it can amplify our feminine energy for the greater good. I have seen it. I have experienced that when women consider themselves to be social catalysts, an unbreakable movement, they begin to see changes in themselves as well as in their communities.

As the global community "westernizes" and imitates an artificial lifestyle of individualism, where the sense of "collectiveness" is more elusive, the relationships that we create are not fluid, and we become stuck. We cannot move. Fear, distrust, and competitiveness get in the way of creating strong *sahwira* relationships. And yet, tapping into one another, the harmonious choir of our feminine energy empowers community building.

Yes, it is that important. My mother believed in the traditional African philosophy of *ubuntu*, which purports that "a person is a person through other persons," and that there exists a common bond among us all despite race, gender, class, backgrounds, and any other forms of difference. This sacred philosophy offers an understanding of ourselves in relation to the world.

My *sahwiras*, our wholeness comes from knowing that we belong, that we are but pieces of a larger community, and therefore the joy of others is our own, and so is their suffering. The heart of the *sahwira* is open to give and receive; it trusts in the knowledge of our connectedness; it does not fear jealousy or competition, but instead basks in the bright light of collaboration and sharing and building.

SACRED RITUAL TO WEAVE YOUR *SAHWIRA*'S WEB

The *sahwira* is all about building an authentic support network, one of mutually supportive connections. These may be found among family, friends, relatives, or others who share goals similar to yours. You might find it through social media. You might find it in a neighbor. The key is to take support and counsel from those who are going to boost you toward your goals rather than from those who doubt you. If you don't have family members who can fill this role for you, seek out others who share the desire to identify, work toward, and fulfill a greater purpose.

As you begin to create your own *sahwira* network, here are a few important things to explore in your journal:

First Ask Yourself Why You Need a Sahwira?

It is important to ask yourself why you need one, and what value will they bring in your life and vice versa, so that you are not just blindly searching around in the dark but have a clear intention and purpose in creating this relationship. In your journal or notebook, explore the questions: What qualities in a mentor and friend will support my vision? What do I bring to the relationship?

Identify Individual Sahwira

Identifying at least one loyal friend and building a relationship of mutual support may mean the difference between achieving your dreams and allowing them to fall by the wayside.

- Who directs my focus toward what is possible rather than what has not yet been achieved?

- Who expands my horizons and helps me see the world through different eyes?

- Who do I feel I can lift up to their highest potential, identifying blocks and blind spots, and offering support?

- What skills and qualities do I have to offer? In what areas do I need support? What will I do in return?

- If you have children or close family members, also think about identifying a *sahwira* who makes your children happy when she is around. The spirit of a *sahwira* and its effect can feel like a "social vaccine" that makes everybody experience joy. Does her presence feel good to the whole family? On the other hand, is she someone who makes your children roll their eyes, cringe, or whisper behind your back?

Expanding the Circle

Grow your web of support one person at a time. Let people around you know your intentions and notice their reactions. If someone tells you it is not possible to do what you want to do, don't be discouraged by them; they are just seeing the world through the limitations of their own filters. The key is to not take their discouragement on board or to judge them, but instead to move on to someone who can lend support as you pursue your dreams.

Remember that it can be more useful to have one or two people who have the same dream than to have an endless number of contacts who half support what you are doing. Go for quality of connection rather than quantity.

- What groups can I join, either face-to-face or online, composed of others whose mission is similar to mine?

- Can I name a second and a third person that fits the descriptions above?

- Are my potential *sahwiras* from a diverse group? Am I looking out for the different roles that people can play or just finding the same qualities in different people? One person might advise you. Another might be a motivator.

Look for mentors who will support your project or mission in both body and soul. There may be people who are willing to give their time to coach you toward your goal, particularly if it is one that benefits the greater good. Invest in quality, authentic mentorship. Ask yourself, What other support networks can I put in place? Do they already exist, and how can they help me? What can I contribute? When you look at creating a connection with others in this way, you take your dream-seeking into a wider playing field.

Once you have explored these questions, it is time to reach out and ask the people and groups you have identified as *sahwiras*. Let them know your sacred dreams journey and discuss the roles you might play in each other's lives. Create special, dedicated time for supporting and mentoring each other. Be intentional about lifting each other up and partnering each other on the road to your sacred purpose.

We belong to a sacred web, and nurturing a *sahwira* relationship allows the continuation of a weaving whose thread makes us stronger. Once one thread becomes weak and pulls off, then the whole web becomes weak. Are we willing to see our shared role in the health of the web? Will we be more intentional in our strengthening of the web? This is what fortifies and bolsters the *sahwira* network of strong women. We are all connected and our survival is bound together with the thread of love.

You are already part of this network. Now you have to do the work of seeing those connections—and this is admittedly no easy task if you live in a culture that privileges individuality over community—

and build on them. Let community and love be your refrain. Set yourself free from the need to do it on your own; reject the myth of toxic female friendships and trust in your essential connectedness.

Beloved *sahwiras*: writers, mystics, activists, and healers have long spoken of the need for community and connectedness. Tap into the poetry of their rhythmic song. Allow yourself to be a *sahwira*, and open your senses to receive the *sahwira* guidance that sings back to you.

Until women can come together and authentically support one another, our communities, and the world, our narratives and dreams will remain disjointed. Remember, *sahwira*-ship is based on deep connectedness: it sustains us, teaches us about the world around us, enriches our lives, and keeps us focused on our dreams.

CONCLUSION: IT IS ACHIEVABLE!

> *The world is round and the place which may seem like the end may also be only the beginning.*
>
> —IVY BAKER PRIEST, *PARADE*

On October 15, 2009, I defended my dissertation to a packed audience of my peers, students from other departments, and professors, including my dissertation committee at Western Michigan University. Thanks to a group of fellow students who grilled me during a mock presentation, I felt ready.

My dissertation was titled "Meta-evaluation of HIV/AIDS prevention intervention evaluations in Sub-Saharan Africa with a specific emphasis on implications for women and girls." Throughout my studies, I worked hard to understand the spread of HIV/AIDS. As I prepared to speak, I thought about Zuda. Our time living together in America was full of tension and strife. The cultural differences in the US only heightened his anger toward me. If a male coworker from my job called using my first name to ask me to cover a shift, Zuda would become enraged.

I lived through physical and emotional abuse even while in America. I was embarrassed to tell anyone that I suffered in this way. I used every trick known to battered women to hide my situation. There were explanations for every cut and scratch on my body. I prayed that

God would transform this man from a wife beater into a good father and loving husband. Though I did my best to hide the abuse, it did not take long for neighbors to complain about the noise coming from our small apartment.

Dr. Ron Beer, a constant source of support for me during my education, soon became aware of my hardship and the risk facing my children. His office and Stillwater's domestic violence program found us temporary shelter while the authorities arrested Zuda for domestic violence. I knew I was finally and forever done with this man. At last, Zuda agreed to voluntary deportation to Zimbabwe at the end of 1999.

Later he contracted HIV/AIDS. He died from this disease in March 2002, one of the first Zimbabweans with a death certificate identifying AIDS as the cause of death and just months after Zimbabwe declared HIV/AIDS a national emergency.

I contemplated Zuda's death as I stood there in front of my dissertation committee. I realized he was a product of his environment, as is everyone. As I found my voice to defend my dissertation, my mind took me back to the years of suffering, and I found myself silently grieving for all the pain and suffering that he brought to my life and the lives of my children as well as his own sad end. I also thought about my own experience with this horrible disease, which greatly influenced my decision to focus on the disproportionate number of women and girls infected by HIV/AIDS in sub-Saharan Africa.

I thought of the year I spent visiting the hospital every three months for more testing, the nights I spent wallowing in self-pity on the bathroom floor of my tiny university apartment. For although Zuda and I had not been intimate while in the United States, there was still a chance that I, too, had HIV. I thought of the shame and guilt that consumed me, my fear of looking in the mirror and seeing a pimple on my face, or how I panicked at every cough or tired feeling, certain that the infection had arrived.

I was lucky; all my tests came back clean. But my quest to understand female exposure to the disease (as well as methods for prevention, especially for those not yet infected) had taken me on quite a journey. Having seen firsthand the pain and resilience of women and girls who have fought and succumbed to the epidemic, these tragedies renewed my energy daily while working on the dissertation.

So much went through my head as I gathered my thoughts on that stage, waiting for my dissertation committee to ask me questions. Looking out over the crowd of students and faculty sitting there, I suddenly envisioned my late brother smiling as he shared a beautifully illustrated geography book that transported me to magical places and made me thirst for more, my first real reading experience . . . I could see my mother handing me a rusty old can in which to secure my dreams.

"Can you describe the difference between meta-evaluation and meta-analysis and how you would apply those in your work?" asked one committee member. Each question is supposed to be answered in a precise manner and within a short space of time. My dissertation adviser asked something next, and I noticed that he is asking some of the hardest questions. I feel intensity building in my body as I am asked one question and then another. I squeeze my rock to get some grounding, concentrating on my breathing as I try to look smart. Yet I feel my legs could buckle at any time.

Soothed by a strong sense of my ancestors holding me forth and the feeling of the small rock in my pocket that I carried since I buried my dreams, I got through my doctoral defense. I was told to leave the room as the committee discussed my performance. Then all there was left to do was to wait for the committee to make a decision. I passed the time in a bathroom worrying about failure rates. I was a nervous wreck. But what else could I do? It was done. I tried to remember what others had told me: Is it good or bad when the committee takes a long time?

Finally, the program coordinator came for me. Examining her for telltale signs, I saw nothing, and so I approached the room holding my breath. The room looked dark and the faces of the doctoral committee members seemed gloomy. *Oh, no, I have failed!* I thought to myself.

Slowly, the committee chair stood up and said, "Please join me in congratulating Dr. Tererai Trent!" Stunned, I barely noticed the tears of joy flowing down my cheeks. I achieved my fourth dream!

It took almost two decades to obtain my doctorate from the day I buried my dreams. One month later, when I walked to the podium to receive my degree, I realized that the two things that brought me to this point were hunger (in this case, for an education) and opportunity. As I was awarded the degree, I felt like a lawyer resting her case. It is achievable!

I arrived at the graduation ceremony armed with a paper containing my list of dreams because I intended to check off my fourth dream during the ceremony. Before I could do this, I discovered that the university president, Dr. John Dunn, had prepared a commencement speech based on my achievements. He agreed to check off my fourth dream during his speech. I was overwhelmed when I received a standing ovation from fellow students, faculty, and strangers. President Dunn's words moved me deeply and made me feel like a giant. As I watched him check off my fourth dream, I thought, "Here I am, a former cattle herder. I came to this country with nothing but a dream. What were the odds that I would one day earn the title of doctor?"

Then it was time to turn to my fifth dream, my sacred dream. My hope was to build a school in my home village to improve the lives of women and children back home. I quickly found myself with limited ideas about how to achieve it.

I desperately wanted to give back to my community, so not knowing where to begin depressed me. Remembering Jo Luck's words, "It is achievable"—"*Tinogona*"—an idea began to percolate. "What if I design a T-shirt with the slogan *Tinogona—It Is Achievable?*" I could sell thousands and with the money, go home to rebuild my elementary school.

As an initial step, I asked a workmate from Heifer to introduce me to her brother, a creative young man who developed my first website. The logo on the splash page was a map of Africa with a wide-branched tree embedded into the map. It was beautiful. With the help of a graphic designer, the logo was transferred onto T-shirts with a mixture of bolded and unbolded letters. The word "is" in *It Is Achievable* looked "swooshy." I loved the whole effect.

Add-on tabs and shopping carts were soon installed on the website, and soon I was ready to make money and start building schools! Little did I know how much more was involved in selling the T-shirts. With limited marketing skills, I only sold about twenty shirts, mostly to my friends. I started to wonder if my fifth dream could be made a reality. I sank into a deep despair.

Then I got a phone call from Harpo Studios, home of Oprah Winfrey's show. I had previously appeared on Oprah's show thanks to Nicholas Kristof and Sheryl WuDunn's book *Half the Sky*, in which my story appeared.

The first time Oprah's people called me, I thought it was a hoax. I almost hung up on the woman on the line claiming to be from Harpo Studios. I thought the caller was a joker or telemarketer. But as the person on the other end continued to talk, I began to believe her. "We are thrilled to tell you that Oprah is sending a team to film your home village and you will get to join them." The voice says this like it's an everyday thing. I'm stunned. Before I could respond, the producer told me to expect another call to make final arrangements for my travels.

It had to be a dream, I thought. I will wake up in the morning and tell my children and friends and we'll all laugh. I knew the name Oprah and had heard of her show, but still I had to Google her. I didn't even know what to look for, I realized, and soon gave up and sat there by my window in disbelief.

Two of my children and my husband, Mark, who I'd met during my graduate studies, arrived home at the same time and found me sitting by the window. "Harpo Studios called," I blurted out. The three of them stood frozen in their tracks. I repeated it again. My last born said, "Wow, you are kidding, right?!" And I could hear one of the kids saying, "Did you tape the call in case you did not understand the conversation?" I'm thinking, Who in the world thinks of taping a call? Mark sat down next to me and said, "Really, this is happening?" All I could do was nod.

A week after the call I received instructions to expect a car to take me to the airport. I arrived in Zimbabwe and met up with a team of producers who had traveled from Chicago to my remote village to tape a program. I was invited to appear on *The Oprah Winfrey Show* to tell my story, on an episode that emphasized perseverance and determination in the fight to educate and empower underprivileged women and girls. I was nervous about appearing on the show, barely sleeping for weeks in advance.

In the end, I enjoyed meeting Oprah and sharing my story. Overnight, I became known as the girl who buried her dreams for an education under a rock where she used to herd cattle. Afterward, I thought of the show as a great experience but nothing more.

This second time I received a call from Harpo Studios, I did not think it was a hoax, but I was surprised. Initially, this second call seemed like a courtesy. The producer and I chatted for a few moments about how things were going. When he invited me to reappear, I declined, as I felt there was nothing more to say since my prior appearance in 2009. I was reluctant because I didn't want my second appearance to simply repeat the first. I didn't want to embarrass myself on television with nothing to say!

As the discussion was coming to an end, the producer asked what I was up to and I told him about my wish to rebuild Matau Primary School. There was silence at the end of the phone, and as though he was clearing his voice, he told me that Oprah's show was coming to an end and she was no longer interested in funding schools as she was moving into a different chapter in her life.

The only new thing I could possibly add to my previous appearance was my new mission: to rebuild my community's school. I could not imagine what we might talk about if I was unable to mention my current project. "Then," I said, "there is no need for me to appear again if I cannot share what's in my heart, rebuilding my now dilapidated school." I could hear the producer's strained voice as he warned never to bring this dream to Oprah because it was the end of her show.

I sat there staring at the phone trying to find a way to end the discussion in a polite manner. Before I could say anything, the producer was insistent and encouraged me to attend the show. Still somewhat reluctant, I nevertheless agreed to reappear. I thought to myself that I am more than my story, and if my story encourages others, especially young women, to achieve their dreams, I can still bring meaning to their lives. At the time, I really had no clear idea how my story inspired other people around the world, or saw why Oprah would want me back on her show.

On a cold morning in February 2011, I arrived at Harpo Studios in Chicago. Not knowing what would happen, I tried to relax, but my mind kept going back and forth about what to say about my goal, if given the opportunity. My response to a producer's enthusiastic greeting was somewhat muted. He again advised me not to bring up my wish to build a school. It saddened me to think that I could not mention what was so close to my heart.

I thought back to my childhood school. The infrastructure was falling apart. The school lacked desks, chairs, books, and skilled teachers. On average, five children shared a math textbook and four shared a seat and desk. Most children completed a seven-year cycle without access to a single textbook. Knowing that Oprah had a school in South Africa, I believed that she understood how such challenges result in poor performance. How could I not bring it up?

I wanted Oprah to know that Zimbabwe's economic crisis has led most children to drop out of school by first grade. She would understand that girls bear the heaviest burden because so many leave school to care for sick parents or marry at a very young age. Oprah's show may be coming to an end, but the situation at my school seemed permanent and she had the reach and the audience I needed to press forward with my mission.

If only I could explain to Oprah and her viewers all of the factors at play. Beyond the crippled economy and a difficult political situation, my country also suffered from a severe "brain drain" of teachers and other professionals who have left Zimbabwe seeking opportunities elsewhere. With little ability to feed their families, the remaining teachers are forced to seek other work to supplement their incomes. How can distracted teachers put forth their best?

Not only did I want to improve the quality of education, I wanted to find ways to increase employment, bolster the local economy, and build a community library. But I was getting too far ahead. I told myself to slow down and stay calm—if I opened my mouth and all of my racing thoughts came pouring out, the Harpo security staff would be forced to throw me off the set!

For the third time, the producer and his team warned me not to bring up the school as they prepped me for the show.

Prior to my invitation, the show ran commercials suggesting names of some people who might be Oprah Winfrey's all-time favorite guest. I had no idea what that meant. I walked onto the stage, and saw Oprah's big smile as she greeted me. As I inched my way toward her, I could not believe what I was hearing. Oprah was announcing that I was her "all-time favorite guest." She threw open her arms and drew me in close, in a sincere woman-to-woman embrace.

It was beyond my imagination to think that after twenty-five years and more than thirty thousand guests, Oprah Winfrey chose me for this honor. I was stunned. Everything around me blurred and I felt as if I was watching someone else's life in a movie. Only Oprah's warm hug and the comforting sound of her voice helped me regain my composure.

Once settled, Oprah asked, "What is your dream now?"

I knew for sure that I did not have permission to speak the words written so heavily on my heart. I paused. I thought, Well, I did not have the permission of my community when I spoke the truth of my dreams to Jo Luck, dreams that were so shocking to them at the time, and I did not have the permission of my husband when I went off to

America to pursue my degree. Yet I did these things and I'd made it this far, and I did so with the conviction that bettering myself would ripple out into a broader healing.

Thus it was that I found myself on national television, telling one of the most powerful women in the world that I wanted to give back to Zimbabwe and to my community. I wanted to build a school so that young girls and adult women can have better lives. I had no external permission to do so, only the strength of my connection to my sacred purpose.

"I feel I need to give back," I told her. "I need to build a school in my village so that the same girls that I see today," I continued, turning my eyes away from Oprah and speaking to the women in the audience, "don't have to go through what I went through."

"When Tererai was here in 2009," Oprah said in response, "we got a glimpse at the horrible conditions of the school." The screens in the studio replayed video footage of the school in my village as she went on. "The buildings are literally falling apart, and most classrooms have no desks, so they do all their reading and writing on the floor. The teachers have no supplies and as a result, there's a dismal fourteen percent pass rate." I nodded my head as she spoke.

"Your story is at the core of everything I believe in," Oprah said. "For that reason I'm going to help you rebuild your school. I'm donating a million and a half dollars."

My mouth opened wide and I instinctively reached for Oprah's hand, completely overcome, my breath caught in my chest. I struggled to get up from my seat, my legs almost giving way beneath me but needing to stand so I could wrap my arms around her. I momentarily turned my back to the audience, my heart racing and my body pulsing, unable to process the power of this miracle gift. My fifth dream! I looked into Oprah's eyes as she looked into mine.

"We are going to build a school," she proclaimed.

Our hands clasped tightly together, I replied, and as I spoke she joined me in my declaration, our voices becoming one, "And it is achievable!"

Once backstage again, I soon realized that this was planned all along. The producer had prepared me for the biggest surprise of my life. The whole Harpo team was in on it from the start. Later I met the producer and he gave me a big hug and congratulated me for the gift I had received. Before I could ask any questions, Oprah came and took my hands for more photos. What a day!

Harpo Studios then arranged for Save the Children, an international humanitarian organization, to manage the whole donation and the construction project. The organization developed a plan that included not only rebuilding Matau Primary School but also repairing the infrastructure of neighboring schools. My school will have a new playground, latrines, and hand-washing stations as well as desks, chairs, and books for every child. Teachers will receive training on how to help young children prepare for school and how to help older children improve their reading skills. More girls will attend class and have greater opportunities to build a better future.

I was numb with joy as I left Chicago and was once again reminded of my mother's words: "Every dream has greater meaning when tied to the betterment of one's community." In my head, I repeated the birth song that my grandmothers sang:

> I, the umbilical cord, I remind you of what is important—the power of your identity, the power of your roots, the power of "we." I call you back home.

The seeds of hope that I had planted almost two decades earlier, my buried dreams, are now bearing fruit for the fifth sacred dream. I never imagined that the universe would help me to achieve more than I had bargained for. I feel the energy of generations of women before me rising up in celebration, chanting, and ululating.

Despite being cautioned three times not to ask, the pull of the umbilical cord and my buried dreams was so strong that I could no longer be silenced by any circumstances. That which is buried energetically connected me from the roots to outward action. I knew the ancient power of what I'd buried in the earth was calling and all I needed to do was to use my voice in the platform I had been given to right the wrongs done to generations of my fellow women and girls. I needed to fulfill my sacred dream. How could I allow myself to be held back by something as inconsequential as waiting for permission when my sacred purpose was calling? Who was I to remain silent in such a powerful arena?

One Brick at a Time

Trust that laying the foundation of your inner authority in the service of your sacred dream is part of a worldwide movement toward building a better world. Fall in love with those moments flickering everywhere, when someone chooses permission over perfectionism, or when someone chooses to pursue her connectedness rather than to linger alone in insecurity.

Know that you are part of a greater whole. Be a part of this revolution by showing up for yourself; know that when you do so, you show up for others, too, and that your actions can and will heal this broken world. Let me show you one way that I've experienced this ripple effect.

Hardly three months after Oprah's initial donation was received, work began on the new Matau Primary School. Students, teachers, families, and local government authorities such as the district administrator gathered at the construction site on the morning of July 1, 2011. Completing a powerful circle from decades before when I buried my dream of this school in the earth, a Matau Primary School student broke ground with a pick commemorating the beginning of the new school.

The local chief and his seventeen headmen mobilized community members to support the efforts of Save the Children. Not long after work had begun, the same headman who had rallied the community to contribute to my airfare so that I could attend school in America again asserted his leadership. Encouraging everyone to support the school project, he organized groups of people to create bricks for the buildings. With no electric power, the community molded almost half a million bricks by hand in less than six months. Using their bare hands and without mechanized support, more than 200,000 bricks failed to meet the construction standards, and yet, the older women never lost hope until the community assembled 450,000 bricks to build a brand-new school, which today accommodates more than 1,200 children.

An elected school development committee organized more than four hundred community volunteers to transport sand, water, and building materials. This is a sight to behold! Every day, groups of women and men gather in different locales to create bricks that are then fired in a kiln at high temperatures. Producing handmade bricks is tedious, backbreaking work. The fact that so many are willing to help is an indication of how much the community wants this school. They understand that they have been given a rare opportunity.

Women were the first to commit to the project. They desperately wanted their children, and especially their daughters, to "be like Tererai"—that is, to break out of the vicious cycle of poverty. The people of my village worked on a common cause in new ways and it brought them even closer together. Rich in spirit, community members proudly "own" the process of building the school from the start, which is a sure marker of success. They set a good example for other communities as they contributed time, labor, skills, and knowledge to the creation of one of the best community-driven rural schools Africa will ever see.

When I returned to America, village women stayed in touch. One morning in December 2012, I received three text messages from some of the grandmothers:

> **Gogo Sande:** A brand-new school is now standing. It seems like a dream!

Gogo Kawocha: Tererai, my daughter could not read or write. She died leaving orphans under my care. Now, those children can read at home and even I am learning to read. That this could happen was unheard of until the Matau Project. It's a miracle!

Gogo Kambuzuma: I saw the new desks and chairs arriving. Now, our children have hope for a better future!

Pleasure mingles with tears as I pictured these grandmothers paying young men with mobile phones to send me these text messages. I cannot stop smiling as I picture Gogo Kawocha participating in her grandchildren's education. It is humbling to know that these women, who have had little to no schooling, are as excited as children preparing for their first day of school.

From 2012 to 2014, more than five thousand preschoolers and school-age children from Matau and neighboring villages participated in early learning and community-wide literacy programs. A comparative study shows that students from our schools are more fluent in English and Shona than children in similar schools. In addition, Matau has instituted a very successful "reading buddy program" in which students join with peers, parents, or grandparents to practice reading. Below is a text I received from another grandmother. Simply signed Gogo, the woman assumes that I will recognize her but I do not.

> I never would have thought it possible to become my granddaughter's reading buddy. While I cannot read or write, my grandchildren give me the eyes I need and a feel for words that I never knew I had.

In May 2013, I returned to the village to see the progress for myself. Walking around campus, I stopped at the new water well and pump. To build it, workers had to drill nearly 140 feet into the ground while volunteers dug trenches for pipes that would connect the water hole to a 5,000-liter-capacity storage tank and pump. The sparkling clean water, now available to all neighboring communities, has for the first time significantly reduced the likelihood of a cholera or typhoid epidemic.

Rounding a corner, I pass colorful paintings of wild animals. Several four- and five-year-old girls are reading new books while others play on swings. Laughter fills the air and the children's smiles are contagious. Besides having fun, I believe that laughter and joy open them up to new learning. The prekindergarten headmistress looks on in wonderment. These little girls are in school, not at home attending to chores and taking care of their siblings. What a different experience they are having compared to my own as a young girl!

Carrying the children's laughter with me, I head toward the newly constructed library, the only library in this area of rural Zimbabwe. As I visualize children concentrating on their books, Gogo Kawocha approaches me. She says, "It is beautiful to be surrounded by these new buildings and to know that our grandchildren are learning." Then she asks, "Tererai, are you coming to our reading camp this weekend?" Here is an old woman who cannot read or write but who knows what is happening in the reading camps. Thirty-six reading camps are shared among six schools in the region, where children read under the guidance of trained mentors. These camps have played a big part in improving literacy in the area.

Despite the fact that Zimbabwe has a high literacy rate in comparison to other African nations, I can easily name all of the adults in my community who can read or count to a hundred. Life for their children and grandchildren will be different, indeed. I think of each one of those handcrafted bricks. This was my dream, yes, but it was built and is enjoyed by an entire community. Now it is a shared dream.

Your dreams are shared dreams, too, my sisters. Your dreams of healing your life, of soothing your heart's aching, will ripple outward to improve the lives of many people and this earth we call home.

When I say that the world is urgently in need of your awakening, I want you to know how very much your inner longings can do when you tie them to a sacred, social purpose. Your sacred dreams are achievable! This world, so full of hurt, broken in so many ways, needs you now.

Sacred Brothers for Sacred Sisters

In my travels around the world, I have seen so many men who go out of their way to celebrate women and promote women's causes, men who are sensitive to the needs of their daughters, sisters, wives, and community members. These men have a massive potential to support and encourage women's global rising. And in many cases, men also need the support and guidance of the teachings that I offer in this book. Gender equality liberates all people from gender stereotypes. We don't change the world for the better without throwing out a net of love and empathy for all living beings.

Unfortunately, social valuing of masculinity over femininity is overwhelming much of the world, breeding a dehumanizing culture in which women's dignity is diminished—and this isn't good for anyone involved: it devalues anything associated with femininity, including the feminine in men. It is not about men versus women, but the ideas and practices that celebrate masculinity over femininity. The world can be a better place if we eradicate this unequal value system and bring more love, more light, and more life into all the places where we experience silencing or invisibility.

After all, it was two men who helped me achieve my dreams: Zuda's uncle, who gave me the key to getting Zuda's permission to go to America, and the headman who rallied my community to help fund my plane ticket. And men mobilized the community in building the school of my dreams so that young girls could be educated. You see, the work we do as sacred dreamers can transform patriarchal communities and ideas. The passion of our dreams and the possibilities they evoke can ripple out into every heart.

We can all learn from one organization in southern Africa working for gender equality: Padare/Enkundleni (Men's Forum on Gender). Based in Zimbabwe, this organization focuses on eliminating violence against women and on HIV and AIDS prevention. This male-led organization has not only used its platform to confront and challenge gender stereotypes that negatively affect women, but also to influence national policy and programs.

How do they do it? Padare/Enkundleni established sixty men's networks across Zimbabwe with an average of fifty men in each group. The organization sits on the Domestic Violence Council, a national body that was established with a mandate to promote the protection and relief of victims of domestic violence through research, information dissemination, and the coordination and monitoring of the implementation of the Domestic Violence Act. It also sits on the Gender-Based Violence Committee supported by UN Women. This is a beautiful, productive framework of both inside-out empowerment and outside-in social organizing; they work with the people on the ground while at the same time reaching out beyond the local all the way to the UN. And it is organized, initiated, and practiced by men for women.

I am also deeply moved by the individual men I've met who are fighting for women. The AIDS pandemic sweeping across the global south most severely impacts those who are economically vulnerable. As a result, older women, widowed grandmothers, and single older women often find themselves joining one of the oldest and most demeaning professions, prostitution, to survive. Robson Zimuto uses his platform to fight for social and economic justice among these women.

As former director of Heifer International in Zimbabwe, Robson had the courage to follow his convictions—what he felt was right—despite intense criticism from friends and allies. With the goal of reducing the spread of HIV, Robson seeks not only to alter deeply rooted ideas about sexuality and gender, but also to challenge gender stereotypes, roles, and practices that prevent men from working with women to end gender discrimination. The only way to resist the gender inequality that exists among commercial sex workers, Robson felt, was to involve men in a meaningful and practical way.

Many thought this director was crazy to pursue prostitutes. After all, those who practiced this trade were shunned by our society. Some people felt strongly that women practicing transactional sex deserved HIV infections as punishment for their behavior. Robson did not agree and defied every warning and criticism even from people close to him. That recruiting prostitutes was not seen as noble or worthwhile did not bother him.

He started by sensitizing his male staff to understand masculinity and privileges that lead to gender inequalities, subsequently denying women access to education and better employment. He understood the role of gender inequality and how it drives women to engage in transactional sex to secure income for food and other family expenses. He also understood that teamwork, a good strategy, and perseverance were needed to convince women to leave behind the one "job" they knew, hard as it was, that provided for their families. Together with his team he set out to coax women commercial sex workers away from the streets.

He searched for them on the streets, in beer halls, and on truck driver routes. Then, he'd bring them to a center offering training in developing business plans and marketing strategies. A group of former prostitutes grew and eventually formed a cooperative that today operates a microfinance project. This venture allows them to make a living by selling vegetables they have grown and livestock they have raised. Soon, more men joined Robson in what he now calls the "Fight for gender equality and dignity."

In 2006, I was sent by Heifer International to evaluate this program's effectiveness. When I asked a group of women to identify changes they'd experienced from their past lives to the present, all agreed that they were not making enough money. As evaluators, especially when dealing with prostitution, we hope that our programs provide enough incentives for participants to move away from life on the streets. So while I was contemplating my answer to their dilemma, one of the older former sex workers looked me in the eyes and said, "My child, when I go home, I look at myself in the mirror and see dignity. Before, I was embarrassed to look into the eyes of my own children after sex activities. I felt dirty and unworthy to be a mother and a grandparent. It's not about how much money we make now; life is about how much dignity we leave behind as a legacy of wealth to our children."

Today, many now see Robson as a true catalyst for change; someone who defied the naysayers and refused to be defined by societal norms. When I asked Robson what made him move away from the path of least resistance, he said, "Gender equality is a social justice issue, and my conscience would not allow me to sleep without at least giving it a try. The war on such inequality could only be won . . ." he continued, "when men join to support women and also become the conscience . . . of gender equality. It's important to realize that men also need the support in understanding their privilege in this society and be sensitized to becoming a collective voice with women to fight gender inequality."

I am inspired by the powerful examples of men and women working together to address gender inequality in other parts of the world as well. When Canada's prime minister, Justin Trudeau, announced he had appointed women to half of his government's cabinet positions, many people asked him why. "Because it's 2015," he replied. And I danced in my living room at the simple, powerful truth of this historical moment.

My mother would often repeat this bit of African wisdom: "If you want to go fast, go alone, but if you want to go far, go with others." My mother knew that no matter the issue, we need collaboration and strong partnerships to fulfill our *ubuntu*—the essence of our humanity. We sacred sisters cannot do it alone. We must also look for those sacred brothers, those men who wear a woman's heart, and rise together.

Being Reborn

I returned to the United States just four days after my mother's burial. Before leaving the homestead on January 9, 2013, I woke up early to visit her grave. There, I promised my mother that I would do all that is within my power to live by her example. I will educate my nephews, Solomon and Tawanda, and make sure they develop into good men, I told her. I will educate my own children, and I will never abandon the community that she so loved.

I was going to be guided by the sacred dream, the fifth dream, the one she helped me find myself. I shared with her my concerns about how to support all that we have undertaken until the community school, canteen, and artisan center become self-sustaining. I felt the burden of leaving my mother's burial grounds, and I knew the journey to healing from grief was going to be difficult. I did not know how to live without my mother, the woman who had given me so much in life, my steadfast compass, always guiding me toward something greater than I was at the time.

As I was about to leave my childhood home, my mother's *sahwira* advised me to shave my head bald. I laughed and reminded her I will scare people in America.

The drive from home to Harare International airport was terrible. Each tear I dropped carried the pain of my unimaginable reality: my mother is dead. Saying good-bye to my mother was utter pain. I imagined my mother being attacked by maggots as her body rots, and I could not bear the thought. I forgot about the Spirit World and the safe journey her spirit took to join her people. Depression seeped into the core of my being.

I caught a two p.m. flight from Harare International Airport to Johannesburg on my way to America. Dozing, I dreamed of my mother hovering over me like an angel. She asked me to move over so that she can sit with me. I even smelled her. When I tried to wake up, she placed a hand on my mouth to silence me. My mother told me that she is fine and that I should let her depart from this world. Then she disappeared. I woke up feeling her presence but she was nowhere to be found. Was my mind playing tricks on me? I was shaken by this experience and wondered if the depression was affecting my psyche. I cried myself to sleep, feeling unbearable sadness.

I am not sure how long I sleep but I am jolted awake by turbulence. The plane is shaking so that it feels as though we are passing through a mountain. I cannot even hear what the pilot is saying. I see fear on the faces of fellow passengers as stewardesses scramble to their seats. My neighbor tells me that the plane is lost in the jungles of Africa and that we must make an emergency landing. While there is panic all around me, I am too depressed to follow what is happening.

When the pilot's voice returns through the intercom, he announces a problem with the engine. Passengers around me seem very upset as an unsettling noise becomes louder. The plane is to land on an island in an hour. Now, fear sets in and I wonder if my mother has been trying to warn me of what is to come.

In a complete daze, as if in a dream, we land in the middle of the night on a volcanic island in the equatorial waters of the South Atlantic Ocean. Ascension Island is 994 miles west of Angola near Saint Helena, almost 1,400 miles from the coast of South America. Closed to commercial planes, it has housed a British Army base since the Falkland War of the early 1980s. They remain a presence on the island, as do the US Air Force, the European Space Agency, and the BBC World Service.

Eventually, passengers are bused to a British Army base to await the new plane from Delta Airlines. We are assigned to various barracks until further notice. I settle into my bunk bed, appreciating the clean white sheets. Without a watch or a working cell phone, I have no way to tell time. I sleep very soundly despite all that is happening, as it has been a long time since I've slept on a bed with a pillow. I feel my mother's presence. She is smiling as she tells me not to worry.

I wake up to the music of all kinds of birds on a beautiful, crisp morning. The hot shower is a luxury. As I scrub my body with soap and water, I feel like a brand-new person. Breakfast is served in a nearby mess hall. I learn that our Delta airplane had lost all power in one of its two engines.

While many passengers scurry around trying to find answers to questions that no one can answer, I take a walk. The trees and grass sway in the wind with such grace. I love the landscape, which reminds me of where I once grazed cattle. This is the first time since my mother's death that I truly enjoy the beauty around me.

During lunch, we are told that a replacement plane will arrive in the evening. I also hear that this morning a British plane landed too close to our plane and accidentally clipped its wing on our broken plane, which is the cause of further delays. Finally, we are off. Upon arriving in Atlanta, Delta Airlines gives each passenger a gift card and a free round-trip ticket to Africa, the Middle East, or India to use within a year. I am so happy because now I can go to visit my mother's grave.

Upon returning to my home in the States, I am haunted by the horrifying image of my mother lying in pain in the hospital. Sleep evades me, and the thoughts of my mother failing to get the medical help she needed, and how that neglect led to her death, start to bother me.

One day I get a call from my mother's relatives, who are concerned about me. I tell them that I am having trouble shaking off my deep sadness. I can't help but feel that I should have done more, and my guilt is eating me alive. My sister says that she feels the same. I then remember a suggestion made by my mother's *sahwira* before I left, that I should shave my head.

I decide to take her advice and cut off all my hair. The long locks that I had nurtured with so much care are gone. I find that being bald and defying convention sets me free, as if I am reborn. In mourning we are reminded of our mortality and what matters most in this life. As a ritual to honor my mother's death, my baldness is a symbolic offering to Nyadenga, the Creator of heaven and human life, and shows my grief for the departed soul. During mourning, hair on my head is an unnecessary vanity, without it I am free to mourn my mother without distraction from my bodily image. In this moment of recognizing human mortality, I am not to be defined by any physical appearance, nor by my ego. The cleanliness I feel paves the way to think only about my mother and to celebrate her life.

With a shaven head that honors my mother, I am invited to speak at the United Nations Global Compact Leaders' Summit, "Architects of a Better World," on September 20, 2013. This is the first time I have spoken in front of global business leaders and heads of state. I feel my mother, my grandmother, and my great-grandmother occupying the room with me; I see their smiles of encouragement and hear their ululations as I tell the listeners in the room about how individual actions count, and urge them to invest in education and create opportunities for the poor by contributing to global priorities and the public good.

How proud my mother would be to know how far her wisdom, along with the wisdom of our ancestors, is now reaching around the globe. The tables are indeed turning. Modern society is embracing indigenous African knowledge, and women are gaining value as equals to men in many parts of the world. I savor the prospect of a future filled with opportunity and abundant possibilities.

In this moment, I celebrate my mother as I recall the day that she handed me a rusty tin can in which to bury my dreams. It's ironic to think the very can that once held nourishment for soldiers who fought to restrict our dignity and civil rights became my vessel to nurture my sacred dreams. My mother's words will forever echo in my mind: "See yourself as the creator of your own destiny—knowing that you have the power to shape your future and that of generations to come."

I began this book with mothers—with my grandmother the storyteller, midwife, and seed keeper—and I end it with mothers, the living legacy of my own mother as she works through me. Why is the image of the mother so important to me and so important to awakening our sacred dreams? Why come full circle?

Remember I said I hoped to be a midwife to this awakening—not to orchestrate it or dictate it, but to support and lift up many women all over the world as they give birth to their sacred purpose, which, as many experts have shown and many wise souls have advised, is a key ingredient to healing the world as we know it. As the old and recently resurfaced women's rights slogan goes: the "Future Is Female."

The metaphor of the midwife who serves the birthing mother is so powerful for me because it beautifully illustrates my own sacred dream. The root word of "education," the heart and soul of all my work, is *educare*, "drawing out." The etymology of this word is often traced back to Plato's image of the teacher as a midwife.[1] Similarly, Socrates preferred to call himself a "midwife of the mind" rather than a "teacher," and he even explained to his student Theaetetus that there will be "pangs of labor" when there is "something within you which you are bringing to the birth."[2]

And so, when I talk about mothers, of course I mean to make us feel a deep connection to our own mothers, the earth's mothers, and the lineage of mothers that connects us to the ancient world, but I do not limit this word to those who have been given the title "mother" by way of child rearing. I am talking about the creative, spiritual, and cosmic birthing potential that we all possess. I am talking about being born.

I come full circle back to mothers because I know that being born, over and over again as you name and imagine and trust your Great Hunger, is important. And you will need to be a mother to yourself in this rebirth, the rising of the feminine worldwide. I also come full circle back to mothers because the awakening of your sacred dreams was never a linear path: there is no one way to start and no one way to finish, and in many ways, the end is also a beginning.

My mother gave me many beginnings: my life, of course, as well as burying my dreams, adding the fifth sacred dream, and many more—and so can her life really be said to have an end, since her vision still lives in me and in the projects we worked on together?

In this same way, you are born and born again to your purpose many times. This may be the most important thing I hope to share with you: in a world that tells women that we have an expiration date—whether it's a certain age, a number of children, a certain position in the company, an economic status, whatever—my message to you, as your loving midwife and seed keeper, from the ancients and the poets and my mother working through me, is this: you can infinitely be reborn. The payday of love is so old, so powerful, that if you choose it, you can be the creator of your own destiny.

Always remember: you are the dreamer, the beacon, and the generous light that enables others to shine.

YOUR SACRED DREAMS JOURNEY: TEN ESSENTIALS

These ten essentials are core elements of the lessons I have learned over time. They are not a declaration of dogma, but rather a vehicle I offer for sharing insights about what helps individuals move forward. Although I did not recognize these key components and the basic questions that help elucidate them until after I had experienced them, I now appreciate the key role they have played in my life. As I reflect on others who have achieved the seemingly impossible, I identify the impact of these same factors.

There are many layers in which you can engage in these core essentials; these lessons can be revisited over and over again. You will probably find that, although for the purpose of this book they have been presented sequentially, as you deepen your journey with them, you will dip in and out of various lessons at different times. There need not be a definite beginning or end—a journey to awaken—and awaken again. Events and occurrences in your external world may trigger a deepening of certain lessons, so that you weave in and out of them with transformed perceptions or new viewpoints as you grow and evolve.

At any stage in your sacred dreams journey, it may be helpful to pick one or more of these essentials and explore the ideas and questions that follow by journaling or reflecting on them to remind yourself of your purpose, abilities, and how to overcome obstacles.

Read your insights aloud, ask questions, and then explore what moves in you. You may want to freewrite or meditate on them, or you may want to use these as touchstones for conversations with your *sahwira*.

1. Identify Your Great Hunger

Remember that your Great Hunger is something you want to attain more than anything, and it is essential to not only keep you going but also to keep you moving in the right direction. Your Great Hunger is fueled by your soul, by your passion, and by your unique gifts and talents. It holds great promise and benefits to you and to others—your family, community, and society. As my mother said, "Your dreams will have greater meaning when tied to the betterment of your community."

2. Recognize Your Unique Talents

The hidden power within you is waiting to emerge to help create your future. When you believe in what you have to offer and decide what matters most, then you will discover your true purpose. There are times when your talents or gifts come naturally, and you can apply them with ease to the situation. Other circumstances are more challenging and encourage you to further develop your skills. Reflect on your natural-born talents and any skills you might want to strengthen in order to achieve your sacred dreams.

3. Understand Your Fears

Or to put it another way: What gets in the way of fulfilling your dreams? Identifying and confronting your fears is the first step in relinquishing their power over you. Speak them out loud, write them down, move and dance to them. Following your Great Hunger and having faith in your unique talents will give you courage to protect your sacred dreams. Always remember that the more difficult the circumstances, the dearer the dream and the bigger the price to be paid for its fulfillment. Tenacity is what sustains you in the fight.

4. Visualize Your Future

According to *Merriam-Webster*, "visualization" is defined as "the formation of mental visual images," or it's "the act or process of interpreting in visual terms or of putting into visible form." Derived from the Latin word "videre," vision means "to see." When applied to your dream, a vision is a mental image of the future that you want to create. I know firsthand the power of redefining "what is" into "what can be." The power of creation begins with imagining or reimagining your future. You have the power to create something bigger than yourself, and, once recognized, the universe will conspire to help make it happen. This vision will be something you can always return to and reflect on for inspiration and motivation.

5. Write Down Your Dreams

This is a simple yet powerful essential that asks you to write what is closest to your heart, allowing you to develop the blueprint of the life you wish to lead. Writing is a magical tool that can make what we hope for seem more real and attainable. Writing is a vehicle for finding your voice, confronting both your past and present while healing yourself. When you write, you connect with something deep inside. Always remember: What's written with intent becomes ingrained in your thoughts. An ingrained thought becomes a deep-rooted belief. Strongly held beliefs can help you to achieve your dreams.

6. Ground Your Faith and Belief

Positive and encouraging words, phrases, or affirmations can be an amazing tool to remind and support your sacred dream journey. Fear can get in the way of your dreams. Fear and lack of confidence can cause you to make excuses for not doing something or for not believing in your greatness. Every day, when I feel an excuse entering my thoughts, I name it and say the positive affirmation that correlates to that excuse. The more you practice listening to your sacred dreams, the more you will recognize its call. Write down the words of your affirmations. Infuse them with passion! With enough repetition and emotion, you *will* come to believe them. Follow your Great Hunger.

7. Cultivate Gratitude

Gratitude is the state of feeling thankful and appreciative. It's not just that we like something that someone said or did; it's deeper than that. Practicing gratitude fires our optimism and encourages us to celebrate the gift of life. It has even been scientifically shown to improve self-esteem, physical and mental health, and the ability to empathize. There is no stronger foundation upon which to build dreams! I encourage you to practice gratitude regularly until it becomes second nature. Practice gratitude for the motivation of your Great Hunger and you will feel that pull of your inner guidance even more. Practice gratitude for all that you *do* have, and your fears about what you *do not* have will fade.

8. Establish Your *Sahwiras*

The power to lift ourselves up by lifting each other up is at the heart of the *sahwira*. To succeed in achieving your dreams, you need to surround yourself or belong to a coalition of sacred sisters who believe in what drives each other's soul without judging. It brings connection to the sister heart in all girls and women; it's a mutually supportive relationship—play, cry, laugh, and always find meaning in the little things you do together. The *sahwira* relationship creates a deep connection as it widens its web of female energy, which sustains your work, family, and how you show up in the world!

9. Commit to Action

Think about what you are willing to do to achieve the specific dreams you have written down. It took me almost eight years from the day I buried my dreams to earn the equivalent of an American GED, but my efforts paid off when I got accepted to Oklahoma State University. Remember: A dream doesn't become reality until you are willing to put in the hard work. Determination, commitment, and self-discipline are supreme to make your dreams come true. And when your dream is tied to something greater than yourself, then sweat becomes the equity for your hard work.

10. Honor the Sacred Laws of the Invisible Ladder

Opening your heart to receive and give is a two-way street. There is a sacred law of reciprocity at work here. In my case, I now realize that as others allowed me to stand on their shoulders in order to achieve my dreams, a sacred expectation had to be fulfilled. It is now my responsibility to allow others to stand on my shoulders as they seek to achieve their dreams. This is how we pass on and reciprocate the gift of humanity—an "invisible ladder"—that creates a meaningful life. Our collective empathy and responsibility toward one another is what awakens our humanity, and therefore each of us is fertile ground that nurtures, inspires, and enables opportunity and growth.

CREATING DREAM CIRCLES OF SACRED *SAHWIRA* SISTERHOOD

In my collectivist culture, the concept of nuclear family does not exist. "Family" includes nephews, cousins, uncles, aunts, grandparents, and totem-related clan members in addition to biological siblings. The circle or semicircle is a powerful symbol of this collective—at meals around the fire, as we listen to stories, during *chinyamusasure* dances, at funeral rituals, or at *dare*, village meetings for solutions to pressing family and community issues—we form circles.

The practice of gathering and moving in circles embodies our unity. In a circle, all members are equal. There is no hierarchy of front or back, higher or lower seats. We believe that the circle has healing power, that within the circle we can solve problems and create peace.

In this spirit, I offer you guidance and inspiration to encourage you to stay on the path toward your sacred dreams by creating your own circles of *sahwira* sisterhood. Beloved sisters, whatever we're experiencing in our lives, one of the best sources of pure joy is to be in tune with our feminine energy. Harnessing our collective feminine energy through the creation of Dream Circles of Sacred *Sahwira* Sisterhood connects us deeply and our pain becomes shared, our fight becomes a symbol of our commitment to our earthly calling.

When we respond to our earthly calling with unity, we all begin to rise with dignity from being wounded souls to joyful and compassionate individuals. Let us become one thread in a web connecting this globe and engaging in a responsible and effective manner for the benefit of the greater good.

These empathic Dream Circles of Sacred *Sahwira* Sisterhood should be based on authentic, healthy, and sacred relationships—starting with how we feel toward ourselves. This is how we band together. This circle allows you to have authentic bonds with other women that are based on trust and respect for each other's values. Otherwise, our narratives and dreams remain disjointed—heartbeats sounding together are unstoppable! Talk can be cheap, let us be real with the way we band and support one another!

Every day I work with global leaders, circles of women, social entrepreneurs, wisdom leaders, and change makers who are dedicated to realigning their goals with a purpose that is harmonious to the needs of others. All the change makers that I connect with are unanimous in one belief: that our dreams give us the most joy when they are aligned to something greater than our individual selves. We help each other dream and develop new possibilities while impacting the lives of others at the same time.

There are many creative ideas around which to form a Sacred *Sahwira* Circle. I offer three possibilities to inspire your own thinking: the Dream Circle, the Healing Circle, and the Reading Circle. I hope the guidance here can help you bring women together to help each other achieve your dreams and, maybe, the circle will grow into a movement.

For each of the suggestions below, it is important to identify and come up with your own rituals that are indigenous to the group. These will help bind the group together. You might want to start your meeting with a ritual done while everyone sits in a circle. Ultimately, Sacred *Sahwira* Circles create an intimate environment that allows trust and honest discussions that enable all *sahwiras* to get to the root of who they are and the expression of the truth they want to see in themselves and the world they live in.

Also always keep in mind that Sacred *Sahwira* Circles allow us to tend to others without sacrificing ourselves for the needs of others or get lost in our own personal endeavors. It's the beauty of our sacredness as women that enables us to balance the two, letting the needs of others motivate and inspire us and be the fuel for our dreams. The success of the group will be its ability to balance the collective good with personal growth.

Sacred Dream Circle

This circle is the intentional coming together of sisters to help each other achieve specific shared sacred dreams. Your sacred circle might reflect on its purpose, and spend time aligning this purpose to something greater.

Invite sisters to brainstorm issues that are important to the group. From that list, identify common issues that are of interest to everyone in the group and act on them.

As you connect with your *sahwiras* in this way, not only will the group's shared dreams be a priority, but an individual's personal dreams will also be strengthened. The beauty of the Sacred *Sahwira* Circle is that it allows women to operate from a true sense of community, and at the same time, we do not ignore our own needs.

Sacred Reading Circle

One of the best ways to feed our Great Hunger is through reading and discussion. There is so much inspiration in the poetry, prose, and prayers to be found in literature. This circle is a group of sisters coming together to read, discuss, and share some lessons from books that inspire them.

Use this circle as an opportunity to learn more about your sacred dream by reading about another culture, a social concern, or activist strategies. Sisters of the circle will also learn about each other's dreams in this way. Make connections between your dreams and that of your *sahwira* as you read, and in your discussions brainstorm plans to move your dreams forward. Be mindful that this is not simply a "book club"—it's a reading circle with the explicit intention of supporting the awakenings of your sisters and exploring the contours of your dreams. You are not just a reader but a sacred dreamer.

Sacred Healing Circle

This is a circle of sisters coming together with the express purpose of healing. Form a group of sisters who are struggling to navigate their lives after or during some trauma or hardship.

Spiritually, the Sacred Healing Circle enables those who are hurting to share with others in the same situation and identify ways to heal. The power of sharing your pain and hurts with sisters not only nurtures our souls, it also heals the body.

A circle of sisters can provide that loving environment for healing, which may be the most powerful medicine. In order to achieve our dream, first we need to look within and identify the pain and hurts that need to happen before healing can take place. We cannot expect to change what's in the world unless we first change the conditionings and its pain that have been deeply ingrained within us. This healing allows the Sacred Healing Circle to help those who are hurting to let go of pain and to live a more authentic and fulfilled life.

Organizers of the group will facilitate leading women through purging past hurts and fear through ritual.

- Establish clear guidelines of the rituals, such as "What happens in this healing circle remains here and it's a taboo for anyone to repeat it." Or perhaps rules for how each participant can listen to the speaker unconditionally, without judgment or the need to solve.

- Enough small pouches or envelopes, papers, and writing utensils for everyone in the group

- Enough tissues to pass around in case they are needed

- A space where all women can sit in a circle, particularly someplace where you can light some sort of fire, a candle in a fireproof bowl/urn or a fireplace

- A call-and-response chant or prayer

The Ritual:

- After sisters are seated around the circle, lead twenty minutes or so of chanting or prayers that everyone follows.

- Begin the discussion by sharing the purpose of the ritual and why it's important to purge the pain and hurt that each feels. This is a very emotional process, so it's important to create a space of trust, honesty, and understanding. We are sacred sisters seeking healing!

- If possible, share your own pain and how you have managed to rise from a wounded soul to a healed one. If that's not the case, then talk about it and the healing needed.

- Pass out the pouches/envelopes, pads, and pencils to the members. I love using little pouches made out of reeds or a piece of colorful cloth.

- While remaining in the circle, have the women take turns talking about what's hurting them and why it affects their dreams.

- Give each person enough time to share their feelings.

- When all have shared their pain and whatever hurt there is, ask the women to take a twenty- to thirty-minute break, and let each find their own space to write down and prioritize the most painful things. They should bring the list either in their pouch or envelope.

- Have everyone take their position in the circle.

- Light the fire.

- Repeat some of the words of the chant or prayer as a group while each woman places her pouch or envelope with her list of hurts and pain in front of them.

- While still remaining in the circle, each woman takes a turn sharing why the final list (prioritized hurts) needs to be purged and in what ways these have impacted the achievement of their dreams. As each woman discusses why the list needs to be purged, they throw the pouch in the fire (please burn carefully in a safe way).

- When all the women are finished, there is need to celebrate. And some may celebrate by having someone massage their body, or holding hands or embracing. This is because this process can be draining and leave your body depleted.

Whatever kind of Sacred *Sahwira* Circle you create, you are fulfilling your sacred responsibility to yourself and to your sisters when you do so. When something is sacred, it comes with certain responsibilities. Many of you probably read the word "responsibilities" and feel it's a heavy weight to bear, but that's not the kind of responsibility I'm talking about here.

We cannot ignore the Great Hunger inside of us, a unique hunger fueled by a gift with which we are all born, which might be a talent, an aptitude, a perspective, a deep burning desire, or some other powerful aspect unique to you. It is indestructible and permanent, even if you have not yet used it (whether by your own choice or because of external circumstances). We have a sacred responsibility to feed our Great Hunger.

Our sacred responsibility also extends beyond the self. When one sister is affected elsewhere, we feel her pain. We are all in this together, intimately and inextricably interconnected and interdependent. Fulfilling a sacred responsibility always carries meaning along with it, even joy in the midst of whatever hard work might be required. Sacred responsibilities lead us to follow dreams with a greater purpose, dreams that not only move and excite us but also positively impact others.

Recently when I was in Zimbabwe I met Susan, an entrepreneur in the clothing industry. Susan grew up in the 1960s under British rule. She never received much education, and the little she did get was limited to home domestic schooling, as was the case for many girls of her time. She learned a great deal about sewing and cooking but was not exposed to math or science.

Susan wanted to further her education, and to do so she needed money to pay her school fees. She decided to perfect her sewing skills and sell clothes, eventually moving into the urban area where her clothing designs became quite popular. Soon she was able to purchase a sewing machine and even hire other women to help her. She was becoming a successful small business owner in her own right.

I asked Susan what gives her joy and what silences her. I expected to hear about local issues such as social and economic challenges, but Susan said, "Western aid silences me more than anything I can think of right now." I was baffled. I asked her to explain. Instead, Susan asked me to go with her downtown so she could show me.

It was a beautiful sunny day when Susan and I went downtown. We sat watching as people walked by doing their normal business. She asked me to observe what people were wearing and the brand of clothes.

I saw young men wearing T-shirts with all kinds of slogans related to brands from the United States, such as baseball and basketball teams, and food shops. Susan must have seen a lightbulb go on in me, because just as I was about to speak, she raised her hand to stop me and then pointed to three old women walking toward us. One woman in her seventies was frail and walked with a limp and a cane. She wore a T-shirt with the word "f*cked" written across the chest. The second woman, maybe the daughter in her early or mid-fifties, wore a woolly pajama top like a blouse. It had a kitten design. The afternoon sun was getting quite warm, heating the already humid air, but the woolly sleeping attire didn't seem to bother her. The third woman, a bit younger than the first two, was wearing an evening gown that looked more like a shiny Halloween costume. They were quite a sight.

As they approached, I greeted them and asked about their day. As our conversation progressed, I couldn't help myself. "Where did you get your clothing?" I asked them. In one voice, they said, "Magaba KuMbare"—"The local market." I asked what attracted them to these dresses and they said the low prices and the colors.

I then asked the oldest woman why she picked her T-shirt and what she liked about what was written. She looked at me blankly. The other women looked at the old woman's T-shirt and then back at me. I realized they could not read it. I glanced at Susan, who had been quietly observing our conversation. She smiled at me, her eyes pregnant with meaning.

The middle-aged woman brought her hand to her mouth and then, letting it rest on her chin, she said, "*Oho, ndosaka*"—"Oh, no wonder why!" The three women exchanged a knowing look and nodded their heads in agreement. I asked what she meant, and in turns they explained that they had met some men who ridiculed them and they had no idea why the men were so rude.

The old woman turned to me and said, "*Mwanagu, zvinorevei?*"—"My daughter, please tell me what these words mean?" In my language there is no word for "f*ck." I was at a loss. Susan spoke for the first time, blurting out, "It's an insult, and you should not be wearing such a T-shirt at your age." Without another word, the daughter looked into her bag and found a piece of cloth, a Zambia, and placed it on her mother's chest to hide the words.

On our way back to Susan's place, she told me she was not only angry about losing business but about how Western aid takes advantage of the country's collapsed economy by sending these culturally inappropriate clothes. "And it's all in the name of 'aid.'"

Susan told me how American charity organizations ship bales of secondhand clothes to poor nations without regard to how those hand-me-downs affect the clothing industry, especially small-scale enterprises, which are normally owned by women like her. Poor women, who struggle their whole lives through a colonial system, overcome hardship to become self-supporting business owners only to have the current aid system silence them once again.

But, I thought to myself, this is the only way the poor can have something to cover their bodies given the economy. Susan must have read my mind—or she is all too familiar with the opposition to her point—because she spoke before I could share my thoughts aloud. "This kind of aid damages the country and escalates poverty among the poor," she said. "You see, if women like me are given a chance, and have access to resources and simple infrastructures to manage our businesses, we have massive potential to grow the economy and help our governments."

I had not thought much about how such donations have a direct impact on the economy and hurt women like Susan. Not only that, I couldn't help thinking about the direct consumers of these clothes, particularly women like the ones I had just met who had their dignity taken away, and yet remain proud of those who donate their clothes.

This is not only a phenomenon in Zimbabwe; used clothes that are shipped in huge bales from overseas is a sore in Africa. I have many friends in the US who donate their used clothes to thrift shops, places like the Salvation Army and Goodwill. These are good people and they donate with good intentions. I soon found, however, that not all used clothes are consumed by locals in the US; in fact, most are bagged in big bales and shipped to developing nations.

As I struggled to understand the plight of Susan and the three women we had met in downtown Harare, a *sahwira* of mine told me to watch the movie *Poverty, Inc.* To say I was left speechless would be an understatement. The movie supported what I have always thought about why aid will not be an effective tool to empower the women we work with. To improve and provide universal access to quality education, my organization works among some of the poorest communities in rural Zimbabwe.

Of the 67 percent of people who live in rural Zimbabwe, 52 percent are poor women. Earlier on, I realized that without economically empowering these rural women, it would be impossible to achieve our mission. We needed to embark on a strategy that focuses on the growth of an education system, which is supported by socially engaged business models that boost local economies while improving community women's livelihoods. Otherwise, rural women in Africa remain poor, while economic freedom is tied to the education of their daughters.

Susan's clothing business, like the efforts of many women in developing countries, cannot compete with cheap secondhand clothing from overseas that floods local economies. As of our last conversation, Susan has had to lay off all her workers. And if the situation continues, she will soon retire and go back to her village and live in abject poverty. She and women like her cannot help themselves, their communities, or their governments to grow economically in this climate.

Susan's story of how women can easily be silenced by "good deeds" can help us to consciously think about our work with women and the unintended impact of our actions. Our intentions may be noble, but if we do more harm than good, what's the use of good intent?

As sacred sisters, what moral responsibilities do we have to right the wrongs of what is happening to our sisters around the world? As we build this global movement, we need to be mindful of how we help and provide spaces to awaken women. We should always be conscious of how we spend our resources and time. Let us be more inquisitive on the path of our own sacred dreams; at every step of our planning, we need to ask ourselves continually: What are the real positive effects on women because of our work? What are the unintended negative effects on women as the result of our work?

While this might be difficult to judge, this is where your Dream Circles of Sacred *Sahwira* Sisterhood come into play. Debate and discuss these issues with your *sahwiras*. Equip yourselves with enough research and knowledge about the issues you intend to work on. More than financial gain, can *ubuntu* and social justice for all also be at the core of your work?

When we act out of authenticity, love, and feeding our Great Hunger, then we know that it is an honor to be of service to the greater good. It's not about our greatness but about serving others. Sacred responsibilities bring collective empowerment, love, ownership, and change.

Our capacity to love and empathize is irreversible. Feeding your Great Hunger will always reveal this. With love as the energy that unites us, we will stop allowing fear and its triggers to silence us.

No pharmaceutical pill can replace the social medicine that comes with our collectiveness. We can break the bondage of an intergenerational cycle together. Our real hope comes from our strengths as global sisters whose humanity is weaved by compassion, love, respect for social justice, and being of service to each other.

In this book, we have formed our own Dream Circle of Sacred *Sahwira* Sisterhood, you and me. We have connected together over a dream you have, and worked through the challenges or blocks that may have so far stood in the way of your achieving it.

By the time you read these words, you may be well on your way to achieving your dream, or you might have just started out, and getting ready to spread the wings of your dream and take off.

It can be easy to read a book like this, be inspired while you are reading it, and then get distracted or disheartened by your immediate external reality or the world around you. There were many times when I lost touch with my own goals or believed they weren't possible. The art is to find people and practices that keep you connected to your dream in the world around you.

It is my hope, even though we may have been raised in different cultures and thousands of miles apart, that this book has closed the gap between us. Perhaps you have found many similarities between my story and your own and realized that although the details of our journey may be different, that which lies in our hearts is the same.

We both had a dream, you and I. We both had challenges that we had to overcome in order to achieve it. It is my hope that this book serves you as part of my fifth goal, to better the lives of others, and that you are able to take it into your heart for yourself and then share its message with the world, so that you touch as many lives as possible with the good that is inherently within you.

I wish you joy, love, and peace as you take the dream in your heart and make it into a reality. We are forever connected, you and I, and I stand by you in times when you forget to stand by yourself and remind you that anything is possible. I will be part of your Sacred *Sahwira* Circle in spirit, holding you forth every step of the way.

RECOMMENDED RESOURCES

ORGANIZATIONS

Alpha Kappa Alpha Sorority, Inc.: AKA's mission is to cultivate and encourage high scholastic and ethical standards, to promote unity and friendship among college women, to study and help alleviate problems concerning girls and women in order to improve their social stature, to maintain a progressive interest in college life, and to be of service. www.aka1908.com.

American Association of University Women: AAUW is a nonprofit organization that advances equity for women and girls through advocacy, education, philanthropy, and research. www.aauw.org.

Chrysalis Foundation: A statewide nonprofit organization focused on education, empowerment, and social and economic equality to ensure that girls and women have the opportunity to contribute to their community in meaningful and lasting ways. www.chrysalisfdn.org.

Delta Sigma Theta Sorority, Inc.: A private, nonprofit organization whose purpose is to provide assistance and support through established programs in local communities throughout the world. www.deltasigmatheta.org.

Emerging Women: A global network that exists to support and inspire women to express themselves authentically through the work they do. Through Emerging Women Live, a premier conference for feminine business leadership, the organization provides the tools, knowledge, and network to help women lead, start, and grow businesses in a way that integrates feminine values such as connection, collaboration, and heart.

Equality Now: An international human rights organization dedicated to action for the civil, political, economic, and social rights of girls and women. www.equalitynow.org.

Girls Who Code: A national nonprofit organization working to close the gender gap in technology and prepare young women for the jobs of the future. www.girlswhocode.com.

Global Fund for Women: An international organization whose mission is to champion the human rights of women and girls by using powerful networks to find, fund, and amplify the courageous work of women who are building social movements and challenging the status quo. www.globalfundforwomen.org.

International Center for Research on Women: The ICRW is the world's premier research institute focused on tackling challenges facing women and girls worldwide. www.icrw.org.

Iowa Women Lead Change: IWLC is Iowa's premier women leadership organization dedicated to the development, advancement, and promotion of women's leadership, their organizations, and to impacting the greater Iowa economy. www.iwlcleads.org.

P.E.O. Sisterhood: An international women's organization of about 250,000 members with a primary focus on providing educational opportunities for female students worldwide. The Sisterhood has chapters throughout the United States and Canada and is headquartered in Des Moines, Iowa. www.peointernational.org.

Tererai Trent International Foundation: An international organization working to improve and provide universal access to quality education to rural communities in Zimbabwe, Africa. www.tererai.org.

Vital Voices Global Partnership: An international nongovernmental organization (NGO) that works with women leaders in the areas of economic empowerment, women's political participation, and human rights. www.vitalvoices.org.

Women for Women International: An organization that supports the most marginalized women to earn and save money, improve health and well-being, influence decisions in their home and community, and connect to networks for support. By utilizing skills, knowledge, and resources, women are able to create sustainable change for themselves, their families, and their community. www.womenforwomen.org.

World Association of Girl Guides and Girl Scouts: This is the largest voluntary movement dedicated to girls and young women in the world. Their diverse movement represents ten million girls and young women from 146 countries. www.wagggs.org/en/.

World Woman Foundation: A nonprofit organization, it provides a platform to give a collectivized voice to women to educate, inspire, and connect with other women; to foster learning so women can have an impact on themselves, their community, and the world at large; and to inspire women leaders. www.worldwomanfoundation.com.

FURTHER READING

A Natural History of Love by Diane Ackerman (Vintage, 1995)

Borderlands/La Frontera: The New Mestiza by Gloria Anzaldūa (Aunt Lute Books, 2012)

Change Me Prayers: The Hidden Power of Spiritual Surrender by Tosha Silver (Atria, 2015)

Communion: The Female Search for Love by bell hooks (HarperCollins, 2002)

I Know Why the Caged Bird Sings by Maya Angelou (Ballantine, 2009)

In Search of Our Mothers' Gardens: Womanist Prose by Alice Walker (Mariner Books, 2003)

Mighty Be Our Powers: How Sisterhood, Prayer, and Sex Changed a Nation at War by Leymah Gbowee (Beast Books, 2013)

Of Woman Born: Motherhood as Experience and Institution by Adrienne Rich (W. W. Norton & Company, 1995)

Outrageous Openness: Letting the Divine Take the Lead by Tosha Silver (Atria, 2014)

Some of Us Did Not Die: New and Selected Essays by June Jordan (Civitas Books, 2003)

Staying Alive: Women, Ecology, and Development by Vandana Shiva (North Atlantic Books, 2016)

Teaching My Mother How to Give Birth by Warsan Shire (flipped eye publishing, 2011)

The Black Unicorn: Poems by Audre Lorde (W. W. Norton & Company, 1995)

The Eros of Everyday Life: Essays on Ecology, Gender and Society by Susan Griffin (Anchor Books, 1996)

We Should All Be Feminists by Chimamanda Ngozi Adichie (Anchor Books, 2015)

Words Under the Words: Selected Poems by Naomi Shihab Nye (The Eighth Mountain Press, 1994)

Zami: A New Spelling of My Name—A Biomythography by Audre Lorde (The Crossing Press, 1982)

ACKNOWLEDGMENTS

This book has come to life with the help of the many who have inspired me, most especially the audiences to whom I speak. For all their diversity, they share a desire to understand how dreams are achieved. I owe them my gratitude.

My mother's wisdom and support has given me the confidence to define what I want my life to be. She encouraged me to peel back layers that hid inborn traits, such as perseverance, an independent spirit, and an instinctive understanding of the world. She helped not only my father but also the men and women in my community to "see" girls with different eyes and to appreciate their potential.

I am grateful to those who helped shepherd the book from inception to publication. I could not have wished for a more reflective and insightful companion along this journey than Colleen Martell. Colleen's feedback was insightful, positive, and constructive. Her editorial contributions were invaluable and her elegant grace is evident on every page. A special appreciation for her insight into some of the background material helped shape this book. A deep bow to Emily Han, who helped me highlight the beauty that lies in the details. Her valuable feedback in the final stages of preparing the manuscript made this a better book.

My deepest gratitude to my literary agent, Stephanie Tade. Her fierce advocacy and her tender heart have greatly supported me through this process. Thank you to my publisher, Zhena Muzyka, for her belief in and commitment to this book and for bringing it to press. Both Stephanie and Zhena have helped me develop a book that I would love my great-grandchildren to read. I am deeply moved by their devotion and respect for this book.

I am forever thankful to Jo Luck, who motivated and inspired me. She lit a fire under me during a very vulnerable time in my life. Her respect for my work and commitment to my success has been humbling. I am grateful to Ron Beer, who never gave up on me. He carried a candle that reignited mine, rallying the Oklahoma community of Stillwater to add a further spark to the light that was my dream.

Heartfelt thanks go to my sister Tariro, my only remaining biological sibling; her encouragement and support have meant so much to me. As the institutional memory of our family, her thoughtful edits have helped me to explain the intricacies of my life. My sister has taught me so much, and in some ways, she has replaced the mother we both lost. On my mother's side of the family, a special thank you to my aunt Rosie, for keeping me grounded and for reminding me of the importance of healing. Rosie's passion and encouragement helped me to stay the course.

I extend sincere gratitude to Oprah Winfrey for her generous donation. She helped to make my final, most sacred dream a reality—that of giving the gift of education to my community in Zimbabwe. I have great appreciation for Save the Children, which skillfully managed project funds and provided educational expertise and guidance to local government officials, and to the leaders and the entire Matau community, who worked tirelessly to produce the bricks for the school building.

More than anyone can possibly understand, this book belongs to my children and to all the children in Matau as much as it does to me. I pray that they do not remain silent when they feel marginalized. I pray that they find their own voices and construct the lives they deserve.

Finally, I am grateful to my husband, Mark Trent, for his unwavering support of this project from the very beginning.

NOTES

Chapter 1: Find Your Great Hunger: The Call to Awaken
1. A. C. Swift, et al., "Oronasal Obstruction, Lung Volumes, and Arterial Oxygenation," *Lancet*, 1 (1988): 73–75.

Chapter 2: The Women the World Forgot: Reclaiming Your Voice
1. Georgia Douglas Johnson, "The Heart of a Woman," *Poetry Foundation*, June 6, 2016, accessed at https://www.poetryfoundation.org/poems-and-poets/poems/detail/52494.
2. Bertice Berry, *Bertrice: The World According to Me* (New York: Scribner, 1996), p. 29.
3. Judith Shulevitz, "The Science of Suffering," *New Republic*, November 16, 2014, accessed at https://newrepublic.com/article/120144/trauma-genetic-scientists-say-parents-are-passing-ptsd-kids.
4. Kit O'Connell, "Native Americans Have 'Always Known': Science Proves Genetic Inheritance of Trauma," *Shadowproof*, August 27, 2015, accessed at https://shadowproof.com/2015/08/27/native-americans-have-always-known-science-proves-genetic-inheritance-of-trauma/.
5. Walidah Imarisha, "Introduction," *Octavia's Brood: Science Fiction Stories from Social Justice Movements*, edited by Walidah Imarisha and Adrienne Maree Brown (Oakland, CA: AK Press, 2015), p. 5.
6. Adrienne Rich, *A Human Eye: Essays on Art in Society, 1996–2008* (New York: W. W. Norton & Company, 2009), p. 35.
7. Muriel Rukeyser, "Käthe Kollwitz," *Poetry Foundation*, accessed June 10, 2016, https://www.poetryfoundation.org/poems-and-poets/poems/detail/90874.
8. Gloria Steinem, "Why Our Revolution Has Just Begun," *Ms. Magazine*,

February 27, 2014, accessed at http://msmagazine.com/blog/2014/02/27/gloria-steinem-why-our-revolution-has-just-begun/.
9. David Smith, "Lindiwe Mazibuko: 'The Insults Are a Signal That We're Having a Huge Impact,'" *The Guardian*, February 9, 2014, accessed at http://www.theguardian.com/politics/2014/feb/09/lindiwe-mazibuko-south-africa-democratic-alliance.
10. Ibid.
11. Derek Hawkins, "The Silencing of Elizabeth Warren and an Old Senate Rule Prompted by a Fistfight," *Washington Post*, February 8, 2017, accessed at https://www.washingtonpost.com/news/morning-mix/wp/2017/02/08/the-silencing-of-elizabeth-warren-and-an-old-senate-rule-prompted-by-a-fistfight/?utm_term=.94e04453a1eb.
12. Smith, "Lindiwe Mazibuko."
13. "This Artist Is Changing the Lives of Domestic Violence Survivors, One Tattoo at a Time," *Huffington Post*, August 31, 2015, accessed at http://www.huffingtonpost.com/jornalismo-de-rede-e-rua/tattoo-artist-domestic-violence-survivors_b_8033004.html.

Chapter 3: Midwife to Your Sacred Dreams: Sowing Fertile Seeds

1. See, for example, Christopher F. Karpowitz and Tali Mendelbergand, *The Silent Sex: Gender, Deliberation, and Institutions* (Princeton, NJ: Princeton University Press, 2014). This study found that women speak much less frequently than men do in meetings, and when they do speak up they are much less likely to be taken seriously. See also Iris Marion Young's "Throwing Like a Girl: A Phenomenology of Feminine Body Comportment Motility and Spatiality," *Human Studies* 3, no. 2 (April 1980): 137–156.
2. Michelle Stronz, chairperson of Women's Leadership Council, United Way, interviewed by author, March 7 and April 16, 2016.

Chapter 4: Be Your Own Storyteller: Creating New Pathways

1. Judith Warner, "Fact Sheet: The Women's Leadership Gap," *Center for American Progress*, March 7, 2014, accessed at https://www.americanprogress.org/issues/women/reports/2014/03/07/85457/fact-sheet-the-womens-leadership-gap/.
2. Ibid.
3. "The Status of Women in the U.S. Media 2015," Women's Media Center, p. 6, accessed at http://www.womensmediacenter.com/pages/2015-statistics.

4   Ibid., p. 31.
5   Ibid., p. 36.
6   Zora Neale Hurston, *Dust Tracks on a Road* (New York: HarperCollins Publishers, 1942), p. 176.
7   Terry Tempest Williams, *When Women Were Birds: Fifty-Four Variations on Voice* (New York: Farrar Straus and Giroux, 2012), p. 86.
8   Amrita Pritam, *Black Rose* (New Delhi: Nagmani, 1967), quoted in Susie Tharu and K. Lalita, *Women Writing in India: 600 B.C. to the Present, Volume II: The Twentieth Century* (New York: The Feminist Press at the City University of New York, 1993), p. 162.
9   Parker J. Palmer, *The Courage to Teach: Exploring the Inner Landscape of a Teacher's Life* (San Francisco: Jossey-Bass, 2007), p. 55.
10 Clarissa Pinkola Estés, *Women Who Run with the Wolves: Myths and Stories of the Wild Woman Archetype* (New York: Ballantine Books, 1995), pp. 472–473.
11 Lissa Rankin, "The Healing Power of Telling Your Story," *Psychology Today*, November 2012, accessed at https://www.psychologytoday.com/blog/owning-pink/201211/the-healing-power-telling-your-story.
12 Ibid.
13 Ibid.
14 Thomas K. Houston, et al., "Culturally Appropriate Storytelling to Improve Blood Pressure: A Randomized Trial," *Annals of Internal Medicine* 154, no. 2 (2011): 77.
15 Sayantani DasGupta, interview with *Business Innovation Factory*, December 22, 2016, accessed at http://www.businessinnovationfactory.com/summit/story/healing-power-story.
16 Ibid.
17 Ibid.
18 Ibid.
19 Audre Lorde, "The Transformation of Silence into Language and Action," *Sister Outsider: Essays and Speeches* (New York: The Crossing Press Feminist Series, 1984), p. 41.
20 Douglas Martin, "Yang Huanyi, the Last User of a Secret Women's Code," *New York Times*, October 7, 2004, accessed at http://query.nytimes.com/gst/fullpage.html?res=9C04E7DE173BF934A35753C1A9629C8B63.
21 Ibid.
22 "The Dialectical Relationship between Children and the Storyteller in

Ngano Aesthetics in Zimbabwe," *The Free Library*, December 29, 2016, accessed at https://www.thefreelibrary.com/The+dialectical+relationship+between+children+and+the+storyteller+in...-a0192351983.

23 Walt Whitman, "Song of Myself," *Leaves of Grass* (New York: The Viking Press, 1959), p. 85.

Chapter 5: Validate Your Body's Knowing: Harnessing Your Sensuality

1 Seynabou Tall, regional gender and GBV adviser, United Nations Population Fund, in discussion with the author, October 2016.

2 "Ending Child Marriage: Progress and Prospects," United Nations Children's Fund, UNICEF, New York, 2014.

3 Ibid.

4 David A. Farenthold, "Trump Recorded Having Extremely Lewd Conversation about Women in 2005," *Washington Post*, October 8, 2016, accessed at https://www.washingtonpost.com/politics/trump-recorded-having-extremely-lewd-conversation-about-women-in-2005/2016/10/07/3b9ce776-8cb4-11e6-bf8a-3d26847eeed4_story.html?postshare=2491475870527101&tid=ss_tw&utm_term=.90b83abaa56c.

5 See Lisa Wade, "The Orgasm Gap: The Real Reason Women Get Off Less Often Than Men and How to Fix It," *AlterNet*, April 3, 2012, accessed at http://www.alternet.org/sex-amp-relationships/orgasm-gap-real-reason-women-get-less-often-men-and-how-fix-it; Paula England, Emily Fitzgibbons Shafer, and Alison C. K. Fogarty, "Hooking Up and Forming Romantic Relationships on Today's College Campuses," *The Gendered Society Reader* (Oxford: Oxford University Press, 2011), 578–591; and Edward O. Laumann, et al., *The Social Organization of Sexuality: Sexual Practices in the United States* (Chicago: University of Chicago Press, 2000).

6 Wade, "The Orgasm Gap."

7 See K. J. Bell, "Wake Up and Smell the Condoms: An Analysis of Sex Education Programs in the United States, the Netherlands, Sweden, Australia, France, and Germany," *Inquiries Journal/Student Pulse* 1, no. 11 (2009), accessed at https://www.inquiriesjournal.com/a?id=40; and Jaclyn Friedman and Jessica Valenti, *Yes Means Yes! Visions of Female Sexual Power and a World Without Rape* (Berkeley, CA: Seal Press, 2008).

8 Kali Holloway, "The Labiaplasty Boom: Why Are Women Desperate for the Perfect Vagina?" *AlterNet*, February 13, 2015, accessed

at http://www.alternet.org/news-amp-politics/labiaplasty-boom-why-are-women-desperate-perfect-vagina.
9. "Violence Against Women in the United States: Statistics," accessed at http://now.org/resource/violence-against-women-in-the-united-states-statistic/.
10. Cheryl Strayed, *Wild: From Lost to Found on the Pacific Crest Trail* (New York: Vintage Books, 2013), p. 143.
11. Zora Neale Hurston, *Their Eyes Were Watching God* (New York: Harper Perennial, 1998), p. 11.
12. Mary Oliver, "Wild Geese," *Dream Work* (New York: Grove/Atlantic, 1986), p. 14.
13. Audre Lorde, "Uses of the Erotic: The Erotic as Power," *Sister Outsider: Essays and Speeches* (New York: The Crossing Press Feminist Series, 1984), p. 54.
14. Ibid.
15. Ibid., p. 55.
16. Ibid.
17. Esther Perel, "The Fluidity of Sexual Desire," Emerging Women Conference, San Francisco, California, October 2015.

Chapter 6: Let Your Spirit Take Root: Believing in Your Dreams

1. See Tara Sophia Mohr, "Why Women Don't Apply for Jobs Unless They're 100% Qualified," *Harvard Business Review*, August 25, 2014, accessed at https://hbr.org/2014/08/why-women-dont-apply-for-jobs-unless-theyre-100-qualified.
2. Rachel Simmons, *The Curse of the Good Girl: Raising Authentic Girls with Courage and Confidence* (New York: Penguin Books, 2010), eBook, introduction.
3. Anat Hoffman, "Why I Was Arrested for Praying at the Western Wall," *Huffington Post*, October 21, 2002, accessed at http://www.huffingtonpost.com/anat-hoffman/arrested-for-praying-at-western-wall_b_1987099.html.
4. Andrea Elliot, "Woman Leads Muslim Prayer Service in New York," *New York Times*, March 19, 2005, accessed at http://www.nytimes.com/2005/03/19/nyregion/woman-leads-muslim-prayer-service-in-new-york.html?_r=4.
5. Psalm 51:7.

Chapter 7: Be Courageous, Not Silent: Inspiring Action and Opportunity

1. Kofi Annan, Keynote Address, International Women's Health Coalition, January 15, 2004, accessed at http://www.un.org/press/en/2004/sgsm9118.doc.htm.
2. Justin Rowlatt, "The Indian Women Who Took on a Multinational and Won," *BBC News*, October 19, 2015, accessed at http://www.bbc.com/news/world-asia-india-34513824.
3. Marian Wright Edelman, "It's Hard to Be What You Can't See," Children's Defense Fund Child Watch Column, August 21, 2015, accessed at http://www.childrensdefense.org/newsroom/child-watch-columns/child-watch-documents/ItsHardtobeWhatYouCantSee.html.
4. Paula Gunn Allen, "Who Is Your Mother? Red Roots of White Feminism," *The Sacred Hoop: Recovering the Feminine in American Indian Traditions* (Boston: Beacon Press, 1992), pp. 209–221.
5. Ibid. Note: Gunn Allen is paraphrasing; the correct proverb reads: "A nation is not conquered until the hearts of its women are on the ground."
6. Jo Luck, former CEO of Heifer International, interview with Colleen Martell, May 12, 2016.
7. Diane Ramsey, CEO, Iowa Women Lead Change, interview with the author, April 2016.
8. Ibid.
9. Ibid.
10. Hope Sadza (Professor and Vice Chancellor, Women's University in Africa), interview with the author, March 3, 2016.
11. Ibid.
12. Ibid.
13. Ibid.
14. Ibid.
15. Stronz, interview with the author, March 7 and April 16, 2016.
16. Shirin Ebadi, Iranian lawyer, former judge, human rights activist, and founder of Defenders of Human Rights Center in Iran, interview with the author, February 8, 2016.
17. Ibid.
18. Leah Campbell, artist and life coach, interview with the author, September and November 2015.
19. Diane Nash, "Black History Month Keynote Speaker: Civil Rights

Leader Diane Nash," Williams Center for the Arts, Lafayette College, attended by Colleen Martell, February 17, 2016.

Chapter 8: The Sacred Sisterhood: Cultivating Your *Sahwira*
1. Brené Brown, "The Power of Vulnerability," TED Talk, Houston, Texas, June 2010, accessed at http://www.ted.com/talks/brene_brown_on_vulnerability?language=en#.
2. Roxane Gay, *Bad Feminist: Essays* (New York: HarperPerennial, 2014), p. 47.
3. Rebecca Traister, *All the Single Ladies: Unmarried Women and the Rise of an Independent Nation* (New York: Simon & Schuster, 2016), p. 105.
4. Ibid., p. 97.
5. Ibid., p. 116.
6. Ibid.
7. Melissa Pandika, "Why Girl Gangs Make for Good Health," *Ozy*, March 10, 2016, accessed at http://www.ozy.com/acumen/ozy-ted-why-girl-gangs-make-for-good-health/66795?utm_source=NH&utm_medium=pp&utm_campaign=pp.
8. Ibid.

Conclusion: It Is Achievable!
1. See Tony Bennett, et al., *New Keywords: A Revised Vocabulary of Culture and Society* (Malden, MA: Blackwell Publishing, 2005), pp. 97–99.
2. Plato, "Theaetetus 148c-151d," *The Dialogues of Plato*, translated by Benjamin Jowett. (Oxford: Oxford University Press, 1892), accessed at http://www.sophia-project.org/uploads/1/3/9/5/13955288/plato_midwife.pdf.

BIBLIOGRAPHY

Allen, Paula Gunn. "Who Is Your Mother? Red Roots of White Feminism." *The Sacred Hoop: Recovering the Feminine in American Indian Traditions*, pp. 209–221. Boston: Beacon Press, 1992.

Annan, Kofi. Keynote Address, International Women's Health Coalition. January 15, 2004. http://www.un.org/press/en/2004/sgsm9118.doc.htm.

Berry, Bertice. *Bertrice: The World According to Me.* New York: Scribner, 1996.

Brown, Brené. "The Power of Vulnerability." TEDxHouston. Filmed June 2010. http://www.ted.com/talks/brene_brown_on_vulnerability?language=en#.

Campbell, Leah. Interview with the author, September and November 2015.

DasGupta, Sayantani. *Business Innovation Factory*. Interview: "The Healing Power of Story." December 22, 2016. Accessed at http://www.businessinnovationfactory.com/summit/story/healing-power-story.

"The Dialectical Relationship between Children and the Storyteller in Ngano Aesthetics in Zimbabwe." *The Free Library*. Accessed December 29, 2016. https://www.thefreelibrary.com/The+dialectical+relationship+between+children+and+the+storyteller+in...-a0192351983.

Ebadi, Shirin. Interview with the author, February 8, 2016.

Edelman, Marian Wright. "It's Hard to Be What You Can't See." Children's Defense Fund Child Watch Column. August 21, 2015. Accessed at http://www.childrensdefense.org/newsroom/child-watch-columns/child-watch-documents/ItsHardtobeWhatYouCantSee.html.

Elliot, Andrea. "Woman Leads Muslim Prayer Service in New York." *New York Times*. March 19, 2005. Accessed at http://www.nytimes.com/2005/03/19/nyregion/woman-leads-muslim-prayer-service-in-new-york.html?_r=4.

"Ending Child Marriage: Progress and Prospects." United Nations Children's Fund (UNICEF). New York, 2014. Accessed at https://www.unicef.org/media/files/Child_Marriage_Report_7_17_LR..pdf.

Estés, Clarissa Pinkola. *Women Who Run with the Wolves: Myths and Stories of the Wild Woman Archetype*. New York: Ballantine Books, 1995.

Gay, Roxane. *Bad Feminist: Essays*. New York: Harper Perennial, 2014.

Hoffman, Anat. "Why I Was Arrested for Praying at the Western Wall." *Huffington Post*. October 21, 2002. Accessed at http://www.huffingtonpost.com/anat-hoffman/arrested-for-praying-at-western-wall_b_1987099.html.

Houston, Thomas K., et al. "Culturally Appropriate Storytelling to Improve Blood Pressure: A Randomized Trial." *Annals of Internal Medicine* 154, no. 2 (2011): 77.

Hurston, Zora Neale. *Dust Tracks on a Road*. New York: HarperCollins Publishers, 1942.

———. *Their Eyes Were Watching God*. New York: Harper Perennial, 1998.

Johnson, Georgia Douglas. "The Heart of a Woman." *Poetry Foundation*. June 6, 2016. Accessed at https://www.poetryfoundation.org/poems-and-poets/poems/detail/52494.

Lorde, Audre. *Sister Outsider: Essays and Speeches*. New York: Crossing Press Feminist Series, 1984.

Luck, Jo. Interview with Colleen Martell, May 12, 2016.

Martin, Douglas, "Yang Huanyi, the Last User of a Secret Women's Code." *New York Times*. October 7, 2004. Accessed at http://query.nytimes.com/gst/fullpage.html?res=9C04E7DE173BF934A35753C1A9629C8B63.

Nash, Diane. "Black History Month Keynote Speaker: Civil Rights Leader Diane Nash." Williams Center for the Arts, Lafayette College, Easton, PA, February 2016.

O'Connell, Kit. "Native Americans Have 'Always Known': Science Proves Genetic Inheritance of Trauma." *Shadowproof*. August 27, 2015. Accessed at https://shadowproof.com/2015/08/27/native-americans-have-always-known-science-proves-genetic-inheritance-of-trauma/.

Oliver, Mary. *Dream Work*. New York: Grove/Atlantic, 1986.

Palmer, Parker J. *The Courage to Teach: Exploring the Inner Landscape of a Teacher's Life*. San Francisco: Jossey-Bass, 2007.

Pandika, Melissa. "Why Girl Gangs Make for Good Health." *Ozy*. March 10, 2016. Accessed at http://www.ozy.com/acumen/ozy-ted-why-girl

-gangs-make-for-good-health/66795?utm_source=NH&utm_medium =pp&utm_campaign=pp.

Plato, "Theaetetus 148c-151d." The Dialogues of Plato. Translated by Benjamin Jowett. Oxford: Oxford University Press, 1892. Accessed at http://www.sophia-project.org/uploads/1/3/9/5/13955288/plato_midwife.pdf.

Pritam, Amrita, *Black Rose* (New Delhi: Nagmani, 1967), quoted in Susie Tharu and K. Lalita, *Women Writing in India: 600 B.C. to the Present*, Volume II: *The Twentieth Century* (New York: Feminist Press at the City University of New York, 1993).

Ramsey, Diane. Interview with the author, April 2016.

Rankin, Lissa. "The Healing Power of Telling Your Story." *Psychology Today*. November 2012. Accessed at https://www.psychologytoday.com/blog/owning-pink/201211/the-healing-power-telling-your-story.

Rich, Adrienne. *A Human Eye: Essays on Art in Society, 1996–2008*. New York: W. W. Norton & Company, 2009.

Rowlatt, Justin. "The Indian Women Who Took on a Multinational and Won." *BBC News*. October 19, 2015. Accessed at http://www.bbc.com/news/world-asia-india-34513824.

Rukeyser, Muriel. "Käthe Kollwitz." *Poetry Foundation*. Accessed June 10, 2016. https://www.poetryfoundation.org/poems-and-poets/poems/detail/90874.

Sadza, Hope. Interview with the author, March 3, 2016.

Shulevitz, Judith. "The Science of Suffering." *New Republic*. November 16, 2014. Accessed at https://newrepublic.com/article/120144/trauma-genetic-scientists-say-parents-are-passing-ptsd-kids.

Simmons, Rachel. *The Curse of the Good Girl: Raising Authentic Girls with Courage and Confidence*. New York: Penguin Books, 2010. eBook edition.

Steinem, Gloria. *My Life on the Road*. New York: Random House, 2016.

———. "Why Our Revolution Has Just Begun." *Ms. Magazine*. February 27, 2014. Accessed at http://msmagazine.com/blog/2014/02/27/gloria-steinem-why-our-revolution-has-just-begun/.

Strayed, Cheryl. *Wild: From Lost to Found on the Pacific Crest Trail*. New York: Vintage Books, 2013.

Stronz, Michelle. Interview with the author, March 7 and April 16, 2016.

Swift, A. C., Campbell, I. T. Campbell, and Tessa M. Mckown. "Oronasal Obstruction, Lung Volumes, and Arterial Oxygenation." *Lancet* 1 (1988): 73–75.

"This Artist Is Changing the Lives of Domestic Violence Survivors, One Tattoo at a Time." *Huffington Post.* August 31, 2015. Accessed at http://www.huffingtonpost.com/jornalismo-de-rede-e-rua/tattoo-artist-domestic-violence-survivors_b_8033004.html.

Traister, Rebecca. *All the Single Ladies: Unmarried Women and the Rise of an Independent Nation.* New York: Simon & Schuster, 2016.

Wade, Lisa. "The Orgasm Gap: The Real Reason Women Get Off Less Often Than Men and How to Fix It." *AlterNet.* April 3, 2012. Accessed at http://www.alternet.org/sex-amp-relationships/orgasm-gap-real-reason-women-get-less-often-men-and-how-fix-it.

Whitman, Walt. *Leaves of Grass.* New York: The Viking Press, 1959.

Williams, Terry Tempest. *When Women Were Birds: Fifty-Four Variations on Voice.* New York: Farrar, Straus and Giroux, 2012.